Jossey-Bass Teacher

Laura VanWallendael
COTA/c

Jossey-Bass Teacher provides educators with practical knowledge and tools to create a positive and life-long impact on student learning. We offer classroom-tested and research-based teaching resources for a variety of grade levels and subject areas. Whether you are an aspiring, new, or veteran teacher, we want to help you make every teaching day your best.

From ready-to-use classroom activities to the latest teaching framework, our value-packed books provide insightful, practical, and comprehensive materials on the topics that matter most to K–12 teachers. We hope to become your trusted source for the best ideas from the most experienced and respected experts in the field.

Life Skills Activities for Special Children

Second Edition

Darlene Mannix

JOSSEY-BASS
A Wiley Imprint
www.josseybass.com

Published by Jossey-Bass
A Wiley Imprint
One Montgomery Street, Suite 1200, San Francisco, CA 94104-4594—www.josseybass.com

ISBN 9780-470-25937-5

Printed in the United States of America

SECOND EDITION

PB Printing   10 9 8 7 6

About This Book

Life Skills Activities for Special Children is a resource for teachers and parents to use with elementary-aged children who have special needs, particularly with regard to developing independence in their home, school, and community environments.

Children with special needs often require specific guidance and teaching techniques to help them grasp the skills needed for success in life. But what skills are essential for children to learn? There are so many things that children today "need" to learn; how can we narrow the focus to choose those skills that are most important? In developing the content of this book, I selected the most basic skills in a number of areas, including basic survival skills (operating a phone, using money, reading and writing), personal independence skills (hygiene, dressing, living a healthy lifestyle), interaction in the community (recognizing and visiting community places), and basic social skills (citizenship, working with others, having a social life). In other words, these skills are necessary to establish and enhance an independent, fulfilled life—our goal for ourselves as well as the children we teach and love.

Content of the Book

The book is divided into four main parts. Part I is Basic Survival Skills. This section focuses on teaching skills that are required for a child to protect himself and handle very elementary transactions. These chapters cover skills for relating basic information, telephone skills, money skills, time skills, and basic reading and writing skills. There are fifty-six lessons in this section. This part has been updated to include lessons on using a cell phone, estimating prices for items on sale, setting personal time goals, and expanding reading skills.

Part II, Personal Independence, teaches skills such as dressing and clothing choices, hygiene, keeping a room clean, food and eating skills, and living a healthy lifestyle. There are forty-two lessons in Part II. This part has been updated to include lessons on self-inspection, what to do when you are sick, organizing a room, eating healthy snacks, and getting enough sleep.

Part III, Community and Independence, includes chapters on community places and people and helpful information that will guide children as they negotiate their way through the community. This part has twenty-seven lessons. Updates on this part include new community places to visit, what to do if you get lost, safe Internet sites, and computer common sense.

The final section, Part IV, is Getting Along with Others. The thirty-one lessons in this part are grouped into chapters on being a good citizen, working with people, and having a social life. This section has been extensively revised, including social skills on speaking up, working with others, knowing when to let something go, friendship skills, and starting up a conversation with others.

Content of the Chapters

Each of the fifteen chapters in this book includes the following features:

Parent Letter. This generic letter is directed to the parent or guardian of the children in a classroom. It can be modified by the classroom teacher to be as specific as necessary. It includes an overview of each set of lessons that will be taught and ideas to implement at home.

Skill Sheet. This basic Skill Sheet can be used to rate or evaluate each student's progress on the skills taught in each chapter. A simple plus, check, or minus symbol is used to score the student's progress.

Lessons. Several specific lessons direct the teacher step-by-step how to teach each skill. Each lesson begins with an objective and includes discussion questions, worksheet directions and answers, and several extension activities that can be implemented in the classroom if desired.

A Final Word

Our hope as teachers is always that by engineering specific learning situations, such as those presented in these lessons, the children we work with will learn to think and respond in a way that they can generalize to real-life situations. It is important that we do not underestimate how important it is to patiently explain, demonstrate, teach, and reteach a skill. Parents and teachers, working together and sharing information, can form a powerful team that will give special children the guidance and encouragement that will truly help them succeed in understanding and living the life skills so necessary for an independent life.

About the Author

Darlene Mannix has worked as an educator for more than twenty years and has taught a wide range of children, including learning disabled, emotionally disturbed, language-disordered, and multiply disabled students. She received her bachelor of science degree from Taylor University and her master's degree in learning disabilities from Indiana University. A past presenter at numerous educational conferences including the Council for Exceptional Children, she has authored many books, including *Social Skills Activities for Special Children, Second Edition* (Jossey-Bass, 2009), *Social Skills Activities for Secondary Students with Special Needs, Second Edition* (Jossey-Bass, 2009), and *Writing Skills Activities for Special Children* (Jossey-Bass, 2001). She currently works as a Title 1 reading teacher at Indian Trail Elementary School in La Porte, Indiana.

Contents

Part One: Basic Survival Skills   1

Chapter 1: Relating Basic Information   3

     PARENT LETTER #1   4

     SKILL SHEET #1: PROGRESS REPORT   6

     Lesson 1.1: Who Are You?   7

     Lesson 1.2: Where I Live   9

     Lesson 1.3: Hello, Anybody Home?   11

     Lesson 1.4: Happy Birthday to Me!   13

     Lesson 1.5: My Family   15

     Lesson 1.6: My Parents and Where They Are   17

     Lesson 1.7: Meet My Teacher   19

     Lesson 1.8: Medical Needs   21

     Lesson 1.9: Emergency!   23

     Lesson 1.10: My Vital Statistics   25

     Lesson 1.11: After School   27

     Lesson 1.12: Lost and Found   29

Chapter 2: Telephone Skills   31

     Parent Letter #2   32

     Skill Sheet #2: Progress Report   33

     Lesson 2.1: Dialing the Number   34

     Lesson 2.2: Using a Cell Phone   38

     Lesson 2.3: Using 911, 411, and 0   40

     Lesson 2.4: Making Emergency Phone Calls   42

     Lesson 2.5: Obtaining Information   44

     Lesson 2.6: Giving Information   46

     Lesson 2.7: Taking a Message   48

     Lesson 2.8: Leaving a Message on an Answering Machine   50

     Lesson 2.9: Using the Telephone Directory: White Pages   52

     Lesson 2.10: Using the Telephone Directory: Yellow Pages   54

Chapter 3: Money Skills   57
        Parent Letter #3   58
        Skill Sheet #3: Progress Report   59

        Lesson 3.1: Coins and Bills   60
        Lesson 3.2: Counting Coins   62
        Lesson 3.3: Recognizing Value of Items   64
        Lesson 3.4: Keeping Money in a Safe Place   66
        Lesson 3.5: Savings Account   68
        Lesson 3.6: Earning Money   70
        Lesson 3.7: Spending Money   72
        Lesson 3.8: Sales and Discounts   74
        Lesson 3.9: Estimating   76

Chapter 4: Time Skills   79
        Parent Letter #4   80
        Skill Sheet #4: Progress Report   81

        Lesson 4.1: Days and Months   82
        Lesson 4.2: Today   84
        Lesson 4.3: Using a Calendar   86
        Lesson 4.4: Using a Clock   89
        Lesson 4.5: Seasons   91
        Lesson 4.6: Planning Ahead   93
        Lesson 4.7: What Happens When?   95
        Lesson 4.8: First Step in a Sequence   97
        Lesson 4.9: Fifteen-Minute Tasks   99
        Lesson 4.10: Setting Time Goals   101

Chapter 5: Basic Reading and Writing Skills   103
        Parent Letter #5   104
        Skill Sheet #5: Progress Report   105

        Lesson 5.1: Words: People   106
        Lesson 5.2: Words: Places   108
        Lesson 5.3: Words: Things   110
        Lesson 5.4: Traffic Signs   112
        Lesson 5.5: Information Signs   114
        Lesson 5.6: Safety Words   116
        Lesson 5.7: Things to Read   118
        Lesson 5.8: Reading for a Purpose   120

Lesson 5.9:   Reading for Pleasure   122

Lesson 5.10: Filling Out a Form   124

Lesson 5.11: Addressing an Envelope   126

Lesson 5.12: Mailing a Letter   128

Lesson 5.13: Making Lists   130

Lesson 5.14: Having Good Handwriting   132

Lesson 5.15: Reminder Notes   134

Part Two: Personal Independence   **137**

Chapter 6: Clothing and Dressing   139

Parent Letter #6   140

Skill Sheet #6: Progress Report   141

Lesson 6.1: What's the Weather?   142

Lesson 6.2: What's the Event?   144

Lesson 6.3: Obtaining Clothing   146

Lesson 6.4: Care of Clothing   148

Lesson 6.5: Washing and Drying Clothes   150

Lesson 6.6: Let's Go Shopping!   152

Lesson 6.7: Final Inspection   154

Lesson 6.8: Fads   156

Chapter 7: Keeping Yourself Clean   159

Parent Letter #7   160

Skill Sheet #7: Progress Report   161

Lesson 7.1: Taking a Bath or Shower   162

Lesson 7.2: Hair Care   164

Lesson 7.3: A Clean Face   166

Lesson 7.4: Taking Care of Your Hands   168

Lesson 7.5: Using a Mirror   170

Lesson 7.6: Care of Teeth   172

Lesson 7.7: Makeup   174

Lesson 7.8: When You are Sick   176

Chapter 8: Keeping Your Room Clean   179

Parent Letter #8   180

Skill Sheet #8: Progress Report   181

Lesson 8.1: Picking Up   182

Lesson 8.2: Making the Bed   184

Lesson 8.3: Floor Care   186
Lesson 8.4: Dusting   188
Lesson 8.5: "Too Much Stuff"/De-Cluttering   190
Lesson 8.6: Organizing a Closet   192
Lesson 8.7: Rules for the Room   194
Lesson 8.8: Sharing a Room   197

Chapter 9: Food and Eating Skills   199
Parent Letter #9   200
Skill Sheet #9: Progress Report   201

Lesson 9.1: Shopping for Food   202
Lesson 9.2: Making a Shopping List   204
Lesson 9.3: Simple Cooking, Easy Meals   206
Lesson 9.4: Table Manners   208
Lesson 9.5: Cleaning Up   210
Lesson 9.6: Washing the Dishes   212
Lesson 9.7: Eating Out   214
Lesson 9.8: Food Groups   216
Lesson 9.9: Healthy Snacks   219
Lesson 9.10: When You Don't Like Something   221

Chapter 10: Living a Healthy Lifestyle   223
Parent Letter #10   224
Skill Sheet #10: Progress Report   225

Lesson 10.1: Visiting Health Care People   226
Lesson 10.2: Getting Exercise   228
Lesson 10.3: Leisure-Time Activities   230
Lesson 10.4: What About Drugs?   232
Lesson 10.5: Avoiding Unhealthy Habits   234
Lesson 10.6: Dangerous Situations   237
Lesson 10.7: Following Safety Rules   240
Lesson 10.8: Getting Enough Sleep   242

Part Three: Community and Independence   245

Chapter 11: Community Places and People   247
Parent Letter #11   248
Skill Sheet #11: Progress Report   249
Lesson 11.1: Restaurants   250
Lesson 11.2: Shopping Mall   252

Lesson 11.3: The Park   254
Lesson 11.4: Houses of Worship   256
Lesson 11.5: Movie Theater   258
Lesson 11.6: Sporting Events   260
Lesson 11.7: The Public Library   262
Lesson 11.8: A Museum   264
Lesson 11.9: The Zoo   266
Lesson 11.10: The Supermarket   268
Lesson 11.11: Barber or Beauty Shop   270
Lesson 11.12: The Post Office   272

Chapter 12: Helpful Information   275
Parent Letter #12   276
Skill Sheet #12: Progress Report   277

Lesson 12.1: Pedestrian Safety   278
Lesson 12.2: Bike Safety   280
Lesson 12.3: Safety After Dark   282
Lesson 12.4: Using a Menu   284
Lesson 12.5: Tipping   286
Lesson 12.6: Locating Restrooms   288
Lesson 12.7: Reading a Map   290
Lesson 12.8: Using a Mall Directory   292
Lesson 12.9: Hours of Operation   294
Lesson 12.10: Television Schedules   296
Lesson 12.11: All About the Newspaper   298
Lesson 12.12: Using a Catalog   300
Lesson 12.13: If You Get Lost   302
Lesson 12.14: Safe Computer Sites   304
Lesson 12.15: Computer Common Sense   306

Part Four: Getting Along with Others   309

Chapter 13: Being a Good Citizen   311
Parent Letter #13   312
Skill Sheet #13: Progress Report   313

Lesson 13.1: Being Polite to Others   314
Lesson 13.2: Having a Good Attitude on a Bad Day   316
Lesson 13.3: Speaking Up   318
Lesson 13.4: Lending a Hand   320

Lesson 13.5: Volunteering   322
Lesson 13.6: Being Courteous   324
Lesson 13.7: At the Movies   326
Lesson 13.8: Helping Others   328
Lesson 13.9: Rudeness in Others   330
Lesson 13.10: Vandalism and Pranks   332

Chapter 14: Working with People   335
Parent Letter #14   336
Skill Sheet #14: Progress Report   337

Lesson 14.1: Working as a Team   338
Lesson 14.2: Understanding the Task   340
Lesson 14.3: Understanding Your Role   342
Lesson 14.4: Matching Skills with Jobs   344
Lesson 14.5: Expressing Your Opinion   346
Lesson 14.6: Being Trustworthy   348
Lesson 14.7: Knowing When to "Let it Go"   350
Lesson 14.8: Another Point of View   352
Lesson 14.9: Having a Discussion   354
Lesson 14.10: Having an Argument   356
Lesson 14.11: Defining Terms   358
Lesson 14.12: Common Sense   360

Chapter 15: Having a Social Life   363
Parent Letter #15   364
Skill Sheet #15: Progress Report   365

Lesson 15.1: Meeting People   366
Lesson 15.2: Understanding That Friends Are Important   368
Lesson 15.3: Knowing How to Treat Friends   370
Lesson 15.4: Having Something to Offer   372
Lesson 15.5: Saying Nice Things   374
Lesson 15.6: Having Good Hygiene   376
Lesson 15.7: Using Conversation Starters   378
Lesson 15.8: Trying Something New   380
Lesson 15.9: Going Places   382
Idea Lists   384

Part One

Basic Survival Skills

Relating Basic Information

PARENT LETTER #1

Relating Basic Information

Dear Parents,

In the next few weeks, we will be discussing and practicing telling basic information about ourselves, such as name, address, phone number, date of birth, family members, and emergency needs. This is not intended to be an intrusion into your private lives, but it is important for your child to be able to identify these items about himself or herself. It would help me a lot to have the correct answers so that I can make sure your child is learning the right information! Please help by completing the form on the next page and return by _____.

You can also help by practicing this information with your child at home.

Thanks for your help!

Sincerely,

_____

Teacher

Child's name:

_____

Name(s) of Parent(s) or Guardian(s):

_____

Who lives in the home:

_____

Address:

_____

Phone number:

_____

Where Parent(s) or Guardian(s) works:

_____

Phone number at work:

_____

Emergency or medical needs:

_____

_____

_____

RELATING BASIC INFORMATION

Skill Sheet #1: Progress Report

| + mastered |
| √ emerging |
| − not mastered |

Student Name	Who Are You?	Where I Live	Hello, Anybody Home?	Happy Birthday to Me!	My Family	My Parents and Where They Are	Meet My Teacher	Medical Needs	Emergency!	My Vital Statistics	After School	Lost and Found	Comments

1.1 Who Are You?

Objective

Upon request or in appropriate situations, the student will state his or her full name.

Discussion

Teacher: Were any of you named after your parents or a particular person? Is there a name that is special for some reason in your family? Names are very important. Can you help me list reasons why someone might need to know your name? (For example, if you're lost, filling out a form, and so on.)

Worksheet 1.1: On this Worksheet, you will see four examples of when you should tell someone your name. I want you to listen while I read the directions, and then finish drawing the student to resemble yourself. In the cartoon "balloon," write how you would tell someone your name.

Answers

(These are examples.)

1. Yes, the card should say (name).
2. My name is (name).
3. My whole name is (name).
4. I'm (name).

Extension Activities

1. *Name Meanings.* Locate a baby name book and have students look up what their first name means. If students know, have them tell the origin of their given name as well as their last name.
2. *Name Posters.* Have students draw and color posters using the letters of their names. Students may shape the letters to form a picture of something that interests them (for example, a skateboard, airplane).

1.1   Who Are You?

Pretend that you are the student in each of these pictures. Fill in the cartoon to tell how you would answer each person in each situation.

Chapter 1: Relating Basic Information

1.2 Where I Live

Objective

Upon request or in appropriate situations, the student will state or write his or her address.

Discussion

Teacher: What kind of mail comes to your house? How does the mail carrier know where to deliver everything? If you were going to send away for something, what information would you need to give the people who were going to send it to you? Your *address* is the directions for where you live. Usually your address includes house number, street, city, state, and ZIP Code. You will need to know all of these parts of your address.

Worksheet 1.2: It is important for everyone to know his or her complete address. On this Worksheet, help the students find the missing parts and use the Help Box at the bottom to complete their address. Then we will work on the directions for your address, including all of the same information.

Answers

1. State—Indiana
2. City—Milwaukee
3. House number—307
4. Street—Lemon Grove Parkway
5. ZIP Code—22901

Extension Activities

1. *Roll Your Address.* Using one die, have students roll and state the part of their address indicated by the following key: one—house number, two—street, three—city, four—state, five—ZIP Code, six—roll again.
2. *My House.* Have students draw or color and cut out a paper house (or apartment, trailer, or other dwelling) with the appropriate information on it. Have students send a letter through the mail to another student, using the address from the paper house. When the letter is received, have the student bring it to school and display it next to his or her paper house.

1.2   **Where I Live**

Something is missing from each of the following addresses. Write the answer on the line.

1. 507 East Main Street
    Bloomington 47401

    _____

2. 300 N. 7th Street
    Wisconsin 53213

    _____

3.   Washington Street
     La Porte, Indiana 46350

    _____

4. 1074 Englewood Cliffs,
    New Jersey 07632

    _____

5. Box 330, Route 7
    Charlottesville, Virginia

    _____

HELP BOX

307	Lemon Grove Parkway	22901
Indiana	Milwaukee	

1.3 Hello, Anybody Home?

Objective

Upon request or in appropriate situations, the student will state his or her phone number.*

Discussion

Teacher: Just last night I talked to a friend of mine who lives a hundred miles away. How did I do that? (Via phone.) What do you need to know to make a phone call? Why might it be important to know your phone number?

Worksheet 1.3: Think about why people would need to know your phone number. On this sheet, you will decide whether or not someone needs to reach you by phone, and you will write down your phone number when it is needed.

Answers

1. Yes   2. Yes (although it could be mailed)   3. No   4. Yes (discuss area codes)   5. No   6. Yes

Extension Activities

1. *Class Phone Book.* If there are no objections from parents or school administrators, compile a class phone/address book. You may want to include other information as well, such as birth dates, pets, favorite activities, and so on.

2. *Call Me.* With prior parent notification, have students assigned to partners within the class. Inform students that they need to state/write their phone number correctly so that their partners can call them on a designated evening. Have students ask specific questions of each other over the phone and discuss the responses at school the following day.

---

* If students do not have a phone in their home, do not embarrass them or pry into reasons why they do not have a phone. Also, some students may have an unlisted number that they cannot divulge. You may adapt this activity by having them learn a parent's number (see Lesson 1.6) or other emergency number. Be sure that releasing this information is OK with all parties involved.

1.3   Hello, Anybody Home?

Which of these people would need to know your phone number to tell you something? Write *yes* or *no* in the space next to each situation. If it is *yes*, write your phone number too.

1. Mr. Pierce wants you to know that football practice has been canceled because of the rain.

2. You just won a free trip to Hawaii! The lady from the travel agency has the details.

3. Your best friend mailed you a birthday card.

4. Your aunt in France wants to wish you happy birthday.

5. Your next-door neighbor dropped off flowers for you while you were sick.

6. A friend wants to let you know what time everyone is going to go bowling.

1.4 Happy Birthday to Me!

Objective

Upon request or in appropriate situations, the student will state his or her birth date.

Discussion

Teacher: Do you know this song? (Hum "Happy Birthday" tune.) What does it mean? What is a birthday? When someone asks for your birth date, they want to know the month, day, and year that you were born. Why would someone need to know how old you are? (Movie tickets, reduced meal rates, class at school, and so on.)

Worksheet 1.4: Here are some examples of people wanting to know some dates. Not all of them need to know your birth date, however. I want you to figure out which ones need to know the date you were born.

Answers

1. Yes   2. No   3. Yes   4. No   5. Yes

Extension Activities

1. *Everybody with This Month Game.* For practice in recognizing their birth dates, have students stand up/touch their toes/turn around, and so on if they have a birth date in a specific month. Go through the months in random order and at a fast pace!

2. *Birth date Helpers.* When you need a classroom helper, instead of drawing the student's name from a hat, use their birth dates. ("I need someone with the birth date of October 16, 1980 to run an errand for me.")

1.4   **Happy Birthday to Me!**

The people shown on this Worksheet want to know some dates from you. Draw a birthday cake if they want to know your birth date, and write the date on the line. If it is another date that they want, leave the line blank.

1.
   I want to get you a wonderful birthday present! When were you born?

   _____

2.
   When did you have your last dentist appointment?

   _____

3.
   Are you old enough to ride the bumper cars? How old are you?

   _____

4. *Your Mother looks so young! What is her birthdate?*

   _____

5.
   I think we were born in the same month and the same year. Tell me your birthdate.

   _____

1.5 My Family

Objective

Upon request or in appropriate situations, the student will name the members of his or her family.

Discussion

Teacher: How many of you have a brother or sister? Who else is in your family? Is a pet dog a family member? There are many ways to describe what a family is. It could be the people you live with, people who take care of each other, or people who are related to each other. We are going to say that a family is a group of people who are together in some way. If we talk about your home family, that will mean the people who live at your house. There may be people who are related to you who do not usually live at your house. Those people are part of your family, too, but not your home family.

Worksheet 1.5: Today you are going to match some students with their home families. Read the clues and see if you can figure out which family the student is from. Match the family group with the student, and write the letter on the line.

Answers

1. Mary—D   2. Marcos—B   3. Frank—E   4. Kelly—A   5. David—C

Extension Activities

1. *Family Portrait.* Have students draw or bring in pictures of family members. They may wish to portray their natural family if this differs from the people who live in their home. They should feel free to include a divorced parent and siblings who do not live in their home. Use a loose definition of "family" for this activity. Have students introduce their families to each other.

2. *Family Awards.* Have a designated Family Day and give awards for the student with the most siblings, youngest sibling, tallest mother, newest in town, and so on. Students may wish to award their own families for some unique attribute they know about.

1.5   My Family

Here are some students who are describing their families. Match each student with the group that is his or her family. Write the letter assigned to that group on the line by the student.

Mary

> I have a big brother, John, and two little sisters, Sandy and Jane. I live with my mother and my grandmother. That's my family!

A

Marcos

> I have a little baby sister and an older sister. We live with my father and my stepmother.

B

Frank

> My parents are divorced. I spend the week with my mother and stepfather. My stepfather has one son. I don't have any other brothers or sisters.

C

Kelly

> I live with my mother and my aunt. I have one sister. There are a lot of women at my house.

D

David

> My parents are away so while they are gone my family is my Aunt Carol and Uncle John. They don't have any other kids.

E

1.6 My Parents and Where They Are

Objective

Upon request or in appropriate situations, the student will state where his or her parents can be reached.

Discussion

Teacher: Have you ever known of anyone who got hurt or sick at school? What happened? (For example, they called a parent.) What would happen to you if you had an accident at school? How could your parents be reached?

Worksheet 1.6: All your students need to reach their parents or another person who can help them. Some of them know enough information to get through, and some of them don't. Write yes or no if the student could or could not locate his or her parent or guardian with the information given. Then discuss what they could do here if they needed to get in touch with someone at their house if there was an emergency or important situation.

Answers

1. No (needs to know which hospital) 2. Yes 3. Yes 4. No (needs to know work schedule)
5. No (needs work phone number)

Extension Activities

1. *Backup Plan.* Have students individually relate what procedure should be followed if the parents needed to be contacted in an emergency. Although this information should be on an emergency card in the school office, students should be able to state the names of a neighbor, friend, or relative who could be called on if necessary.

2. *School Nurse.* Have students role-play situations in which one has an ailment (they can be creative as to the various maladies) and the other is the "school nurse." Have students practice giving appropriate information clearly and completely.

1.6 My Parents and Where They Are

These students need to get in touch with their parents. Some of them do not know the information to contact them. If students have enough information, write yes on the line. If they need more information, write no on the line.

1. My leg really hurts. Could you call my dad? He works at the hospital, but I don't remember which one.

_____

2. I forgot my math book! It has all of my homework in it! My mother is at home and our phone number is 367-2440.

_____

3.  It's raining — I wonder if my stepfather can pick me up after school. Let's see.. he works at Smith's Service Station and the number is 274-3093.

_____

4. I need to tell my grandmother about the meeting at school tonight. I know she's at her job, but I don't know if she works today or not.

_____

5.  I'm supposed to call Dad when I'm ready to come home. My home number is 324-5827 but Dad's at work right now.

_____

1.7 Meet My Teacher

Objective

Upon request or in appropriate situations, the student will state the name of his or her teacher, grade or class in school, and/or the name of the school he or she attends.

Discussion

Teacher: Pretend you have a friend from far away who is coming to visit you for a day at school. What information would you need to give him or her so that you could be located? Why do you think it is important to know the name of your teacher? (So someone would know what class you're in.)

Worksheet 1.7: Here are some students who need to know the name of their teacher and what grade they are in. Use the clues to figure out whose class they are in. Write your answers on the lines.

Answers

1. Mrs. Martin   2. Miss Alexander   3. Mr. King   4. Mrs. Martin   5. Mrs. Martin
6. Mr. King   7. Miss Alexander   8. Miss Alexander   9. Mr. King (some assumptions were made here)
10. Miss Alexander

Extension Activities

1. *Teacher Hall of Fame.* Locate pictures of all the teachers in your school. Assign students to find out the names, grades, or classes taught by the teachers. Put that and other interesting information on posters and arrange them for display.

2. *Guest Visitor.* Have teachers drop in for a five-minute interview by your class. Assign students to prepare some questions for the teacher. Teachers may wish to display or tell something interesting about themselves to share with your class as well.

1.7　　　　　　　　Meet My Teacher

Below are students from the classes of Mr. King, who teaches fourth grade; Mrs. Martin, who teaches fifth grade; and Miss Alexander, who teaches sixth grade. Help the students get to the right class. Write the name of the teacher next to the student who is in his or her class.

Mr. King

Mrs. Martin

Miss. Alexander

1. Jason is in fifth grade this year. _____

2. Mark was in fifth grade last year. _____

3. Jenny likes having a man for a teacher. _____

4. Kim had Mr. King last year. _____

5. Fred does not have Miss Alexander or a man for a teacher. _____

6. Ramon has to repeat fourth grade this year. _____

7. Angel has the same teacher that Mark has. _____

8. Zac is a year ahead of Jason in school. _____

9. Kara's teacher is not married. Kara is not in sixth grade. _____

10. Karin was in fourth grade two years ago. _____

1.8 Medical Needs

Objective

Upon request or in appropriate situations, the student will state what medication or medical needs he or she requires.

Discussion

Teacher: Sometimes people need special medication to help themselves stay healthy. Can any of you give some examples of why special medicine may be required? (Seizure control, blood pressure, and so on.) *Medication* is a big word that refers to the medicine that a doctor has told you to take. It is not the same thing as taking drugs in a bad way. This is something that assists a person who needs extra help. Why is it important for someone to be able to tell what medication he or she needs? (To get help in a hurry.) Suppose someone needs immediate medical attention. Can you think of any examples? (Nosebleeds, seizures.) How do glasses help someone?

Worksheet 1.8: Here are a few examples of students who have specific medical needs. Read about their situations and decide what the best thing to do is in each case. Circle the letter of the best answer. Then we'll discuss your choices.

Answers

1. d   2. a   3. c

Extension Activities

1. *School Nurse Visit.* Invite the school nurse to stop in and explain some basic medical situations and how they are handled, such as the need to wear glasses, epilepsy, or specific handicaps. Emphasize that medication or medical advice is to be followed specifically.

2. *Book Reports.* Check out books from your school or local library dealing with children who have specific medical conditions, such as diabetes or leukemia. Read them to your class or have capable students do book reports on them and discuss as a class.

1.8   **Medical Needs**

Each of the following students has a medical need. Show what that student should do by circling the best answer in each story.

1. Kim often gets nosebleeds at school. Her mother told her to pinch her nose tightly when it bleeds. The next time it happens, what should Kim do?

   a. Call her mother and go home from school.

   b. Let her teacher know.

   c. Rush to the bathroom with several friends.

   d. Pinch her nose.

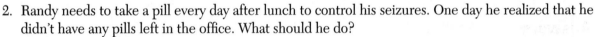

2. Randy needs to take a pill every day after lunch to control his seizures. One day he realized that he didn't have any pills left in the office. What should he do?

   a. Let the school nurse know to call home.

   b. Hope that he doesn't have a seizure.

   c. Take someone else's pill.

   d. Go home.

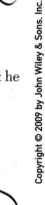

3. Jeff had an operation on his leg and is supposed to keep his leg raised for a few hours each afternoon. One afternoon he wanted to play outside with his friends. What should he do?

   a. Call his doctor and ask if he can go out this time.

   b. Tell his teacher that it is OK to go out.

   c. Keep his leg raised.

   d. Have his friends play football inside the classroom.

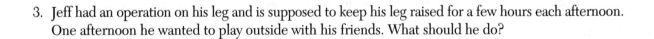

1.9 Emergency!

Objective

The student will recognize an emergency situation and follow appropriate procedures.

Discussion

Teacher: What is an ambulance for? (To help in emergency situations, accidents.) Who are the people on board the ambulance? What kind of training do you think they have to have? An emergency is a situation that needs attention right away. Can you give me some examples of emergencies? (Accident, fire, and so on.) Unless you know exactly what to do, it is best to call someone who can help with the situation. Who are some people you can call? (Adults, police, firefighter, doctor, and so on.)

Worksheet 1.9: Here are some examples of emergency situations and some students who have ideas as to what to do. Decide in each case which students are doing the best thing. We will discuss your answers.

Answers

1. A   2. C   3. B

Extension Activities

1. *Red Cross.* The Red Cross publishes numerous easy-to-understand pamphlets dealing with basic first aid and emergency situations. As a class project, list common emergency situations and come up with viable solutions. You may wish to show a filmstrip or video on basic first aid. Be sure students are aware of their limitations. (CPR, for example, should be performed only by trained persons.)

2. *Larry the Loser.* Have students write a silly story about a careless person who gets into dangerous situations (walking down the middle of a street, throwing matches around, and the like) and causes numerous emergencies. Invent a superhero ("Carlos the Careful"?) who teaches Larry some safety skills. Identify the emergencies created and appropriate action to be taken in each.

1.9   **Emergency!**

Here are some situations that need attention right away. Circle the letter assigned to the student who you think is doing the best thing.

1. Situation: There is smoke coming from the trash can in your garage.

2. Situation: A strange dog bit a little girl on the arm.

3. Situation: Your friend fell while playing and his head is bleeding.

                                              Chapter 1: Relating Basic Information

1.10 My Vital Statistics

Objective

Upon request or in appropriate situations, the student will state his or her current height and weight.

Discussion

Teacher: How tall do you think I am? How much do you think I weigh? Well, I'm not going to tell you how much I weigh, but I bet you can tell me how to find out. What tools could you use to find out these things? (Scale, height chart.) Why is it important to know how tall you are? (Buying clothes, getting into rides at the fair.) Why is it important to know how much you weigh? (Monitoring health, staying in shape.) Your height is how tall you are in feet and inches. Your weight is how many pounds you weigh on a scale.

Worksheet 1.10: This Worksheet shows four students and their heights and weights. Sometimes rides and exhibits at fairs have restrictions or limits for your height and weight. Write the names of the students who could go on the rides or exhibits shown on the Worksheet.

Answers

1. Fred, Jason   2. Sandy, Maria   3. None   4. Sandy, Maria   5. Sandy, Fred, Maria

Extension Activities

1. *My Height and Weight.* Take your students to the nurse's office and have each measured and weighed. Have them write the numbers on a picture or drawing of themselves. If you do this at the beginning of the year, repeat the activity after a few months to note changes.

2. *My Day at the Fair.* After students know their height and weight, have them figure out which rides or exhibits they could participate in using the Worksheet.

1.10   # My Vital Statistics

Here are the numbers for the height and weight of some students. Write the names of the students who could do the activities shown on the lines below the pictures.

Sandy
Height : 4ft. 3 in.
Weight : 75 lbs.

Fred
5ft. 1 in
100 lbs.

Jason
5ft. 11 in.
130 lbs.

Maria
4ft. 1½ in.
67 lbs.

1. Roller Coaster

You must be at least 5feet tall to ride this ride!

_____

2. Swinging Bridge

Don't go on this if you weigh more than 90 pounds!

_____

3. Fun House

Only people shorter than 4 feet can go in the Fun House!

_____

4. Teeter-Totter

This is for people under 80 pounds!

_____

5. Narrow Pass

You'll get stuck if you weigh more than 120 pounds!

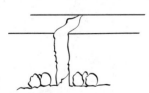

_____

         Chapter 1: Relating Basic Information

1.11 After School

Objective

Upon request or in appropriate situations, the student will give information regarding pick-up, care, or transportation plans for after school.

Discussion

Teacher: When school is out, I bet a lot of you go home to your parents. But a lot of students don't go home after school. What are some things that might happen after school? (Go to a friend's house, daycare at babysitter's house, child care at school, practice for a sport, Brownies.) Some kids are not picked up by their parents because the parents work or may not be able to drive to school. Who are some other people who might pick up students after school? (Relatives, a designated adult, older sibling.)

Worksheet 1.11: Which of these students is giving clear information about what will happen to them after school? Put a check mark next to each good example.

Answers

1. Check mark   2. No   3. No   4. Check mark   5. No   6. Check mark

Extension Activities

1. *Prepare Your Partner.* Have students gather in pairs. Take turns having the students ask each other specific after-school questions, such as: How are you getting home tonight? What days do you stay after for practice/meetings? What bus do you ride?

2. *Change of Plans.* Your school may have a specific procedure for handling the cancellation of programs or late-arriving parents. Make sure that students are familiar with their backup plan if a parent is late, there is bad weather, a bus has changed routes, and so on. Some students get very upset if there is a change in routine; preparing them for this possibility will pay off in the future.

1.11   After School

Which of these students is giving clear information about what will happen to them after school? Put a check mark next to each good example.

1. My dad has to work late tonight, so my Uncle Bob is picking me up. Here's the note.

2. I'm supposed to ride a different bus home, but I don't know which one.

3. Do I have a meeting for Cub Scouts tonight? I can't remember if I'm supposed to stay or not.

4. I'm supposed to ride bus #37 home tonight. My mom called the office already.

5. I want to go to Makayla's house tonight. Can I just ride with her on the bus?

6. My babysitter is picking me up after the basketball game, so I am not riding the bus home tonight. I have a pass from the office.

1.12 Lost and Found

Objective

The student will provide a plan for returning or locating a lost item.

Discussion

Teacher: Everybody loses things sometimes. What are some things that you have lost? (Homework, clothes, book, camera.) Did you get the items back? How? (Ran an ad in the paper, talked to people, retraced steps.) Have you ever found something that belonged to someone else that was probably pretty important? (Medicine, homework, iPod.) What happened? We are going to talk about what to do if you have lost something, and also what you can do if you find something that is important to someone else.

Worksheet 1.12: These students have lost or found something. Write what each student could say or do to get help.

Answers

1. Talk to a teacher or coach.
2. Ask the bus driver if anyone found a book.
3. Take the phone to the office.
4. Ask friends if they have seen his sweatshirt.
5. Talk to the lunch people about finding it.
6. Give the bag to the bus driver.

Extension Activities

1. *"Missing" Ads.* Have students select an item that they would miss if it became lost. Write an ad describing the article so that someone could easily identify it. Students may wish to attach a picture. Alert them to pay attention to unique details that will help identify the article.
2. *"The Day I Found…"* Have students write a short story in which they find an unusual item. (A talking dog, a flying carpet, a robot.) Write about what they would do with it for the day and how they eventually would try to return it to its owner or destination.

1.12   Lost and Found

These students have lost or found something. Write what each student could say or do to get help.

1. William found a wallet with $30 in it under the bleachers at a basketball game in the gym.

    _____

2. Sydney can't find her reading book. She thinks she might have left it on the bus.

    _____

3. Lauren found a cell phone on the playground.

    _____

4. Dylan took off his Chicago Bears sweatshirt while he was playing with friends after school. When he was getting ready to leave, it was gone.

    _____

5. Victoria left her retainer on a napkin while eating her lunch. She realized it was gone about an hour later.

    _____

6. Noah felt something by his feet on the bus. It was a little plastic bag with a prescription bottle in it for medicine.

    _____

Telephone Skills

PARENT LETTER #2: TELEPHONE SKILLS

Dear Parents,

Our next survival skill is that of using the telephone for routine calls, finding specific information, and handling emergency situations. We will be discussing how to operate a phone (regular touch-tone phones and cell phones), how to ask for and give information over the phone, and how to use a phone directory to locate information in the White (residences) and Yellow (businesses) Pages.

Some of these activities may ask you to help your child make supervised phone calls to practice dialing and requesting information. They may be asked to call another student in the class to pass on a message or to call a specific business to find out more information for a class assignment. Please allow your child supervised access to your phone if possible.

Some children have cell phones. Please go over your specific rules for using the cell phone with your child and be sure that he or she knows how to operate the basic functions.

Thanks again for your help!

Sincerely,

_____

Teacher

Skill Sheet #2: Progress Report

| + mastered |
| √ emerging |
| − not mastered |

Student name	Dialing the Number	Using a Cell Phone	Using 911, 411, and 0	Making Emergency Phone Calls	Obtaining Information	Giving Information	Taking a Message	Leaving a Message on an Answering Machine	Using the Telephone Directory: White Pages	Using the Telephone Directory: Yellow Pages	Comments

2.1 Dialing the Number

Objective

The student will correctly dial, press, or use a short-cut key to access a phone number.

Discussion

Teacher: If I wanted to contact your parents at home, what would I have to do? (Go to a phone and dial the number.) Of course, I would have to know what the correct phone number was and I would have to know how to operate the phone. There are many different kinds of phones these days. Who knows what a touch-tone phone is? (Has buttons.) Does anyone know what a rotary dial phone is? (You have to find the number and turn a wheel.) And, of course, what is a cell phone? (A smaller phone that you can carry with you.) Each of these phones operates a little differently. It is good to know how to work them so that you can use them properly.

Worksheet 2.1: These three pages show examples of three different kinds of phones: a touch-tone phone, a rotary dial phone, and a typical cell phone. Practice accessing each phone number on each phone. Put a check mark next to each number after you have finished.

Answers

You may wish to have students work in pairs to monitor each other.

Extension Activities

1. *Phone Chain.* If appropriate, make a phone book of numbers for students in the class. Start a message with a designated student (perhaps in alphabetical order?) and have each student repeat the message to the next student. It could be something as simple as "Wear green to school tomorrow" or "Bring something to eat for Read-N-Munch."

2. *Practice Calls.* With parent approval and supervision, assign students practice in making local calls at home. The purpose can be as simple as finding out what time the zoo opens, what the weather report is for the next day, or how much it costs for a haircut.

Name _____ **Date** _____

2.1   Dialing the Number

The first page shows a touch-tone phone. The second page shows a rotary dial phone. The third page shows a cell phone. Show how you would dial the phone numbers on each type of phone. Check off each number when you are finished.

1. 324-5827 ☐

2. 871-3992 ☐

3. 641-0044 ☐

4. 788-2387 ☐

5. 632-8114 ☐

6. 322-0388 ☐

2.1 (*Continued*)

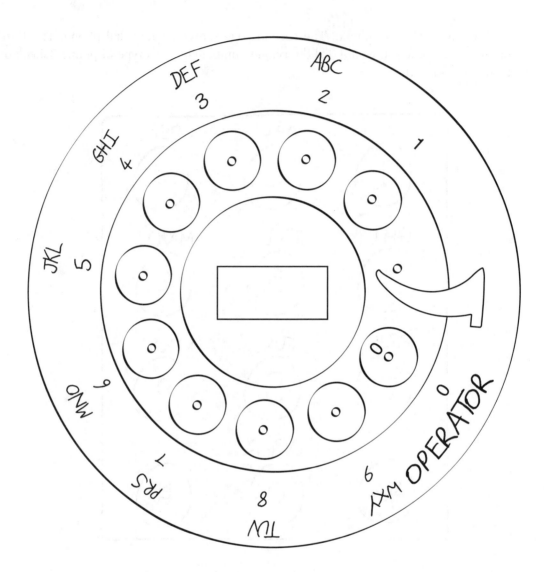

1. 324-5827 ☐

2. 871-3992 ☐

3. 641-0044 ☐

4. 788-2387 ☐

5. 632-8114 ☐

6. 322-0388 ☐

1. 324-5827 ☐

2. 871-3992 ☐

3. 641-0044 ☐

4. 788-2387 ☐

5. 632-8114 ☐

6. 322-0388 ☐

2.2 Using a Cell Phone

Objective

The student will demonstrate knowledge of basic cell phone operational skills, such as on/off, silencing, and clear.

Discussion

Teacher: How many of you have used a cell phone to make calls? How is a cell phone different from a regular phone? (Small, portable, can take pictures, play games.) You might not have your own cell phone, but you might need to use one that belongs to someone in your family. There are all kinds of cell phones, so you will have to make sure you know how to operate the one that your family has. Some things are pretty basic to all cell phones, so we will go over just a few basic things.

Worksheet 2.2: Here is an example of a simple cell phone. Read the instructions for the features of dialing, silencing, and clearing. Then answer each question on the lines provided.

Answers

1. Turn the phone on.
2. Use the CLR key to erase your mistake.
3. Press the SEND key.
4. Turn the volume to high.
5. Turn the volume to low.
6. Turn the phone off.

Extension Activities

1. *Phone Chain.* If appropriate, make a phone book of numbers for students in the class. Start a message with a designated student (perhaps in alphabetical order?) and have It could be something as simple as "Wear green to school tomorrow" or "Bring something to eat for Read-N-Munch."

2. *Practice Calls.* With parent approval and supervision, assign students practice in making local calls at home. The purpose can be as simple as finding out what time the zoo opens, what the weather report is for the next day, or how much it costs for a haircut.

2.2   Using a Cell Phone

Welcome to Super-Simple Cell Phone!!

ON/OFF: To turn the cell phone ON, press the appropriate key for three seconds. To turn the cell phone OFF, press the same key for three seconds.

Dialing: After the phone is ON, press the number buttons to make your call. Then press the appropriate SEND key to complete the call.

Clearing: If you make a mistake while pressing the numbers, press the CLR key to erase your mistake.

Volume: The button on the side shows how LOUD your phone will ring. Press the top of the key to make it ring louder; press the bottom of the key to make it ring softer. The final setting will turn the ring to SILENCE.

1. You are supposed to call your mother after school. What is the first thing you should do?

   _____

2. You dialed the first four numbers, but you realize you made a mistake on the third number. What should you do?

   _____

3. You dialed all of the numbers, but nothing happened. What button should you press next?

   _____

4. Your mother says she will call you back in five minutes. You want to make sure you hear the phone ring, so what should you do with the volume key?

   _____

5. After your mother calls, you are going to wait for her in the school office. The secretary looks very busy and you don't want to interrupt her. What should you do with the volume key?

   _____

6. You get home and are done with the phone for the day. What should you do?

   _____

2.3 Using 911, 411, and 0

Objective

The student will identify situations in which he or she should use the 911, 411, or 0 calls on a phone.

Discussion

Teacher: There are a few special numbers that you can use from a phone to help you in certain situations. For example, if you are in an emergency situation, such as a fire or a car accident, you should call 911. This will connect you to a special operator who can send the right kind of help. If you just want to get some information about finding a phone number for a person or business, you can call 411. If you are having problems with your phone or have another nonemergency question, you can call the operator by dialing 0.

Worksheet 2.3: Which number—911, 411, or 0—should you use for the following situations?

Answers

1. 911   2. 911   3. 0   4. 411   5. 911   6. 0

Extension Activities

1. *Emergency!* Write examples of emergency situations on index cards. Have students select a card at random and practice dialing 911 and explaining the situation to the operator. Remind students to speak slowly, give their name and address if appropriate, and relay information correctly.

2. *Information, Please.* With parent supervision, have students practice using the 411 information line to obtain specific information/phone numbers. You may wish to make a list of examples for students and parents to use as practice. ("What is the number for Mr. Green on Washington Street?" "I am looking for the number for Flower Power Florists, but I am not sure of the address.")

2.3   # Using 911, 411, and 0

1. You light a candle in the kitchen and suddenly the paper towels are in flames! Your parents are not home, and the fire is starting to spread! _____

2. It is late at night and you hear someone in the yard trying to break open a door. Your father tells you to call for help. _____

3. You dialed a phone number but the line keeps going back to a dial tone. You keep trying, but your call doesn't go through. _____

4. Your best friend moved to a new neighborhood and you would like to call him. All you know is that he lives on James Street. _____

5. You are taking your dog for a walk and hear a loud crash! Two cars collided at an intersection. You can't tell if anyone is hurt, but the cars look pretty bad! _____

6. There was a storm and your phone has a lot of static on it. You wonder if someone is going to fix it or not. _____

2.4 Making Emergency Phone Calls

Objective

The student will identify what information should be relayed in an emergency situation.

Discussion

Teacher: Remember we talked about emergency situations? What are some examples? (Fire, accident, poisoning.) Instead of calling the operator, who could you call for specific help with emergencies? (Fire department, police department, poison control.) Many cities use 911 for emergencies. What would happen if we dialed that number? (Talk to an operator who would direct your call to the proper source.) What would you tell the person you talk to about the emergency? What would they need to know? (Who you are, your problem, address, phone number.)

Worksheet 2.4: This shows some examples of emergency calls. The caller got through to someone, but look at the messages. Something is missing from each one. Before the caller can get help, more information is needed. Supply the information needed on the line next to each situation. In some examples, several parts are missing.

Answers

1. Complete name, where, phone
2. Phone
3. Phone
4. Where, phone
5. Name, where, phone
6. Name, what, where, phone

Extension Activities

1. *Help!* Compile emergency situations and randomly distribute them to students. Have students work in pairs to practice giving complete information to relay to someone for help.
2. *Emergency Helpers.* If possible, have a police officer or emergency medical technician (EMT) visit your class and discuss why giving correct information over the phone is important. Ask them to relate some incidents in which a phone call and a good message saved someone's life.

Discussion

Teacher: Let's review some emergency situations in which you might need to make a phone call. Can you give some examples?

Name _____ Date _____

2.4 Making Emergency Phone Calls

These students are calling for help in an emergency. But there is a problem. What is missing from each of the phone calls? Write what information is needed on the line next to each situation.

WHAT   NAME   WHERE   PHONE

1. Help, help, help! I think the house is on fire! Get over here right away! My name is Sally and I'm scared!

   _____

2. My name is Eric Smith, I live at 201 North Street, and I think there is a car accident in front of my house.

   _____

3. Is this the police? There is a growling dog running around the neighborhood. My name is Jane Blayne, and I live at 300 W. Apple Grove.

   _____

4. I need to talk to someone at the hospital! My grandmother fell down and I think she's hurt. My name is Juan Ricardo. Hurry!

   _____

5. Doctor? My little sister swallowed something and she's turning green. What should I do?

   _____

6. Fire department? Help!

   _____

2.5 Obtaining Information

Objective

The student will use an appropriate source to obtain information about a specific situation.

Discussion

Teacher: If you wanted to find out what the weather is going to be like, how could you use the phone? Would you call the operator? (No, use prerecorded service.) What if you wanted to find out a friend's number if that person moved to another city? The phone company offers a service called directory assistance that will give you phone numbers without using the operator. (Check with your local phone company to determine the procedure.) What are some other numbers you can call for information?

Worksheet 2.5: Here are some situations where people need to call for information about something. Match each situation with the source that will help them out. Write the letter on the line.

Answers

1. e   2. d   3. f   4. b   5. g   6. h   7. a   8. c

Extension Activities

1. *I Want to Know.* Have students list three questions that they want to find out about (similar to those on the Worksheet). Have them exchange questions and work on each other's situations to find an appropriate source to find the answer.

2. *Now I Know.* As a follow-up to the first activity, have students actually call one of their sources to find out the answer (for example, a time, a place, a quantity).

2.5   Obtaining Information

The students want to find out some information using the phone. Match each student with the source that will help them find out what they want to know. Write the letter on the line following each situation.

1. Alex wants to know what the weather will be like this afternoon. _____

2. Bridget wants to know the phone number of a friend who just moved to a new city. _____

3. Carl wants to know what time the zoo opens on Saturday. _____

4. Tara wants to order a pizza. _____

5. Michael wants to call his favorite radio station to ask them to play his favorite song. _____

6. Randy wants to know if the bike he ordered has come in yet. _____

7. Debbie wants to know if the library has the latest mystery story by her favorite author. _____

8. Keith and Chad can't wait to see the horror movie at the local theater, but they don't know what time it starts. _____

a. Greenville Public Library

b. Hank's Pizza Store

c. Town and Country Movies

d. Directory assistance

e. Local weather

f. Westville Zoo

g. WZQD radio station

h. Center Street Sporting Goods

2.6 Giving Information

Objective

The student will provide appropriate and accurate information to a caller.

Discussion

Teacher: When you pick up the phone after it rings, what happens next? (Say "hello.") Then what? (Find out what the person wants.) What are some reasons why people call you or your home? (Talk to someone, ask a question, and so on.) Usually people call with a specific reason; they want to know something or tell something. If someone wants to know something, how can you help that person? (Tell them what they want to know.) How much should you tell a stranger? Would you tell them that you are home alone? Why? Is there a polite way to give information? What words could you use? (Please.)

Worksheet 2.6: This Worksheet shows students giving out information over the phone. One student in each situation is doing a much better job than the other. Circle the student who is giving information appropriately. Then we will discuss your answers.

Answers

1. B   2. A   3. A   4. B   5. B   6. B   7. A

Extension Activities

1. *It's for You.* Have students monitor the number of calls to their home after school and the purpose of the call. Compare responses. Try to conclude what types of information are most commonly requested.

2. *Service with a Smile.* Have students practice giving information in a polite versus an offhand or surly manner. Discuss the importance of a friendly telephone voice. (Good impression.)

2.6   Giving Information

These students have just answered the phone. Someone wants some information. Circle the student who you think is giving the best information to help the caller.

A   B

1. Hello, I want to speak to your father, please.
   - What do you want to know? Am I in trouble?
   - I'll get him. Just a minute, please.

2. What time will your sister be home?
   - She'll be home in about an hour.
   - Beats me.

3. Is this the Johnson home?
   - Yes, it is.
   - Why do you want to know?

4. Is this the Smith home?
   - Boy, do you have a wrong number.
   - No. I'm sorry you must have the wrong number.

5. Would you like to contribute $100 to our charity?
   - Sure, why not?
   - You will have to talk to my father about that.

6. Good morning! I am selling magazines. Would you like to hear about them?
   - I hate to read.
   - You should probably talk to my parents. They will be home at five o'clock.

7. Could I please speak to your mother?
   - I'm sorry, She's not available right now. Could you call back at 3:00?
   - She's not here. I'm in the house all alone.

Chapter 2: Telephone Skills   **47**

2.7 Taking a Message

Objective

After hearing a brief message from a (hypothetical) caller, the student will accurately state or write down the message.

Discussion

Teacher: When someone calls your home for a parent or brother or sister and they aren't home, what usually happens? Do your parents get mad when they find out you forgot to tell them that someone important called? Have you ever missed any important calls? How does taking a message help? A message is simply writing down who the caller is and what he or she wants to know. It doesn't always have to be written down, but how could that help? (Less likely to forget, get mixed up.) What information should you include on a message? (Who called, phone number, message content.)

Worksheet 2.7: Here are some phone call messages that need to be written down. On the side of the paper, jot down what you think is the important part of the message. Remember to include who called, his or her phone number if necessary, and the important part of the message (not every single word).

Answers

(Examples)

1. Dad, Mr. Richardson will meet you at usual time.
2. Sis, Randy called and will call back.
3. Mom, call Phyllis at 877–2004.
4. Brother, Bob will call you at 9:30.
5. Aunt, watch news on Channel 10 tonight.
6. P.O. called—get package before 5.

Extension Activities

1. *Need More Information.* Prepare similar phone messages, but omit certain pieces of information, such as the caller's name or phone number. Have students ask questions to obtain the complete message.
2. *Message Sheets.* Obtain or have students create small message pads. Discuss what information should be included. Have students use them at home and bring them in to school (if the messages aren't too personal) to discuss.

2.7   **Taking a Message**

Here are some phone calls from people who want you to take a message. What could you write down so you wouldn't forget to give the message to the right person?

1.

Tell your father that I will meet him at the usual time. My name is Mr. Richardson. Thank you. Good-bye.

2.

This is Randy. I'll call your sister later.

3.

Have your mother call me at 877-2004. My name is Phyllis.

4.

I'm Bob. I don't have a phone, but I will call your brother back at nine-thirty.

5.

Tell your aunt to be sure to watch the news tonight on channel 10.

6.

This is the post office. You have a package to pick up before 5 o'clock.

2.8 Leaving a Message on an Answering Machine

Objective

The student will appropriately give information to an answering machine after making a phone call to a number.

Discussion

Teacher: Many people aren't home during the day and miss some important phone calls. Or some people are gone a lot and don't have anyone at home to take messages. What do those people do? (Get an answering machine.) How does an answering machine work? (Has recorded message, lets people record a message.) What does the answering machine tell the caller? (Probably who he has reached, what kind of message to leave.) What should the caller do if he wants to leave a message? (Talk after the beep.) What should the caller say in the message? (Brief point—not long conversation.)

Worksheet 2.8: Here are some answering machine messages to you, the caller. How would you respond to them? Write your answer on the cartoon next to the answering machine.

Answers

(Examples)

1. Hi, this is (name) and my number is (number).
2. I'm (name), today is (date), it's (time). Call me!
3. This is (name). I need to know what time you're coming over.
4. My name is (name). I'm calling for (name), and I wanted to let you know that (message).

Extension Activities

1. *Recorded Conversations.* If you have an answering machine or know of someone who does and who wouldn't mind participating in this activity, have students call and listen to the recording. If possible, have them leave a message.
2. *Funny Recordings.* Some people are quite creative in their recorded messages. Locate some and tape them for the students. You may wish to have students use a tape recorder and design their own recorded answering message.

2.8   Leaving a Message on an Answering Machine

These are some recordings from an answering machine. How would you answer them? Write what you would say in the balloon next to each machine.

Good morning! I'm not here to answer the phone, but I'd like to know who called. Leave your name and phone number after the beep and I'll call you back.

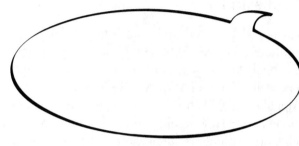

Hello, you have reached the Smith house. Please leave your name, the date and time that you called, and I'll call you back when we return.

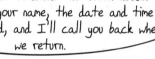
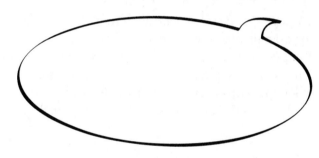

This is 874-3261. We're not able to answer your call right now, but leave your name and a short message. Thank you.

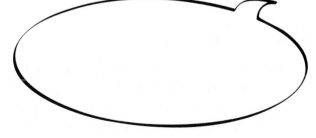

Hello! I'm sorry we can't come to the phone right now, but we'll be happy to call you back later. Tell us who you are, who you want to talk to and leave a message. Bye!

2.9 Using the Telephone Directory: White Pages

Objective

The student will identify phone numbers located in the White Pages of the directory and locate important personal numbers.

Discussion

Teacher: If I wanted to call each of you tonight after school, would I have to memorize all those phone numbers? Why would that be difficult? (So many.) What would I have to do to find your numbers? (Look in school directory, telephone book.) What could I use to look up numbers of people I may not know very well? (Phone book.) Are the numbers just scattered around in the book? How are they organized? (Alphabetically.) Why? (Easier to find, systematic.) How many of you know if your phone number is in the phone book? How would you go about finding it? Are there only families listed in the phone book? (No.) What other numbers are in there? (Schools, businesses, services.) In general, though, the White Pages is a list of people in a community, their phone numbers, and addresses.

Worksheet 2.9: (Decide ahead of time on eight names that have some meaning or interest to the students; for example, names of other teachers, the mayor, a local celebrity, people in the class, and so on.) Today I am going to have to work on finding the phone numbers and/or addresses of several people. You will have to use the phone book to find this information. Remember to use letters at the top to help you know where to start looking. (You may wish to have students work in pairs or use a small portion of the phone book and Xerox a few consecutive pages to make this more manageable.)

Answers

(Prepare an answer key ahead of time, using the names you selected.)

Extension Activities

1. *White Pages Races.* Obtain multiple copies of the local phone book of whatever source you are using. Divide students into two teams and have students race against each other (two at a time) to locate the name you call out.
2. *White Pages Addresses.* Students will realize that not only phone numbers but also addresses are printed in the phone book. Have students identify two or three neighbors who live on the same street or same apartment complex and look them up in the phone book. They should find that the same street is listed for the neighbors.

2.9   Using the Telephone Directory: White Pages

Your teacher will help you identify several names to look up in the phone book. Find the name; then write down the phone number, address, or page where it is found in the phone book.

	Phone number	Address	Page
Name 1			
Name 2			
Name 3			
Name 4			
Name 5			
Name 6			
Name 7			

2.10 Using the Telephone Directory: Yellow Pages

Objective

When asked to find a general service or business, the student will correctly locate and identify an advertiser in the Yellow Pages to fit the description.

Discussion

Teacher: There is another part of our phone book that we need to look at besides the White Pages. What is it? (Yellow Pages.) What kind of information is included there? (Business.) The Yellow Pages book contains numbers and information about businesses in town. But companies are not arranged in alphabetical order by the name of the business at first; they are arranged according to the type of business they are in. Who can give me some examples of businesses in town? (List on board.) If I would want to know of all the service stations, for example, what would be included? (List several local stations.) If I wanted to know of places where I could buy a refrigerator, what places of business might be included? (List several.) To use the Yellow Pages, you first have to decide what you are looking for, and then use the Yellow Pages to find all your choices. Remember, after you have your key word, you can use alphabetical order to find the names of different businesses.

Worksheet 2.10: Here are situations in which someone needs to use the Yellow Pages. The first thing is to find the key word so you will know where to look up the companies in that business. For the examples on the Worksheet, circle the best answer.

Answers

    1. Jewelry 2. Motels 3. Restaurants 4. Refrigerators 5. Shelter   6. Churches
    7. Dentists 8. Music stores

Extension Activities

1. *Give Me a Name.* For each situation on the Worksheet, have students use the Yellow Pages to look up the key word and find at least one business that could help with that service.

2. *Christmas (Holiday) List.* Have students make an early Christmas (Holidays) list of items that they would like to obtain. Then decide on a key word (toys, bicycles, camping equipment) for each item and proceed to have the student look up businesses in the Yellow Pages that could supply that item.

2.10   Using the Telephone Directory: Yellow Pages

To use the Yellow Pages, think of the best word or two that would help you find the business or service you need. Read each of the following situations, and decide which words would best help each person find the business that they need. Circle your answer.

1. Mrs. Smith wants a new diamond necklace. She wants to know where to look for one.

    Printers   Jewelry   Photographers

2. Mr. Riley is staying overnight in a city. He needs to find a place to stay.

    Laundry   Mobile homes   Motels

3. John and Marcia want to go out to eat.

    Restaurants   Florists   Radio Stations

4. Max has a broken refrigerator.

    Refrigerators   Pizza   Firewood

5. Sally would like a new puppy for a pet.

    Zoos   Shelter   Schools

6. The Robinson family just moved and are looking for a church close by.

    Hotels   Child care   Churches

7. Ben broke a tooth playing hockey and needs to see a dentist.

    Doctors   Bowling   Dentists

8. Peter wants to get new strings for his guitar.

    Lawn Mowers   Music Stores   Locksmiths

Chapter 3

Money Skills

PARENT LETTER #3: MONEY SKILLS

Dear Parents,

Our next group of lessons centers on money—counting it, using it, and saving it. If your child does not get an allowance, this may be a good time to talk about jobs he or she can do around the house in return for some spending money. On the other hand, earning some "saving money" is not a bad idea, either! Your child is old enough to accompany you to the bank to open a savings account for him- or herself. It is very motivating (for all of us) to set a goal and then save up the money to finally go out and get it! Whether it's a skateboard or designer jeans, a goal of saving up enough money to get something you really want is a great incentive to learn about saving.

Also consider letting your child help you count your change, hand you the correct coins from time to time, and see if you have enough money to get him or her a candy bar or other treat. Certainly it's easier for you to do it yourself, but it's an excellent opportunity for your child to practice real-life money situations.

Happy counting!

Sincerely,

_____

Teacher

Skill Sheet #3: Progress Report

	+ mastered
	√ emerging
	− not mastered

Student Name	Coins and Bills	Counting Coins	Recognizing Value of Items	Keeping Money in a Safe Place	Savings Account	Earning Money	Spending Money	Sales and Discounts	Estimating	Comments

3.1 Coins and Bills

Objective

Given examples of real and printed coins and bills, the student will identify the coin/bill.

Discussion

Teacher: I saw something at the store that I really wanted to buy. What would I need to get it? (Money, charge card.) Why do people use money? (To buy things.) Money is something used for payment, to buy something. Who knows what the different kinds of money in our country are? I'll give you a hint—one is a dime. Can you think of others? (Penny, quarter, nickel, half dollar.) A piece of metal money is called a coin. Paper money is called a bill. Can anyone think of the kinds of bills that we have? (One-dollar bill, five-dollar bill, and so on.)

Worksheet 3.1: On this Worksheet, you are going to practice looking at coins and bills and figuring out what they are. Here you will only have to match the coins and bills with the names of them. Then we will do some other activities with money. Write the letter next to the coin on the Worksheet.

Answers

1. f 2. c 3. j 4. g 5. h 6. b 7. i 8. a 9. d 10. e

Extension Activities

1. *Coin Flash Cards.* Have students make series of flash cards bearing a coin print on one side and the name on the other side. Pair students with a partner and have races in which the object is to identify the coins (ten to fifteen) in a stack without missing any.

2. *I'm Thinking Of.* Allow students to handle and observe actual coins (and bills, if desired). Have them think how they can remember which coin is which. Students find all sorts of cues to help them (the direction the person is facing, Jefferson's ponytail, the color of the coin, the ridged edge of the dime and quarter, and so on). Then have students take turns giving clues as to which coin they are thinking of.

3.1   Coins and Bills

Match the groups of coins and bills on the left with the description on the right. Write the letter of your choice on the line after the coins and bills.

1. (1¢) (5¢)

   a. Two quarters, a one-dollar bill _____

2. (1¢) (10¢)

   b. A one-dollar bill _____

3. (25¢) (5¢)

   c. One penny, one dime _____

4. (10¢) (25¢)

   d. A one-dollar bill, two dimes _____

5. (10¢) (10¢)

   e. Two one-dollar bills, two nickels, one dime _____

6. [$ 1 $]

   f. One penny, one nickel _____

7. [$ 5 $] (25¢)

   g. One dime, one quarter _____

8. (25¢) (25¢) [$ 1 $]

   h. Two dimes _____

9. [$ 1 $] (10¢) (10¢)

   i. One five-dollar bill, one quarter _____

10. [$ 1 $] (5¢) (5¢) (10¢)

11. [$ 1 $]

   j. One quarter, one nickel _____

3.2 Counting Coins

Objective

Given amounts of coins, the student will correctly count out the total amount.

Discussion

Teacher: Let's see what you know about counting money. If I wanted to have ten cents, what are some ways I could get that using coins? (One dime, two nickels, one nickel and five pennies, ten pennies.) What about twenty cents? Or thirty cents? You see, there are lots of ways I can get the amount I need. What if I gave you two nickels and three pennies? What would that amount be? (Thirteen cents.) How did you figure that out? If I gave you one quarter and one nickel, what would that be? (Thirty cents.)

Worksheet 3.2: On this sheet, you are going to practice counting the amount of money you have in coins. Remember to put the cents sign after your amount, because all of these are less than one dollar, so we call them cents. Some of you have probably figured out shortcuts to counting coins, so we'll have you tell us your secrets when we discuss the answers.

Answers

a. 12 cents b. 30 cents c. 27 cents d. 41 cents e. 60 cents f. 37 cents
g. 46 cents h. 40 cents i. 35 cents j. 51 cents

Extension Activities

1. *Counting Relays.* Divide into several teams and distribute coins to each. Call out an amount (under one dollar) or write it on the board. When you say "Go," a designated player from each team will use the coins to count out the amount. First one wins a point for their team. Then change amounts and change players.

2. *Handful of Coins.* Again using teams, place various coins into jars or cups. Players from each team pick four coins randomly from their cup. The player with the highest value (four quarters would be the most) wins a point. Then mix the coins up and repeat with the next player.

Name _____ **Date** _____

3.2   Counting Coins

Here are some groups of coins. Count the value of each group and write the amount in cents on the line next to each group.

_____ 1. (5¢) (5¢) (1¢) (1¢)

_____ 2. (25¢) (5¢)

_____ 3. (10¢) (10¢) (5¢) (1¢) (1¢)

_____ 4. (25¢) (10¢) (5¢) (1¢)

_____ 5. (25¢) (25¢) (10¢)

_____ 6. (25¢) (10¢) (1¢) (1¢)

_____ 7. (25¢) (10¢) (5¢) (5¢) (1¢)

_____ 8. (10¢) (10¢) (10¢) (10¢)

_____ 9. (25¢) (5¢) (5¢)

_____ 10. (10¢) (10¢) (10¢) (10¢) (5¢) (5¢) (1¢)

3.3 Recognizing Value of Items

Objective

Given an item or picture of an item, the student will estimate the item's approximate value in terms of dollars or cents.

Discussion

Teacher: If you had $100, could you buy a ruler from the office? Could you buy a brand-new car? What could you buy with only $1? What can you buy for a dime? Why do some things cost more than others? (Bigger, better.) How much do you think a pair of new jeans costs? What about a pencil? How do we know how much to pay for things? (Familiar with the items, advertising.)

Worksheet 3.3: Today you are going to be a detective. Your job is to find out how much these items cost. You can use pretty much any helpful source. Some examples are the newspaper, magazines, or going to a store. When we're all done, let's compare findings and see who found the cheapest and most expensive items. Write down where you found the cost. That can affect the price.

Answers

(Will vary according to your area.)

Extension Activities

1. *Ordering the Items.* Once you have established a median or average price, have students list the items in order from least expensive to most expensive. It may take them more than one try.

2. *If I Had $100.* Tell each student that they have just been given $100. They must spend all of it, without going over the amount. They must also have at least five items on their list. See what they come up with! They must list the item, the price, and the total spent. (It's harder than it seems!)

3.3   Recognizing Value of Items

Find out about how much the following items cost. You can use magazines and newspapers, real stores, or other people to help you. Compare your answers with those of other people.

How Much Is . . .	Where I Found It	Price
1. A sports car		
2. A banana		
3. A T-shirt		
4. A paperback book		
5. A pencil		
6. A candy bar		
7. A bar of soap		
8. A half gallon of ice cream		
9. A living room couch		
10. A dog from a shelter		

3.4 Keeping Money in a Safe Place

Objective

The student will identify places where money can be kept safely.

Discussion

Teacher: If I had some change, where would I most likely keep it? (Purse, pocket, wallet.) Why wouldn't I keep it in my hand? (Hard to hold.) Why not in a pocket with a hole? (Lose it.) If I had a lot of money, where would be a safe place to keep it? (Bank.) Why would keeping money in a place like a bank be safer than just letting it lie around the house? Don't people rob banks? (Still fairly safe, insurance.) How do I know I can get my money back if I leave it in a bank? (Bank book, checking account.) Name some other safe places to keep money.

Worksheet 3.4: Here are some examples of students who keep their money in various places. Decide which places you think are safe and which are not. Then we'll discuss why you picked certain ones as safe. Write *safe* or *not safe* on the line.

Answers

1. Not safe 2. Safe 3. Not safe (probably) 4. Not safe 5. Safe 6. Safe 7. Not safe
8. Safe 9. Safe 10. Safe

Extension Activities

1. *Token Economy.* For fun and experience, try using chips or paper money from construction paper to "pay" students for various activities at school. See what they do with the tokens they have accumulated. Some will probably be careless; others will devise elaborate means to safeguard their loot.

2. *Bank Search.* Using the Yellow Pages or other community resources, have students list all the banks in the community. This could also include savings and loans or any other institutions that provide a savings service for customers.

3.4   Keeping Money in a Safe Place

These students have some money. Some of them are keeping their money in safe places; others are not. Write *safe* or *not safe* after each example.

1. Frank keeps his money in his desk at school.

_____

2. Susan got a dollar from her dad. She put it in her piggy bank in her room.

_____

3. Amy is using her five-dollar bill as a bookmark in her library book.

_____

4. Ben keeps his milk money in his back pocket with a hole in it.

_____

5. Sharon has a coin purse inside her larger purse for her coins.

_____

6. Darla keeps her money in a savings account at the local bank.

SAVING Book no: 14116

_____

7. Steve gives his money to his little brother to keep for him.

_____

8. Joy keeps her change in a wallet.

_____

9. Rick gives his money to his mother to keep for him in her bank account.

SAVINGS BANK

_____

10. Ramon has a small safe with a padlock for his money.

_____

3.5 Savings Account

Objective

The student will explain how a savings account works to give the customer interest on his or her money.

Discussion

Teacher: If I borrowed some money from you, let's say $10, how much do you think I should pay you back? Does anyone think I should pay back more than $10? Why or why not? (Pay for the privilege of using the money.) We talked about a bank being a safe place to keep money. One way is to open a savings account. That's a special record of the money that you put into the bank. But there's another reason why a savings account is good for you. Does anyone know why? (Interest.) The bank will pay you interest for letting them keep and "borrow" your money. Interest is extra money for the customer, depending on how much you have in your savings account.

Worksheet 3.5: Sara is a student who wants to save $100 before Christmas. This Worksheet tells some of the things that happen to her and her money, including being paid interest on the money she keeps in her savings account. Work through each problem and see if you can figure out how much she saved before Christmas.

Answers

   1. $25   2. $37   3. $39   4. $51   5. $81   6. $86   7. $96   8. $102

Extension Activities

1. *Interest Rates.* Have students look through local newspaper bank ads to find out what they are paying for interest on savings accounts. Discuss what this means (simply) and show how a single percentage point makes a difference.

2. *Interest on Token Economy.* If you started a token economy in the classroom, begin paying "interest" on the amount that students have saved. Set up a fixed payment schedule, such as every Friday, for the interest to be paid out to students.

Name _____ **Date** _____

3.5   Savings Account

Sara the Student opened a savings account at her local bank. Solve the following problems in order and see if you can figure out how much money she has saved before Christmas. Did she reach her goal of $100?

1. Sara's aunt gave her $25 for her birthday. She immediately put it in a savings account. What's her total? _____

2. A few days later, she got $5 from her uncle in Chicago and $7 from her cousin in the next state. How much does she have now? _____

3. Sara got a note from the bank that said she had earned $2 in interest. How much money is in her savings account now? _____

4. Sara did some babysitting for her little cousin next door and earned $2 an hour. She worked for six hours. She put all of it into her savings account. How big is the account now? _____

5. Later, Sara sold her bicycle for $35. She spent $5 on candy and a book, but the rest went into the savings account. How much is in the account now? _____

6. A bank note came for Sara, telling her that she had earned $5 interest on her savings account that month. Now how much does she have? _____

7. Sara's dad told her that if she had saved at least $75 by now, he would give her $10. What do you think happened? _____

8. Sara's money earned another $6 in interest. If this is the last payment before Christmas, did Sara reach her goal of $100? _____

3.6 Earning Money

Objective

The student will list at least three ways that an adult can earn money and three ways that a student can earn money.

Discussion

Teacher: Suppose I wanted to open a savings account and earn some interest on the money to save up for something. First, I would have to get some money. How do people get money? (Someone gives it to them, they find it, they work, they invest.) Most people get their money by earning it. To earn money means to work for or provide a service for someone and then receive money as payment. How do people that you know earn money? Can people your age earn money, too? How? Sometimes people earn money by providing a service. A service is something that you do for someone to help him. What are some services that you could do for people in your neighborhood? (Wash car, mow lawn, rake leaves, babysit.)

Worksheet 3.6: Here are some services that adults or students could do to earn some money. Write down whether you think the job could be done by only an adult, or whether a student could do it. (Clarify that they should write *Student* even if an adult could perform the service, but most likely a student-aged person could earn money in this capacity.)

Answers

1. Student 2. Adult 3. Student 4. Student 5. Adult 6. Adult 7. Student 8. Adult
9. Student 10. Student

Extension Activities

1. *At Your Service.* Have students page through the local Yellow Pages ads in the phone book and list at least ten services that are described. Continue the project by having students list the title of the person most likely to perform the service (such as car repair—mechanic, weeding—gardener).

2. *Job List.* Have students compile a list of jobs that they could potentially do to earn money. Then have specific students indicate which jobs they actually have performed. They could also estimate how much each job is worth in terms of dollars per hour. Does dog-sitting pay more than babysitting? When is the best time to have a lemonade stand?

3.6   Earning Money

Here is a list of some services that people could do to help earn money. Write *Adult* if you think the service should be done by an adult. Write *Student* if someone your age could help with this service.

1. Mow the lawn for the people who live next door. _____

2. Repair an engine in a car. _____

3. Walk a dog every day after school. _____

4. Babysit the children who live in your neighborhood. _____

5. Put a new roof on a two-story house. _____

6. Put a cast on a broken arm. _____

7. Deliver newspapers. _____

8. Drive a school bus. _____

9. Rake leaves. _____

10. Sell lemonade in the summer in your front yard. _____

Chapter 3: Money Skills

3.7 Spending Money

Objective

The student will identify at least three appropriate items or ways that he or she could spend a designated amount of money.

Discussion

Teacher: After I have saved money for a while, I may decide that I wish to spend it. What are some things I could spend my money on? (Vacation, clothes.) What do you think I should consider before I spend my hard-earned money? (What I really want, my overall needs, how much I have, and so on.) Let's make a list. (Include have, need, want.)

Worksheet 3.7: Today you are going to give advice to five students who are thinking about spending some money. Read each situation and think about what you would advise each of them. There is no real right or wrong answer, but be able to tell me why you picked yes or no for each situation.

Answers

(Explanations may vary.)

1. Yes—he'd enjoy the purchase
2. Yes—if she doesn't have too many other people to buy for
3. No—he should get the bike repaired first
4. Yes—she really loves the cat
5. No—he can't buy a car for $15

Extension Activities

1. *Where My Money Went.* Have students keep track of how much money they spend in a typical week, what their purchases are, and what the largest expense is. Compare answers. Do girls spend more than boys?

2. *Comparison Shopping.* Have students research the price of a certain item (such as a popular DVD or CD, name-brand jeans or shoes) at several stores around town. Which places will give them the most for their money?

Name _____ **Date** _____

3.7   Spending Money

These students want to spend some money. Keep in mind how much each has to spend, how great the student's need is, and how badly the student wants the item. Decide whether or not you think the student should spend the money. Circle YES or NO next to each situation. Tell Why/Why Not?

1. Randy has $20. He is crazy about computers and knows that there is a sale at the store. Do you think he should spend his money on a computer disk?

   YES　　**NO**

   Why/Why Not?

   _____

   _____

   _____

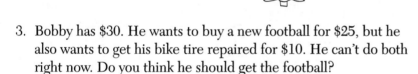

2. It's almost Christmas. Jenny would like to buy her mom a bottle of perfume for $10 and some stationery for $5. She knows her mom would really like the gifts. She has $50 to spend. Do you think she should do this?

   YES　　**NO**

   _____

   _____

   _____

3. Bobby has $30. He wants to buy a new football for $25, but he also wants to get his bike tire repaired for $10. He can't do both right now. Do you think he should get the football?

   YES　　**NO**

   _____

   _____

   _____

4. Amy has $60. Her cat needs to have an operation that will cost $50. Amy can give the cat away to a neighbor who will take care of it, or she can take it to the vet for the operation. Amy loves the cat. Should Amy spend the money on the cat?

   YES　　**NO**

   _____

   _____

5. Juan has $15. He is thinking about buying a new car. He would like a car, but he would also like other things more. Should he spend his money on a car?

   YES　　**NO**

   _____

   _____

Chapter 3: Money Skills   **73**

3.8 Sales and Discounts

Objective

The student will correctly calculate the price of an item that has been discounted or is on sale.

Discussion

Teacher: What does it mean to buy something "on sale"? (Less expensive than the regular price.) What are some things that you can get on sale? (Books, clothes, toys.)

Sometimes you might see a sign that says you can get a "discount." That means the price is lower by a certain percentage. For example, a 50% discount means half price. What would half of $10 be? ($5.) Why do you think stores offer a discount? (To get you to buy more of an item, to get rid of items that they don't want anymore.) This is a good way to save some money on things that you might need. Watch for some sales!

Worksheet 3.8: Read each situation involving a sale or discount. Write your answer on the line next to each item.

Answers

    1. $4   2. 6 movies   3. $5   4. 22 candy bars   5. $15   6. $70

Extension Activities

1. *Big Sale!* Bring in the sales pages of your local newspaper and have students find items that interest them. Have them work in pairs to write out a story problem involving the item(s) and the sale. Have students exchange their story problems.

2. *Go Crazy Sale!* Using the same sales pages for #1, tell students that they have $100 in pretend money to spend on a sale. Have students list the items that they would purchase without going over $100. You might want to add to the frenzy by giving them a ten-minute time limit to spend all of their money!

3.8   Sales and Discounts

Read the following situations involving a sale or discount. Write your answer on the line next to each item.

1. Meagan bought a shirt for $8.00. She can get a second shirt for half price. How much will she pay

   for the second shirt? _____

2. Zachary went to a big sale at the video store. He could buy one movie for $5 or three movies for

   $10. How many movies could he buy if he spent $20? _____

3. Lauren went to a book store that was having a 50-percent-off sale. She found a book about mermaids that was originally priced at $10. How much did she pay for the book?

   _____

4. Noah wanted some candy bars that were on sale for $1.00 each. The sign said if he bought ten candy bars, he could have one for free. He paid $20 for the candy. How many candy bars did

   he get? _____

5. Ella bought some jeans for $30. She noticed that the zipper was broken, so she returned it to the store. The clerk told her that she could have the jeans for half price if she wanted to fix them herself.

   How much would the jeans cost Ella? _____

6. Logan wanted some basketball shoes that normally cost $80. He found out that there would be a sale for $10 off if he waited until the weekend. How much would the shoes cost then?

   _____

3.9 Estimating

Objective

The student will correctly choose an estimated answer for the value of a common item.

Discussion

Teacher: How much do you think my shoes cost? Do you think I paid $500 for them? (Probably not.) Do you think it is more likely that I spent $30 on them? (Yes.) Why did you guess $30 rather than $500? ($500 is a lot of money; they are not really nice shoes!) Sometimes it helps to estimate what something will cost. That means you come up with an approximate number and not an exact number. How much do you think a car would cost: $100 or $10,000? ($10,000 should pay for a decent car.) We are going to do a little activity involving guessing or estimating how much some common items probably cost. Remember, use common sense to guess a good price. You do not have to be exact!

Worksheet 3.9: Read each of these situations and circle the number that would probably be closest to the answer.

Answers

1. a   2. b   3. a   4. b   5. b   6. c

Extension Activities

1. *Guess My Price.* Collect pictures of common objects and glue them on index cards with the actual selling price on the back of the card. Have students estimate what they think the object might cost at the store. You can have two teams and play a version of *The Price Is Right*.

2. *What Can You Get For . . .* Give students a dollar amount ($50 to $100) and have them search the sales circulars to find out what single items they could purchase for approximately that amount of money. Students might find that $50 would be enough to buy a chair, a special book, a pair of jeans, or a season's collection of a favorite TV show. You might want to assign a different amount of money to pairs of students.

Name _____ Date _____

3.9   Estimating

Read each situation below and circle the price that would probably be closest to the answer.

1. A comic book

    a. $2   b. $20   c. $2,002

2. A backpack

    a. $3   b. $15   c. $100

3. An ice cream cone

    a. $2   b. $10   c. $40

4. A bicycle

    a. $10   b. $100   c. $500

5. A pair of jeans

    a. $2   b. $30   c. $900

6. A trampoline

    a. $10   b. $50   c. $150

Time Skills

PARENT LETTER #4: TIME SKILLS

Dear Parents,

The activities covered in the next unit involve basic time concepts, such as awareness of the days of the week and months of the year, planning ahead for events, and becoming familiar with measuring time by using a clock and calendar. You can help your child at home in the following ways:

1. Post a monthly calendar in the kitchen. Each morning before school, check off the previous day and note any appointments written there.

2. Purchase an inexpensive watch (digital is fine) for your child to wear. Ask him or her often to tell you the time.

3. As daily events occur (getting up, getting ready to go to school, anticipating dinner, watching television), have your child locate and tell you the time. Help him or her pair up significant daily events with the times they occur.

4. On a yearly calendar, mark all the significant family events such as birthdays, anniversaries, vacations, and holidays. Have your child take special note of what is going to happen each month.

5. Take pictures of your child and display them in a prominent place. Show that time changes him or her also, and note changes in height, weight, and appearance.

6. When you and your child do things outside, take particular note of the signs of each season. Discuss what will happen next as you approach the next season.

Time passes so quickly—enjoy the time that you can spend with your child!

Sincerely,

_____

Teacher

TIME SKILLS

Skill Sheet #4: Progress Report

+ mastered

√ emerging

− not mastered

Student Name	Days and Months	Today	Using a Calendar	Using a Clock	Seasons	Planning Ahead	What Happens When?	First Step in a Sequence	Fifteen-Minute Tasks	Setting Time Goals	Comments

4.1 Days and Months

Objective

Upon request, the student will state the days of the week and months of the year in chronological order.

Discussion

Teacher: How did you know to come to school today? Why didn't you come on Sunday? If it were the middle of July, would you be in school? (If summer school or all-year school.) If it were Wednesday today, would it be a long time until the weekend? What if it were January? Would it be a long time until Halloween? Help! We need to get the days and months organized! When I ask you to tell me the days of the week, I want you to say, "Monday, Tuesday, Wednesday, Thursday, Friday, Saturday, Sunday." When I ask you to tell me the months of the year, I want you to say, "January, February, March, April, May, June, July, August, September, October, November, December."

Worksheet 4.1: These students are playing a game that we will play in our class later. Each has a tag with a day or month named on it. Put the students in order by numbering the boxes below them 1 to 7 or 1 to 12.

Answers

6-2-5-1-4-3-7

5-8-1-3-9-12 and 4-2-11-7-6-10

Extension Activities

1. *Relays.* Assign students name cards with days or months, similar to the Worksheet. Tell them that when you say "Go" they must find their place in a lineup. Time them on their trials to see how fast they are. Switch cards often.

2. *Before and After.* Using the same cards, alter the strategy by having students tell the day/month preceding and following their day or month. Toss a beanbag among the students to select who goes next. Keep the pace quick!

4.1   Days and Months

The students on the top part of the page are playing the Days of the Week game. The students on the bottom are playing the Months of the Year game. Both groups want to get the players in the right group.

Row 1

Row 2

4.2 Today

Objective

The student will be able to relate the present day, month, number, and year.

Discussion

Teacher: What day is it today? How did you know? If I asked you what the date is today, what would you say? How is the day different from the date? (One is the name of the day of the week; the other is three parts—month, number, year.) What was the date five days ago? When I ask you for the day, tell me the word that ends with "day." When I ask you for the date, tell me the three parts: the month first, then the number, then the year.

Worksheet 4.2: On this Worksheet the teacher is asking students to tell her the day or the date. You are to circle the student in each group who is giving her the correct answer. You don't have to know which day or date is the actual one, because we don't know when the stories happened. But look for all parts of the information needed in each situation. Don't worry about what the actual months or days are. We'll do that for real very soon.

Answers

1. Second   2. First   3. Second   4. Second   5. Second   6. Second   7. First   8. Second

Extension Activities

1. *What's Today?* Each day, preferably in the morning, have students recite the day and date. At frequent times during the day, question students as to the current date.

2. *Find a Date.* Have students be on the lookout for places in which a date is used; for example, library due dates, newspaper, and future doctor's appointments. You may want to introduce using numbers to indicate months (as in 10/16/53 for October 16, 1953).

4.2   Today

The teacher is asking the students questions about the day and the date. Circle the student in each situation who is answering correctly.

1.  What day is it today?  March.  Thursday.

2. 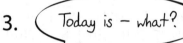 What is today's date?  April 1, 2010.  April.

3. 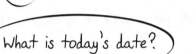 Today is — what? 1992.  Monday.

4. 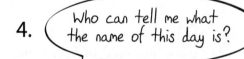 Who can tell me what the name of this day is? February.  Tuesday.

5. 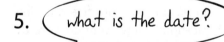 what is the date?  September 2. September 2, 2010.

6.  Who knows what today's date is?  Monday. October 16, 2010.

7.  What 's today? Wednesday.  March.

8. Do you know what today's date is? Yes, December 2010. Yes January 2, 2010.

4.3 Using a Calendar

Objective

Given a specific day and/or date, the student will use a calendar to locate the requested information.

Discussion

Teacher: Who can tell me what the day is today? Who can tell me today's date? How did you know? (Heard someone, looked at paper or calendar.) Does anyone know what an orderly arrangement of days is called? It's a calendar. It's a way of showing how all of the days go together to make up months and a year. Remember how many months in a year there are? (Twelve.) Usually a calendar shows all of the days in one year. There are 365 days, and usually a calendar shows one month at a time.

Worksheet 4.3: Use the calendar on the second Worksheet to help you answer the questions on the first page. Write your answers on the line following each question.

Answers

1. July 2. 31 3. 2010 4. July 4, 2010 5. Sunday 6. Tuesday 7. Friday 8. 1 9. 12 10. Four 11. Four 12. June 13. August 14. July 17, 2010 15. July 27, 2010 16. July 19, 2010

Extension Activities

1. *Calendar Puzzle.* Hand out old calendars (monthly sheets may work best at first) cut into jigsaw-like shapes. Have students put the calendar together. Ask what clues they used to help them. (Numbers, days of week, and so on.)

2. *Questions by Students.* Hand out calendar sheets to students and have each write five questions similar to the ones on the Worksheet. Exchange calendars and questions. How accurate were the questions? (Students should also provide an answer key.)

Name _____ **Date** _____

4.3   **Using a Calendar**

The following worksheet shows a month from a calendar. Use it to answer the following questions. Write your answer on the line next to each question.

1. What month is it on the calendar? _____

2. How many days are in the month? _____

3. What year is it on the calendar? _____

4. What day is Independence Day? _____

5. What day of the week is Independence Day on? _____

6. What day of the week is July 27? _____

7. What day of the week is July 16? _____

8. What is the number of the first Thursday? _____

9. What is the number of the second Monday? _____

10. How many Wednesdays are in this month? _____

11. How many Tuesdays are in this month? _____

12. What month came before this one? _____

13. What month comes after this one? _____

14. What is the date of the day with the *? _____

15. What is the date of the day with the $? _____

16. What is the date after July 18, 2010? _____

JULY 2010

SUNDAY	MONDAY	TUESDAY	WEDNESDAY	THURSDAY	FRIDAY	SATURDAY
				1	2	3
4 Independence Day	5	6	7	8	9	10
11	12	13	14	15	16	17 *
18	19	20	21	22	23	24
25	26	27 $	28	29	30	31

4.4 Using a Clock

Objective

Given a clock (traditional face or digital), the student will identify the correct time.

Discussion

Teacher: It's (state present time). How did I know that? (Looked at watch, clock.) Why is it important to know what time it is? (Don't miss appointments, stay on task.) What time do you get up in the morning? What time is school over? What's on television at 8:00 tonight? What are some other important times for you?

Worksheet 4.4: Here is a list of some events that are going to happen. On the right side are clocks that show the time. Circle the clock that shows the correct time that the event will happen.

Answers

1. First clock 2. First clock 3. First clock 4. Second clock 5. Second clock 6. First clock 7. Second clock 8. Second clock 9. First clock 10. Second clock

Extension Activities

1. *What Was That Time?* Have students use the Worksheet to practice reading the times on the clocks that were the incorrect times for the event listed. You may also wish to make flash cards of clocks set at various times, with the correct time written on the back.

2. *My Time Card.* Have students list various important events that occur in their lives, such as bus times, sports events times, television programming, and so on. Using a blank clock face, have students draw hands on the clock to indicate their important times.

4.4   Using a Clock

Match the events on the left with the correct clock on the right. Circle the clock that shows the correct time.

1. You want to watch a football game on television that starts at 8:30.

2. The bus is coming to pick you up at 7:25.

3. Your best friend is coming over at 4:15.

4. Your mother is going to call you from her office at 3:30.

5. You are supposed to pick up your sister from the babysitter's house at 5:05.

6. Your dog has an appointment at the vet at 6:00.

7. You are supposed to be home for dinner at 5:45.

8. If you leave home at 7:35, you will get to school on time.

9. Your friends are meeting you at the hamburger place at 4:30. Don't be late!

10. Your library book is due today, and it closes at 1:00. Plan ahead!

4.5 Seasons

Objective

The student will identify the four seasons and state characteristics of each.

Discussion

Teacher: It's snowing outside! Just kidding (unless, of course, it *is* snowing)—but is that likely to happen today? If you keep track of the temperature and the weather conditions for a long time, you'll find out that there are four basic patterns. These are called the seasons. Can anyone name all four? The seasons are spring, summer, fall, and winter. What is it like outside in the spring? How about the other seasons?

Worksheet 4.5: There are certain characteristics, or patterns, for each season. Read over the list of things you might feel or do, and then write each item under the name of the season in which you might feel or do that thing.

Answers

(Answers will vary.)

Spring: May be good time for an umbrella, gets very wet, plant flowers, fly a kite, may be windy

Summer: Gets very hot, a good time for playing outside, use sunscreen, mow the lawn, good time for swimming

Fall: May be windy, rake leaves

Winter: Gets very cold, wear your mittens, have snowball fights, shovel snow

Extension Activities

1. *Month by Month.* Have students consider each month and categorize it into a season, weather and temperature pattern, and typical events for that month (including holidays). You may want to pick a theme (such as Spring Fever or Winter Fun) and have students draw pictures or write stories to illustrate events specific to that season.

2. *Changing Leaves.* As the seasons change, have students change the leaves (construction paper or real, if possible) on a large cutout tree (trunk with long branches). In winter, the tree should be bare or snow-covered. Outlining a hand makes a good pattern for cutting out leaves from colored construction paper. Each student may want to contribute his or her handprint to the "class tree." (You could accessorize the tree by adding a wayward kite, a squirrel, an apple, and so on)

4.5   **Seasons**

Here is a list of weather conditions and events that may occur during the seasons of the year. Your part of the country may be a little different, so you may want to change or add to this list. Write each characteristic under the name of the season.

Gets very hot	A good time for playing outside	Wear your swimming suit
Gets very cold	Good time for swimming	Use sunscreen
May be windy	Good time for an umbrella	Rake leaves
Gets very wet	Wear your mittens	Have snowball fights

SPRING

SUMMER

FALL

WINTER

4.6 Planning Ahead

Objective

Given a calendar and real or hypothetical events, the student will anticipate and plan events in a reasonable order.

Discussion

Teacher: Would you like to hear my list of what I'm going to do next week? On Monday, I'm going to fly to Alaska. On Tuesday, I have a dentist appointment. On Wednesday, I'm having my tonsils out. On Thursday, I'm meeting the president and his cabinet to talk about educational programs. Do you see a problem with this schedule? What? (Transporting self around the country quickly, surgery complications.) Of course, that's not my real schedule, but what if it were? Any suggestions for changing things around? (Allow time, change order.) When you plan events, you should keep in mind (1) how long it may take and (2) what might happen that will affect other plans.

Worksheet 4.6: Sometimes you can make plans for things to happen because most of the time nothing goes wrong. These students are making plans. Help them by circling the answer that you think is the best plan for their time. Then we'll discuss what could go wrong (although we hope that nothing will).

Answers

1. Take the dog out
2. Saturday or Sunday
3. In winter
4. Get a haircut
5. Thursday before Sally's party
6. Friday night . . .

Extension Activities

1. *What Could Go Wrong?* In each situation on the Worksheet, have students discuss what could possibly happen to make their choice unworkable. For example, in situation #4 perhaps David would have to wait a week to get an appointment with the stylist he wants. In #5, perhaps Sally's house is so huge that they would need to start cleaning up on Monday—being careful not to mess up the house during the other days!

2. *How Long Does It Take?* Have students estimate how long certain events usually take. Examples may include going to a movie, going to the dentist, cleaning a room, doing homework, taking out the garbage, building a model, brushing teeth, and so on. Students may be surprised at how much (or how little) time is actually involved in these tasks.

4.6   Planning Ahead

These students are making plans. Help them decide what to do when. Circle your answer.

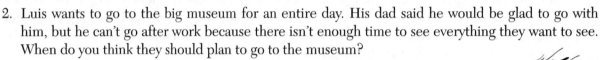

1. Mandy is supposed to clean her room before her cousins come over to play. She is also to walk the dog and feed him. What should she do first?

   Take the dog out   Clean her room

2. Luis wants to go to the big museum for an entire day. His dad said he would be glad to go with him, but he can't go after work because there isn't enough time to see everything they want to see. When do you think they should plan to go to the museum?

   **When his dad doesn't work   Saturday or Sunday
   anymore and is retired**

3. Maria wants to go skiing. Sometimes the ski slopes are closed when there isn't enough snow. When do you think Maria should plan to go skiing?

   In fall   In winter

4. David wants to get a haircut and go to the ballpark with friends and go to the movies. Today was a very busy day and he only has time to get one thing done. What should he plan to do?

   See a movie   Get a haircut   Play ball with friends

5. Sally is having a birthday party Friday night. Sally's father is having a party Saturday night. When would be a good time to clean up the house?

   Thursday before Sally's party   Monday before Sally's party

6. Randy can have a friend stay overnight one night this week. He wants to spend as much time as he can with his friend. Which night do you think he would choose?

   **Friday night with no other   Tuesday night before school on Wednesday
   plans for Saturday**

4.7 What Happens When?

Objective

Students will answer "time" questions appropriately and accurately by giving the day, date, time, month, year, or season.

Discussion

Teacher: What day is it today? What's the date? What time is it? What season is it? All of these questions are about time and knowing when something happens. They are all asking about today, but they all were different answers. It's Monday, but it's also October. Listen for what exact question I am asking, so you will know how to answer my question. In what month is your birthday? In which season is your birthday?

Worksheet 4.7: This Worksheet reviews the different ways to look at time that we have talked about: the day, the date, the month, year, season, and clock time. Be sure to read each question carefully so you are answering the question. Write your answer on the line next to each situation.

Answers

1. Will vary
2. Will vary
3. December
4. Will vary
5. Summer (other seasons acceptable)
6. Will vary
7. Will vary
8. Will vary

Extension Activities

1. *On Target.* To help students conceptualize how our measurement of time can become increasingly more specific, use a target poster with several concentric circles, labeled YEAR, SEASON, MONTH, DAY, NUMBER. Have the arrow point touching the "number" circle and change information on the target (daily for the inner circle) as the time changes.

2. *New Month Holiday.* Create a holiday for the first day of each new month. Students may wish to start a special tradition or festival (such as November Leaf Dance, February "Send-the-President-a-Valentine" tradition) to kick off the new month.

4.7   **What Happens When?**

Each of these students wants to know when something happens. Read each question carefully and write the best answer on the line next to the item.

1. Alissa What time do you go to lunch?

_____

2. Mark What is the day after tomorrow?

_____

3. Richard What month is Christmas in?

_____

4. Claudia When is your birthday?

_____

5. Max In which season do you go sailing?

_____

6. Kim When would be a good day for us to get together to play after school?

_____

7. Linda What time do you have to go to bed?

_____

8. Ben This library book is due to tomorrow. What is the date?

_____

Chapter 4: Time Skills

4.8 First Step in a Sequence

Objective

The student will identify a first step in completing a sequence or a task.

Discussion

Teacher: Sometimes the hardest part about getting something done is taking that first step. For example, maybe it seems overwhelming to have to clean out the garage, but if you can pick out one thing that will get you started, you can ease into the job. What might be a good first step toward getting a garage cleaned out? (Collect all of the cleaning supplies, get everything sorted into sections, sweep the floor.) When you find yourself looking at a job instead of doing it, try coming up with the first step—then do it!

Worksheet 4.8: Read the following tasks with some possible first steps. Pick the best step to do first and put a check mark next to it.

Answers

1. Putting your homework on a table

2. Picking everything up off the floor

3. Finding clean clothes and putting them in the bathroom

Extension Activities

1. *Many Steps, One Task.* Assign students in pairs or small groups the job of breaking tasks into smaller steps. Have groups compare the sizes of their steps and the sequence involved in completing a larger task.

2. *"First I Will . . ."* When students are presented with a task to complete, have them begin by stating out loud: "First I will . . ." and finish the sentence with the first thing that they will do. By identifying and stating that first step, students are on their way toward task completion. This helps them take ownership of the task as well, instead of waiting for an adult to tell them what to do.

4.8   First Step in a Sequence

For each of these tasks, pick out the first step that would need to be done. Put a check mark next to that step.

1. Doing Your Homework

   _____ Checking over your answers

   _____ Putting your homework in your book bag for tomorrow

   _____ Feeding the dog

   _____ Putting your homework on a table

2. Cleaning Your Room

   _____ Looking around the house for a broom

   _____ Picking everything up off the floor

   _____ Finding a book under the bed and starting to read it

   _____ Calling your friends to tell them that you can't play right now

3. Taking a Bath

   _____ Draining water out of the tub

   _____ Getting soap all over your body

   _____ Finding clean clothes and putting them in the bathroom

   _____ Looking around for a toy boat

4.9 Fifteen-Minute Tasks

Objective

The student will identify at least three tasks that can be completed within fifteen minutes.

Discussion

Teacher: How long is fifteen minutes? Is that long enough to watch your favorite television show? (No.) Is it enough time to eat an ice cream cone? (Yes.) There are many tasks that can be completed in a relatively short time—just fifteen minutes. If you are careful not to let that time get away from you—by staying on task—there is a lot you can accomplish in just a short amount of time.

Worksheet 4.9: Which of these tasks could probably be completed in a short time, such as fifteen minutes? Circle each answer.

Answers

(Answers may vary.)

2, 3, 4, 6, 8, 11, 12, 14

Extension Activities

1. *Timer Tasks.* Get a kitchen timer and set it for fifteen minutes. Assign a classroom task (cleaning out desks, completing a worksheet, and so on) and challenge students to complete the job before the timer goes off. Discuss how staying on task helps, rather than leaving the original job to wander around, talk, or get involved in other distractions.

2. *Personal Choice.* At a convenient time during your day (before lunch, after lunch, before recess, and so on), assign a fifteen-minute block for students to engage in a chosen activity. Inform them that they must stay with the same activity for the entire fifteen minutes and not go over the fifteen minutes. In other words, focus on the idea of staying with something and stopping when told to do so. If students have some options in picking the activity (doing a jigsaw puzzle, silently reading, drawing, and so on), they have now committed themselves to their own choice.

4.9   **Fifteen-Minute Tasks**

Which of these tasks could probably be completed in a short time, such as fifteen minutes? Circle each answer.

1. Painting your room

2. Brushing your teeth

3. Walking the dog

4. Reviewing your spelling words

5. Reading a complete book

6. Reading a story in a book

7. Riding the bus to school

8. Making your bed

9. Going to church

10. Watching a movie

11. Washing dishes

12. Talking to a friend on the phone

13. Helping your parents shop for food

14. Vacuuming your room

15. Eating a meal with your family

4.10 Setting Time Goals

Objective

The student will estimate how long a task will take and complete the task within that amount of time.

Discussion

Teacher: We have been talking about how long it takes to complete some jobs. Now it is time for you to see how accurate you can be! I would like you to estimate how long you think some common tasks might take, and then you can time yourselves to see if you were on target or not! For example, how long do you think it takes you to eat lunch at school? (Thirty minutes? Ten minutes?) How long do you think it should take you to clean out your desk? (Times will vary.) Let's do some predicting and find out.

Worksheet 4.10: How long do you think it would take you to complete each task? Write your answer in minutes or hours on the lines.

Answers

(Answers will vary.)

Extension Activities

1. *I'm on the Clock.* Go through some of the activities on the Worksheet and ask students to select two or three that are convenient for them to do either at school or at home. Allow for three trials before you have them come up with an answer. Were they accurate at predicting how long the task took?

2. *My Personal Goal.* While stressing that students should always strive for quality work, continue to focus on setting realistic goals for a task. Before having students complete a routine task, have them set a time goal for how long it will take. Emphasize that faster is not always better; indeed, rushing through something may only result in having to do it over. You want students to make a good time estimate and then live up to their personal goal.

4.10   **Setting Time Goals**

How long do you think it would take you to complete each of these tasks? Write your answer in minutes or hours on the lines.

1. Taking a bath _____

2. Setting the table for a meal _____

3. Playing a video game with your friend _____

4. Putting clothes into the dryer _____

5. Riding your bike to the store, an errand, or someone's house _____

6. Completing your homework _____

7. Getting ready for school _____

8. Taking the dog for a walk _____

9. Writing a book report _____

10. Doing yard work _____

Chapter 5

Basic Reading and Writing Skills

PARENT LETTER #5: BASIC READING AND WRITING SKILLS

Dear Parents,

The ability to read and write are basic skills that everyone can learn and improve upon throughout one's life. They are skills that are necessary for many tasks in life, and the better someone is at reading and writing, the more opportunities he or she will have as far as education, jobs, and personal pleasure.

This unit focuses on basic reading and writing skills that your child will need to get along in life. Reading skills include recognizing important everyday words, traffic signs, and informational signs, and discovering sources of reading material. Writing skills include completing forms and lists, and personal tasks such as keeping a log or homework journal.

Both reading and writing can be improved by practice! As you have the opportunity at home, encourage your child to read. Take him or her to the library, to book sales, or even a comic book exchange. Ask questions that can be found by reading the local newspaper, the TV guide, or popular magazines. Let your child see how important writing is by having him or her help you make a grocery list, write a letter or e-mail to a relative, and keep a family journal of vacations.

Working with you,

_____

Teacher

BASIC READING AND WRITING SKILLS

Skill Sheet #5: Progress Report

	+ mastered
	√ emerging
	− not mastered

Student Name	Words: People	Words: Places	Words: Things	Traffic Signs	Information Signs	Safety Words	Things to Read	Reading for a Purpose	Reading for Pleasure	Filling Out a Form	Addressing an Envelope	Mailing a Letter	Making Lists	Having Good Handwriting	Reminder Notes	Comments

5.1 Words: People

Objective

Given prompts, the student will read or write words depicting people (such as family, occupations, important others).

Discussion

Teacher: I'm going to write some words on the board, and I'd like you to tell me who I am writing about. (Write: Teacher, your full name, your first name if desired.) These words all refer to me! Who are some of the most important people in your life? (Parents, family, friends.) We are going to be working on the skills involved in reading and writing the words that refer to people. There are many ways to group people. We could group them by family, by friends, by workers, and all kinds of other groups. (See accompanying "Idea List.")

Worksheet 5.1: On this Worksheet, I want you to think about people who are familiar to you. Everyone's answers may be quite different on this sheet this time. Write down your own people and we'll talk about the many different answers that we find.

Answers

(Answers will vary.)

Extension Activities

1. *People Magazine.* Have students create and produce their own personal copy of a magazine with interviews, articles, drawings, and/or collages of important people. They may wish to include a type of glossary at the end, listing the name of the person, some statistics, and a brief explanation of why that person is important to him.

2. *Word Bank (People).* Have students brainstorm and see how extensive a list they can produce for each category of person listed (such as famous people, characters, workers). Have them read and/or write the ones that you feel are most important.

Idea List

asssistant	grocer
aunt	mother
author	policeman
brother	principal
bus driver	sports figure
chef	teacher
doctor	uncle
fireman	veterinarian

Chapter 5: Basic Reading and Writing Skills

5.1   **Words: People**

Think of the name of a person who would fit the following description. Write his or her name on the line.

A person in my family _____

A person who laughs a lot _____

A person who is tall _____

My best friend _____

A person who helps me _____

A person who works in my town _____

A person who is a woman _____

A person who is famous _____

A person who is in the news _____

A person who can do something I wish I could do _____

A person who is not real _____

A cartoon person _____

A person on television _____

A person at school _____

A character in a book or story _____

5.2 Words: Places

Objective

Given prompts, the student will read or write words depicting places in the community, their state, and the country.

Discussion

Teacher: Where would you like to go if I gave you the next hour off? Where would you go if you could go anywhere in our state? Now let's say you have a free airplane ride to any place in the country. Where would I find you? All of those are important places. It's important to be able to read and write the names of those places. Let's group your ideas by community, state, and country. (See accompanying "Idea List.")

Worksheet 5.2: Here is a Worksheet that will help you practice reading and writing words that tell about places. There may be more than one correct answer for the places described, so think about other choices, too.

Answers

(Answers will vary.)

Extension Activities

1. *Community Map.* Have students locate important community places on a map (enlarged, if possible) of your town. They may want to draw or find a picture depicting the place and draw an arrow from the spot on the map to the picture. Arrange for a "walking tour" if your community is close and easily accessible.

2. *Welcome to My State.* Spend some time discussing the noteworthy points of interest in your state. Collect and display brochures, view filmstrips or videos, and if possible take a field trip. Read and review the words associated with these places often.

Idea List

Possible answers could be:

emergency room, doctor's office; playground, zoo; video store, movie theater; pizzeria, park; pool, restaurant; animal shelter, pet store; tourist attractions; post office; library, book store; Disney World; historical sites; bakery, food store; appliance store, furniture store; White House, Washington D. C.; shopping mall, clothing store.

For more place words, see page 384

5.2　　　　　　　　　**Words: Places**

Think of the name of a place that would fit each of the following descriptions. Write the place on the line.

A place to get help if you get hurt _____

A place to have fun _____

A place to see a movie _____

A place to go to with a friend _____

A place to go to with a parent _____

A place to get a pet _____

A place to show friends who are visiting from far away _____

A place where you can get a postcard _____

A place to get books _____

A place where you'd like to visit for a day _____

A place where you'd like to visit for a week _____

A place where you could get something to eat _____

A place where you could get something for your house _____

A place where you could find the president of the United States _____

A place where you could get something to wear _____

5.3 Words: Things

Objective

Given prompts, the student will read or write words depicting things (such as animals, clothing, tools).

Discussion

Teacher: I am going to give you a category, and I want you to help me list as many words as you can think of that would go in that group. (Give categories such as animals, furniture.) These are other words that are important to know how to read and write. (See accompanying "Idea List.") The words that you choose are important, because they are important to you.

Worksheet 5.3: Here are students who want to get some things. Help them list possible items that might be what they are looking for.

Answers

(Answers will vary.)

Extension Activities

1. *Twenty Questions.* Give students a general category; then have them ask questions (limit to twenty) to try to ascertain what the specific object or item is. Write their choices on the board for practice in reading and writing the items. When the answer is reached, reread the guesses and discuss why they were good guesses but not the correct answer.

2. *"Fish."* Make word cards for items in several categories. Deal seven cards randomly to each player. When a player has four words from the same category, he or she can "retire" them and draw new cards from the fishing pile. Winner is the player who has the most sets of word cards when all cards from the fishing pile are gone. (This game may be adapted as needed to fit the number of categories used, players, and words to be learned.)

Idea List

Possible answers could be:

cat, dog, turtle; coloring book, doll, paint set; pants, dress, skirt; scarf, homemade card, drawing; backpack, pencil, notebook; spaghetti, milk, eggs.

For more object and thing words, see page 385

Chapter 5: Basic Reading and Writing Skills

5.3 Words: Things

Help these students make lists of things that would go into the categories.

I would like a new pet for my birthday. What are some pets that I might enjoy having?

_____

_____

_____

My aunt gave me $15 for my birthday. What are some things I might want to buy?

_____

_____

_____

I'm going to a party this weekend. What clothes should I get ready?

_____

_____

_____

It's my mom's birthday. What would make a nice gift for her?

_____

_____

_____

It's the first day of school. What do I need?

_____

_____

_____

I'm so hungry! What might make a great meal?

_____

_____

_____

5.4 Traffic Signs

Objective

Given a list of common traffic signs, the student will read and explain each one's use.

Discussion

Teacher: When you are out walking or riding your bike around town, what are some signs that you see that help you get around? A traffic sign is a sign that helps move people or things by showing them which way to go. Why do you think we need signs like that? (Might be a lot of traffic, helps everyone know which way to go to avoid accidents.)

Worksheet 5.4: Here are the words and pictures to ten common traffic signs. Some you would see if you were on your bike or in a car; others you would see if you were walking. Match the sign with the words that tell you what you should do if you see the sign in traffic.

Answers

1. i	6. a
2. c	7. h
3. d	8. f
4. e	9. g
5. j	10. b

Extension Activities

1. *Traffic Walk.* If possible, take a community walk and note which traffic signs are common in your area. Have students watch pedestrians and cars and notice whether or not people are following the instructions carefully.

2. *Driving Course.* Have students bring in small toy cars and maneuver them along a student-made "driving course" with traffic signs to direct them. Include a stop sign, a one-way sign, pedestrian crosswalk, and other signs that appear locally.

Idea List

Traffic Signs:

bicycle crossing	don't walk/walk	school crossing
curve left/right	keeep left/right	stop
detour	one way	yield
do not enter	pedestrian crossing	rest stop
do not pass	railroad crossing	For more safety words, see page 386
	S curve	

Name _____ Date _____

5.4   Traffic Signs

Match the traffic sign with the description of what the sign means. Write the letter after the picture of the sign.

1. Bicycle crossing _____

2. Curve left _____

3. Don't walk _____

4. Detour _____

5. Railroad crossing _____

6. Stop _____

7. One way  _____

8. S curve _____

9. School crossing _____

10. Yield   **YIELD** _____

a. You must come to a complete stop.

b. Go slowly and if there is someone coming to the intersection, let them go first.

c. The road ahead is going to the left.

d. Don't cross the intersection while this is flasing; wait.

e. The usual road is not the way to go; follow the signs for directions to go a different way.

f. The road ahead is going to curve first one way and then another way.

g. Be careful ahead because children will be crossing the street to get to school.

h. You can only go in one direction on this street.

i. Be careful ahead because people on bicycles will be crossing the street.

j. Be careful ahead because you will be crossing railroad tracks; watch for a train.

5.5 Information Signs

Objective

Given a list of common information signs, the student will read and explain each one's use.

Discussion

Teacher: Let's say you safely took a bicycle ride through town and wanted to get something to eat. What is a sign that you might see on the door of a restaurant that would help you make a decision about eating at that restaurant? (Open/closed; hours.) How would you get in the door? (Push/pull.) What is a sign that you might look for if you needed to wash your hands? (Restroom.) Today I want you to think about information signs—signs that tell you something you need to know.

Worksheet 5.5: Here are some situations that you may encounter and some signs that may help you by giving you some information. Read each situation and decide what you will do. Circle Yes or No for each situation.

Answers

1. Yes   2. No   3. No   4. Yes   5. No   6. No   7. Yes

Extension Activities

1. *Information Posters.* Driver's manuals have color pictures of traffic and information signs used along roads. Have students work in teams and draw, enlarge, and color posters to depict helpful signs. Display them around the room and allow students time to explain their use.

2. *Walk Through School.* Have students carefully observe information signs that are displayed throughout the school building. Discuss the purpose of the signs and the information that is conveyed. How many of the signs incorporate pictures to get the message across? (No Smoking, Handicapped Access, and so on.)

5.5   Information Signs

Here are some situations that you may encounter and some signs that may help you by giving you some information. Read each situation and decide what you will do. Circle Yes or No for each situation.

ELEVATOR

1. You want to go to your doctor's office on the tenth floor of a building. Will this sign help you get there?

   Yes   No

OUT OF ORDER

2. You are trying to make a phone call to your mother to have her pick you up after school. Will you use this phone?

   Yes   No

PUSH

3. You want to go inside the video store, but the door won't open. Are you pushing on the door?

   Yes   No

SELF-SERVE

4. You are in line to get a drink and a sandwich at a cafeteria. You are waiting for the man behind the counter to help you, but he isn't even looking at you. Are you supposed to reach in and get your own food?

   Yes   No

NO TRESPASSING

5. Your toy airplane flew over the fence and landed in a yard with this sign in front. Will you climb the fence to get your plane?

   Yes   No

EXACT CHANGE NEEDED

6. You want to buy a 75-cent candy bar from a vending machine. All you have is a dollar bill. Can you get a candy bar here?

   Yes   No

CLOSED

7. You want to play pinball at the arcade, but the door won't open. Should you come back at a different time?

   Yes   No

5.6 Safety Words

Objective

Given a list of common safety words, the student will read and explain each one's use.

Discussion

Teacher: There is one more group of words that we are going to make sure you understand and can read. These are safety words. Safety words help you stay out of danger. Can anyone think of any helpful safety words? (Beware of dog, poison.) When would you see these words?

Worksheet 5.6: See if you can figure out what the message is from these safety words. On the lines, write what you think might happen if someone didn't read or understand the safety words.

Answers

(Answers will vary.)

Examples: Might touch something that would shock them; Might get hit by a car; Might get trapped in a building on fire; Might not be able to put out a fire in time; Might eat or drink something that could make you very sick; Might get bitten by a dog; Might get paint all over your hands or clothes; Might not notify fire department in time; Something might catch on fire if you aren't careful with matches; Might get lost or stuck in the wrong place; Might burn yourself; Might trip down the steps

Extension Activities

1. *The Safety Match Game.* Make two copies of each of the safety words on durable cards. Flip the cards over and scatter them on a flat surface. Have students take turns turning over two at a time. If the cards match, the student takes them and takes another turn. The winner is the student with the most pairs of cards.

2. *Safety Coloring Book.* Assign each student a safety word to write carefully and to illustrate with a simple picture or cartoon depicting someone not following the safety instruction. Reproduce and collate everyone's contribution and assemble into a class coloring book of safety words.

5.6   **Safety Words**

Here are some safety words. What could happen if you didn't read or understand the words? Write your answers on the lines.

1. Danger—Keep Out   _____

2. Don't Walk   _____

_____

3. Exit   _____

_____

4. Fire Extinguisher   _____

_____

5. Poison   _____

_____

6. Beware of Dog   _____

_____

7. Wet Paint   _____

_____

8. Fire Alarm      _____

_____

9. Flammable   _____

_____

10. Do Not Enter   _____

_____

11. Hot   _____

_____

12. Watch Your Step   _____

_____

5.7 Things to Read

Objective

The student will identify at least five examples of sources of reading materials.

Discussion

Teacher: Look around the room. There are examples of many different things to read. What do you see? (Books, encyclopedia, bulletin board, games.) Think about things in your home that you can read. What are some ideas? (Cereal boxes, comics, newspaper.) Now think about things that you can read while you are in a car or bus on your way to school. What are some examples of these? (Billboards, signs on buses, advertisements in front of businesses.) There are things to read almost everywhere you look!

Worksheet 5.7: Here is a list of some things that a person might read in a typical day. Add items to the list that you can think of.

Answers

(Answers will vary.)

Examples: instructions for games, birthday cards, e-mails from friends, notes from your teacher

Extension Activities

1. *Pick Five.* Assign students the task of finding and reading from at least five different sources over a period of a day or two. They should list the five reading materials that they used. This could include books, newspapers, and typical reading materials, but also encourage them to find unusual, creative reading sources by looking carefully around them.

2. *Book Report but Not a Book.* Instead of the typical book report, have students take turns giving reports on completely different types of reading materials. For example, how about a "Recipe Report" on a good recipe from Grandma, or sharing a funny Shel Silverstein poem that they discovered, or a report on the ingredients in their favorite candy bar or health food bar. Let the audience know what information they discovered by reading about it!

5.7   **Things to Read**

Here is a list of some things that a person might read in a typical day. Add items to the list that you can think of.

Library book

Shopping list

Comic book

TV listings

The back of the cereal box

_____

_____

_____

_____

_____

Chapter 5: Basic Reading and Writing Skills   **119**

5.8 Reading for a Purpose

Objective

The student will match a purpose for reading with an appropriate reading source.

Discussion

Teacher: Sometimes people read just for fun, but other times people read because they are looking for some information about something they are going to do that day. What kinds of things do you think people might read to find out something? (Newspaper, magazines, horoscopes.) People might also read because they want to learn about a certain topic. What are some things that would be interesting for you to learn about? (Shipwrecks, magic tricks, sports figures.) We are going to investigate some different purposes for reading.

Worksheet 5.8: Match the item on the left with a purpose for reading on the right.

Answers

  1. e 2. a 3. d 4. c 5. f 6. b

Extension Activities

1. *Scavenger Hunt.* Write a list of questions that can be answered by using reading resources. Provide each student or team with the list and turn them loose to complete the hunt by searching through the books, magazines, cards, and other reading sources to find the answers. The first team to complete the list correctly wins!

2. *How To . . .* Make a classroom book by having each student contribute at least one page explaining how to do/make/achieve something. Encourage students to include drawings, pictures, or photos for their page to create interest. Explain that this is an example of a resource that has the purpose of offering explanations for student topics.

5.8   **Reading for a Purpose**

Match the item on the left with a purpose for reading on the right.

1. Weather report in the newspaper

   _____

2. A joke book _____

3. Instructions for building a model car

   _____

4. List of supplies for art _____

5. Sunday comics _____

6. A baseball card _____

a. To have something funny to tell your friends

b. To find out how many home runs a player hit

c. To know what to buy at the store

d. To know what to do first to put the model car together

e. To know what to wear

f. To read a continuing story about your cartoon friends

Chapter 5: Basic Reading and Writing Skills

5.9 Reading for Pleasure

Objective

The student will identify several sources of reading for pleasure.

Discussion

Teacher: Some people are book-lovers. What does that mean? (They enjoy reading books.) If you could read anything you wanted to, what kind of books would you read? (Horse stories, mysteries, Harry Potter books.) What are some other things that you might read for enjoyment? (Comics, poems, joke books.)

Worksheet 5.9: There are many things a person can read simply for enjoyment! Help these students choose something that they would enjoy. Circle your choice.

Answers

1. a   2. b   3. b   4. a   5. b

Extension Activities

1. *Reading Corner.* Set up a reading nook or corner in your classroom in which students can bring favorite things to read. This might include a collection of paperbacks, puzzles, stories written by the students, and anything else that your class enjoys reading. Add a beanbag chair and some pretzels!
2. *Revisit the Library.* Arrange for a classroom tour of your school or local library. Have a worker or volunteer show students around and point out new books, magazines, or other items that would interest the students. Take notice of book displays, posters, and other promotional items.

5.9   Reading for Pleasure

There are many things a person can read simply for enjoyment! Help these students choose something that they would enjoy. Circle your choice.

1. Mia loves mysteries! What could she read?

   a. A book a.bout hidden treasure   b. A book about penguins

2. Jose likes to do word puzzles. What could he read?

   a. A joke book   b. A crossword puzzle book

3. Natalie wants to learn about zoo animals. What could she read?

   a. Information about when the zoo opens   b. An encyclopedia about animals

4. Jeremiah thinks the quarterback on the pro team in his town is awesome! What could he read?

   a. An interview with the quarterback in the paper   b. A book about football

5. Brandon enjoys Batman, Superman, and other superhero stories. What could he read?

   a. Reviews about animal movies coming up   b. Comic books about these and other superheroes

Chapter 5: Basic Reading and Writing Skills   **123**

5.10 Filling Out a Form

Objective

Using a sample form requesting basic information, the student will clearly and accurately complete the form.

Discussion

Teacher: Earlier, we talked about being able to tell someone what your name is, your address, and other important information. Why is it important to be able to do that? (To get help, keep careful records.) Why do you think it might be important to read and write that information too? (Don't have to keep repeating it, send it to someone through the mail.) What are some examples of when you might have to fill out a form that needs that information? (Going to camp, sending away for something, school records.)

Worksheet 5.10: Have you ever won a million dollars? Someday maybe that will happen to you, so to prepare you for that, you are going to fill out a practice form. If you are unsure of some of the information (area code, school address), think about how you could find the answers. (Ask, use phone book, school secretary.) Remember to write clearly. Why? (So people at the other end can send the prize to the correct address.)

Answers

(Answers will vary.)

Extension Activities

1. *Forms and More Forms.* Have students begin collecting forms that require writing their address and other basic information. They may include send-away forms from cereal boxes, comic books, and other sources.

2. *Raffle.* Have students complete a class-made form for a chance at winning a (small) raffle prize. Students may include information that they think is important to know, such as favorite movie character, shoe size, number of pets, and so on. Make it fun!

5.10   Filling Out a Form

You have just been given a chance to win $1,000,000! The specially-marked box of cereal that you enjoyed this morning has a winning ticket inside. Fill out the following form clearly and correctly!

My name is _____.

My address is _____
                                (number)   (street)

_____ (ZIP) _____
             (city)   (state)

My phone number is _____
                          (area code)

My date of birth is _____
                    (month)   (day)   (year)

My parent's names are _____
                         (father)

_____
                         (mother)

I go to school at _____
                   (name of school)

_____ (ZIP) _____
             (city)   (state)

This is what I would like to do if I win the $1,000,000 prize:

5.11 Addressing an Envelope

Objective

Given appropriate information, the student will correctly address an envelope.

Discussion

Teacher: What information is needed to send a letter to someone? (Name, street, state, ZIP Code.) Do you think the people who work at the post office care how you write the information as long as it's somewhere on the envelope? (There is a standard way to write the information, helps them sort the mail faster.) Who are some people you might send a letter to? (Family member, someone having a birthday, invitation to classmates.)

Worksheet 5.11: Look at the sample envelope. Then complete the practice envelopes using the information given.

Answers

(Answers will vary, but the envelopes should contain three lines for the return address and three lines for the recipient's address.)

Extension Activities

1. *I'm Your Biggest Fan.* Track down the addresses of celebrities who may be likely to respond to student fan letters. Have students write to a famous person of their choice and complete the envelope. Send them and see what happens!

2. *A Letter to Myself.* Have students write themselves a letter and address the envelope. Put the letters in a safe place and keep them out of sight and out of mind for as long as is feasible. (Maybe six months?) Send the letters to the students and have them let the class know when they were received. Discuss what events have changed over the past few months.

5.11   **Addressing an Envelope**

Look at the sample envelope. Then complete the practice envelopes using the information below.

Annie Body
123 Main St.
Detroit, MI 48220

Joe Schmoe
321 Any Ave.
San Francisco, CA 94110

1. Use your own name and address for the return information. Address an envelope to Mr. Fred Black who lives on 1435 Windy Street in Lexington, KY 40511.

2. Use a friend's name and address for the return information. Address an envelope to your teacher, using his or her school information.

3. Use the school's return address. Address an envelope to your parents using your own information.

4. Use your own return information. Address an envelope to the President of the United States. His address is 1600 Pennsylvania Avenue, NW, Washington, D.C. 20500.

5.12 Mailing a Letter

Objective

The student will correctly address an envelope, apply a stamp, and mail a letter to a recipient.

Discussion

Teacher: Has anyone received their prize of $1,000,000 yet? Why not? (Didn't send out forms.) What do you think we should do next to make sure you get your prize? (Send the form.) If we wanted to mail a letter, is it enough to just stick it in a mailbox? What else do we need to do? (Stamp, and so on.) The steps for mailing that letter include (1) address the envelope, (2) put your return address, (3) put on a stamp, and (4) mail the letter.

Worksheet 5.12: These students are all sending away for something or writing a letter that they wish to mail. Each, however, has run into a problem. Look over the steps for mailing a letter and write down the number of the step that is a problem. Then we'll discuss how to correct it so the students can get their letter in the mail.

Answers

1. 2 (return address)
2. 3 (stamp)
3. 4 (mail the letter; she placed it in a trash can)
4. 1 (address)
5. 3 (stamp)
6. 2 (return address)

Extension Activities

1. *Mail Call.* Have students complete one of the forms from the previous lesson and actually send it through the mail to obtain something or some information. (You may wish to find some inexpensive items or free information that would be interesting for them to receive.) Walk to the post office or nearest mailbox and deposit each letter.

2. *Letters to Someone Famous.* Have students select one of several cartoon characters, sports heroes, or someone appealing to the student. After writing a letter, have students complete an envelope (possibly including a sticker for a stamp if you don't intend to actually mail them), and "mail" them. You may wish to have students answer each other's letters (in character, of course).

Name _____ Date _____

5.12   Mailing a Letter

Each of these students wants to mail a letter, but each has a problem with one of the four steps. Write the number of the problem that needs to be corrected.

> 1 = address the envelope
> 2 = return address
> 3 = stamp
> 4 = mail the letter

1. Ron sent away for a set of comic books. He filled out the form, put it in the envelope, wrote the address, put on a stamp, and took it to the post office. He didn't get his comic books. What was the problem? _____

2. Sandy wrote a letter to her best friend. She carefully put her address in the top corner, wrote her friend's address on the front, and put it in her mailbox with the flag up. What was wrong? _____

3. Jennifer sent away for a set of coloring markers. She put a label on that had her address printed on it, wrote out the address, put on a stamp, and put the letter in a large metal box. What was the problem? _____

4. Randy put a stamp on his letter, wrote his return address, and put the letter in the mailbox on the corner. What was the problem with this letter? _____

5. This is the letter that Debbie sent to a toy company. What was the problem? _____

6. Maria was in a hurry to get her order for a new game in the mail. What was wrong with this letter? _____

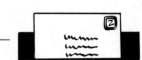

Chapter 5: Basic Reading and Writing Skills   **129**

5.13 Making Lists

Objective

Given a category or situation, the student will compose an appropriate list of needed items or people.

Discussion

Teacher: I'm having a party at my house, and I want you to go to the store and get me these things: two quarts of milk, eight pounds of hamburger, 6 bananas, one quart of strawberries, two cans of whipped cream, eight hot dogs, one loaf of bread, three bags of potato chips—wait! How are you going to remember all that? (List.) Unless you've got a memory like a tape recorder, you might need to make lists of things that you need to remember.

Worksheet 5.13: Now you are going to pretend that you are in some situations where you will find a list helpful. Write your answers in the space after each situation.

Answers

(Answers will vary.)

Extension Activities

1. *How Many Can You List?* Call out a topic (or choose one randomly from a pile) and have students list as many items that would go with that topic in sixty (or thirty) seconds. Topics may include animals, girls' names, words that start with "b," kinds of dogs, kids in the class, baseball teams, and so on.

2. *Rotating List.* A variation on the first activity is having one student begin the list, passing the list to the next student, and continuing on until each student has had at least one turn. How many items can you include for a given topic? If a child is stuck, you could have students with other ideas give clues, so that everyone is still thinking (even when it isn't their turn). The student with the list should call out his or her answer before writing it down to make sure the group agrees that it belongs on the list. Good discussions may follow!

5.13   Making Lists

Here are some situations for which you may have to make a list. Write down the items that would be on your list.

1. You just got a check for $100 in the mail with instructions that you have to spend it *today* or lose it all! Quick! Make a list of at least five things that you're going to buy.

2. You turned into Santa Claus for a day and have to make a list (and check it twice) of what you're going to get for all of the members of your family. What's on the list?

3. Your teacher wants you to list as many zoo animals as you can think of in sixty seconds. *Go!*

4. You're going shopping for food for that birthday party you're having. What are you going to get?

5. Your rock group, The Ninja Cows, is going on tour. You want to line up some important places to play. Make your list of where you'll be playing.

6. You are having a birthday party at your house. Your mother wants to know who you would like to invite. Who's on your list?

5.14 Having Good Handwriting

Objective

The student will critique and grade examples of handwriting, based on legibility and neatness.

Discussion

Teacher: I have pretty good handwriting, don't you think? But what do you think my handwriting would look like if I decided to write with my foot? Do you think you would be able to read it? (Probably not.) Whenever you write something for someone else to read, it has to be clear enough so that the person can actually read what you wrote. Why else is it important to write clearly? (So you will remember what you wrote later, so other people won't have to bother you to figure it out, so others will be able to read an important message quickly.) We are going to take a look at some examples of handwriting and let you be the teacher to give out the grades this time!

Worksheet 5.14: Today, YOU are the teacher. Give these writing samples a grade and be ready to discuss why you gave the grade your did. Use A, B, C, D, or F.

Answers

(Answers will vary, but look for these key points.)

1. C – The student didn't form letters correctly, didn't space or pay attention to the lines.
2. C – The handwriting is fair, but there are capital letters everywhere and sometimes the writing is in cursive.
3. A – Everything is easy to read.
4. B or C – Lots of cross-outs, difficult to read.

Extension Activities

1. *Class Checklist.* As a class, come up with a writing checklist that you and your students can use to reflect the important things to remember about writing. Decide which items are the most important and list them first. Then have students copy the checklist in their best handwriting!
2. *Handwriting Detective.* Collect samples of students' handwriting (without names). Have students evaluate them and note areas that could be improved. Use the Class Checklist to help give the sample a grade. Remember to keep the samples anonymous.

5.14   Having Good Handwriting

Today, *you* are the teacher. Give these writing samples a grade and be ready to discuss why you gave the grade you did. Use A, B, C, D, or F.

1. ~~Are~~ Our capital city is Washington DC.

2. On THursDay we will SEE the capitol.

3. Abraham Lincoln was born in Illinois.

4. Our class visited the White House.

5.15   Reminder Notes

Objective

The student will use given information to write a reminder note correctly.

Discussion

Teacher: You have probably noticed colorful little notes all over my desk. What are these little notes? (Sticky notes, reminders of things.) Since I have been telling you that writing is so important, why wouldn't I get my pen out and write a nice paragraph to myself that says something like the following? "Dear Self, It is important to keep track of what story we are on. Please remember to start on page 37 and stop on page 41. Sincerely, Self." (That would take a long time, a lot of unnecessary information.)

When I use a reminder note, it is a shortcut. I am going to write down only the very important thing that I need to remember. What do you think I might write instead of the long example I gave you? (Pages 37–41.)

Worksheet 5.15: Use the information to write a reminder note for yourself or someone else.

ANSWERS

(Answers will vary, but look for these key points.)

Dentist – 3:30 on Monday

Mom, call Dr. Smith

Send card to Aunt Julie for her birthday on 10/16

Spelling test Friday

Gym shoes – tomorrow

18 cupcakes

Extension Activities

1. *Sticky Note Home.* Have students decide where they will "park" their sticky note reminders. If you have them use a homework folder, you may want them to put them inside the front cover. Decide on a place where reminder notes should always go, so they don't have to write a reminder note to go looking for the reminder notes! You can label the place their "home."

2. *Color-Coded Notes.* To give students practice in using shortcuts, use color-coded sticky notes for each day of the week with an assignment for each day. For example, on Monday you might remind students to bring gym shoes; on Tuesday, use a different color and remind students to study for their practice spelling test; and so on.

5.15   **Reminder Notes**

Use the following information to write a reminder note for yourself or someone else.

1. You have a dentist appointment at 3:30 on Monday. _____

2. Your mother got a phone call from Dr. Smith and should call him back. _____

3. Your Aunt Julie's birthday is on October 16. Send her a card. _____

4. You have a spelling test on Friday. _____

5. You need to bring your gym shoes to school tomorrow. _____

6. You are supposed to bring eighteen cupcakes to school for a party.(Handwriting: lots of cross-outs) _____

Part Two

Personal Independence

Clothing and Dressing

PARENT LETTER #6

Dear Parents,

Part of personal independence is knowing how to dress, when to dress a certain way, and how to care for clothing. We will be working on skills related to clothing appropriate for particular situations.

There are several ways you can help your child as we progress through this unit. First, if your child can dress himself or herself, allow him or her to do so (even if the clothes don't always match!). You may want to provide the final once-over to make sure your child is presentable. Give your child choices as to what he or she will wear, reminding him or her to think about the weather, the temperature, the conditions of the place that he or she will be going to (inside? heated? muddy?), and how careful he or she needs to be to keep his or her clothes clean.

Cleanliness! Another thought! When you are doing the laundry, let your child watch and help, even if it's just a matter of pairing up socks or pouring in the detergent. Children need to see the complete process of wearing, cleaning, putting away, and wearing again.

When you shop for clothes, ask your child's opinion about the clothes you get for him or her. Make your child think about warmth and style, of course, as well as cost. Expose your child to your own thoughts about buying something to wear—what goes through your mind?

Happy shopping!

Sincerely,

_____

Teacher

Chapter 6: Clothing and Dressing

CLOTHING AND DRESSING

Skill Sheet #6: Progress Report

| + mastered |
| √ emerging |
| − not mastered |

Student Name	What's the Weather?	What's the Event?	Obtaining Clothing	Care of Clothing	Washing and Drying Clothes	Let's Go Shopping!	Final Inspection	Fads	Comments

6.1 What's the Weather?

Objective

The student will identify appropriate clothing suitable for weather conditions.

Discussion

Teacher: It's snowing outside, so I better get my swimming suit and my umbrella. What are you laughing at? Is there something wrong with my choice of clothing? We are going to be talking about clothes for a few days. One thing that you should keep in mind about clothes is the weather. What kinds of clothing would you wear in very cold weather? (Warm, sweaters, extra layers.) What would you wear in hot weather? (Shorts, T-shirts, swimsuits, and so on.)

Worksheet 6.1: What you wear each day depends a lot on the weather. Read the weather reports on the worksheet and circle each item that you could wear on that day.

Answers

Shorts, tennis shoes

Raincoat, light jacket

Shorts, T-shirt

Jacket, hat, boots

Shoes, mittens, jacket

Heavy jacket, socks

Sweater, long-sleeved shirt, pants

Extension Activities

1. *Weather Forecaster.* Have students listen to the weather report on the evening news. Does the weather forecaster give advice on what to wear? You may bring in a large doll (or mannequin) and have students "dress" the prop according to the weather.

2. *Season Sort.* Collect numerous pictures from magazines of people dressed in seasonal clothing. Mount them on construction paper, shuffle them, and have students sort them according to their dress for the seasons.

6.1   What's the Weather?

Here is the weather report for certain days in your city. Circle each item that would be appropriate to wear on that day.

1. Today will be very hot, with a high near 92 degrees. It will be sunny and sticky.

   mittens   boots   shorts   tennis shoes

2. It is going to rain most of the day.

   ear muffs   raincoat   light jacket   thermal underwear

3. It will be pleasant and sunny today, about 75 degrees. No rain in sight!

   shorts   winter coat   T-shirt   scarf

4. Today will be cold, windy, and snowy. Expect two to four inches of the white stuff!

   shorts   jacket   hat   boots

5. No snow today, but it will be very windy and cold.

   shoes   mittens   sunglasses   jacket

6. It will be about 20 degrees today and cloudy.

   light jacket   heavy jacket   socks   shorts

7. Today will be sunny, windy, and cold, with a high temperature of 40 degrees.

   sweater   long-sleeved shirt   flip-flops   pants

Chapter 6: Clothing and Dressing   **143**

6.2 What's the Event?

Objective

The student will identify appropriate clothing suitable for social events.

Discussion

Teacher: Do you remember the story of Cinderella? What was her problem with going to the ball? (Didn't have any fancy clothes.) Why was it important to her to have a nice dress? (Look right.) Would Cinderella wear that dress to a baseball game? It's a ball gown, right? (No, not that kind of ball.) Why do people have different kinds of clothes for certain events? (Feel more comfortable, look better, and so on.)

Worksheet 6.2: On this Worksheet, you are going to match each student who is going to an event with the proper clothing that he or she should wear. Think about why certain clothes are all right for some places, but not for others, such as school.

Answers

   1. d   2. f   3. h   4. c   5. a   6. g   7. b   8. e

Extension Activities

1. *Fouled-up Fairy Tale.* Have students rewrite familiar fairy tales, only have them mix up the clothing that the characters wear. For example, how would Cinderella have ended up if the Fairy Godmother had dressed her in Halloween clothes? What if the Seven Dwarves wore baseball uniforms? Or if Little Red Riding Hood's red coat was at the dry cleaner's one day and she wore a policewoman's uniform?

2. *Spirit Week.* Schools often have a "spirit week" in which each day of the week calls for some sort of specific dress; for example, Clash Day (wear items that do not go together), Twin Day (wear identical clothes with a friend), Colors Day (wear all of one color), and so forth. Designate one week as such and include Sports Day, Dress-up Day, Favorite Character from a Book Day, and so on.

Name _____ **Date** _____

6.2   What's the Event?

These students are going to attend certain events. Match each student with the clothing that would fit each occasion. Write the letter on the blank next to each situation.

1. Alberto is going to play football with the team after school.   _____

2. Cynthia is going to her cousin's wedding.   _____

3. Benjamin has been invited to a swimming party.   _____

4. April is going to a slumber party.   _____

5. Danny is going horseback riding.   _____

6. Vincent is going to a Halloween dance at school.   _____

7. Ricky is hiking around the lake.   _____

8. Maria is going biking in the country.   _____

a.

b.

c.

d.

e.

f.

g.

h.

6.3 Obtaining Clothing

Objective

The student will specify several appropriate places where clothing may be obtained.

Discussion

Teacher: Why do people have to get new clothes from time to time? (Outgrow them, rip them, seasons change, fads change.) Why don't you wear clothes like your mother or father wear? Do any of you ever hear complaints from older people about the clothes you wear? Sometimes you really do need to get new or different clothes. Where do they come from? Does everyone get clothes from a store? Do people ever get clothes from each other? (Handing down within a family, thrift shop, trading with a friend.)

Worksheet 6.3: The students on this sheet are all wearing something that is new or different for them. Each got some item of clothing at a different place or source. Write on the line the place where each got clothing.

Answers

1. Sisters
2. Gift from relatives
3. Retail store
4. Sporting event
5. Sew one herself

Extension Activities

1. *Did People Really Dress Like That?* Bring in pictures from the "olden days" such as the early 1900s, showing the ornate hats the women wore, elaborate clothing (especially the women's), and ties. Check out a book from the library on how styles have changed over the years. Ask students how they would feel about wearing something like that today!

2. *Fashion Fads.* Each generation has had its own clothing fads. Have students ask their parents about bell bottoms, Nehru jackets, go-go boots, and other fashion fads from an earlier time. Old yearbook pictures are another source of some good laughs and discussion.

Name _____ Date _____

6.3   Obtaining Clothing

These students got some of their clothes from different sources. Read each situation and write on the line the place where each got clothing.

1. I am the youngest of three girls. When I outgrow my sweater, I sometimes can get different sweaters without even going out of my house. Where did I get my sweaters?

   _____

2. It's my birthday! My aunt and uncle really came through with a great present! Guess where my new jeans and jacket came from?

   _____

3. I've got $20 in my purse. My friend and I are heading to the mall to look at some skirts. Where do you think I will get one?

   _____

4. Dad and I went to a football game at the county stadium to watch a professional team. I wanted a sweatshirt with the name of my team on it. Where did I get this?

   _____

5. I have a sewing machine. Next time I want a new vest, what do you think I'll do to get one?

   _____

Chapter 6: Clothing and Dressing   **147**

6.4 Care of Clothing

Objective

The student will identify several appropriate ways to care for clothing items to ensure longer wear.

Discussion

Teacher: Why does your mother tell you to take off your good clothes after religious service and put play clothes on? (So they won't get them dirty, torn, and so on.) Do your parents ever yell at you for not picking your clothes off the floor? Why? These are ways that you can take care of your clothes so they will last longer and give you more years of wear. Can you think of other ways?

Worksheet 6.4: Some of the students on this Worksheet are showing ways to take care of their clothes. Others are being careless. Circle the student in each pair who is being careful.

Answers

> Second student
> First student
> First student
> Second student

Extension Activities

1. *How Much Does It Cost?* Have students calculate the average price of a pair of jeans or casual outfit. Then estimate how long the average outfit is worn. What does the daily, weekly, or monthly cost come out to? Is it greater or less than students thought?

2. *Real Practice.* Give students a demonstration and practice time in clothing care habits such as washing in a washing machine, sewing on buttons, and folding and hanging up clothes. They may be surprised to find that it is not as hard as it seems. And practice makes perfect.

6.4   Care of Clothing

These students were told to take good care of their clothes. Circle the student in each pair who is doing something to help take care of his or her clothes.

6.5 Washing and Drying Clothes

Objective

The student will identify the appropriate cleaning procedure for different types of clothing articles.

Discussion

Teacher: If you fell on a day when the snow was melting and your winter coat got all muddy, how would you clean it? Would you throw it in the washing machine? (Probably too big, bulky.) Would you hang it out on the line to dry? (Too cold to dry it.) Different kinds of clothing articles require different kinds of cleaning methods. But all kinds of clothes need to be cleaned when they are dirty or have been worn for a while. Let's think about different ways to wash and dry clothes to get them clean.

Worksheet 6.5: This Worksheet shows some items that would need to be cleaned and different ways that you could clean them. Read the clues carefully to find the answer that matches and write the letter on the line.

Answers

1. d 2. g 3. e 4. c 5. f 6. a 7. h 8. b

Extension Activities

1. *Visit to Dry Cleaners.* If possible, arrange a visit to a local dry cleaning establishment and have the personnel explain the dry cleaning process to the students. Ask how different types of stains are removed and how cleaning is achieved without water.

2. *Laundry Experiments.* Have students identify laundry products that claim to get rid of common stains. Set up and carry out simple experiments in class, comparing different products and their performance in getting out the same stain. Use old towels or T-shirts to receive stains such as mud, grass, Magic Markers, and so on. Be sure to have students keep accurate records and carry out comparison procedures carefully.

Name _____ Date _____

6.5   Washing and Drying Clothes

Match each item below with a good way to get it clean. Read the clues carefully to find the best matches. Write the letter of your choice on the line.

_____   1.   Heavy wool sweater

_____   2.   T-shirt

_____   3.   Jeans

_____   4.   Towels

_____   5.   Delicate socks or pantyhose

_____   6.   Very nice suit

_____   7.   Sweat socks

_____   8.   Sneakers

a. Take it to a dry cleaner; they will clean it without damaging it and probably put it on a hanger.

b. They can be cleaned by hand with a rag and some polish.

c. They can be put in a washing machine and then a dryer, then folded and stored in a closet or the bathroom.

d. This should be taken to a dry cleaner so that it can be cleaned without shrinking, because this material tends to shrink.

e. This material can shrink too, but after the first washing, it usually will be the same size; you can wash these in a washing machine and then put them in a dryer or hang them out to dry.

f. Wash these by hand in a sink or tub; the washing machine could rip them up.

g. Because you probably wear this over and over, just throw it in a washing machine and then a dryer for cleaning; it's easy to care for.

h. These are tough too, and can be cleaned the same way as (g).

6.6 Let's Go Shopping!

Objective

The student will state which characteristics are important when shopping for clothing items.

Discussion

Teacher: When you go shopping for something, why can't you get anything you want? (May not have enough money, not your size.) If your mom or dad sent you to shop for shoes for school, what might you come home with? (Name-brand sneakers, loafers.) What would they say if you came home with ski boots? (Go right back.) So when you go shopping for clothing, what are some things you should keep in mind? (Cost, size, value, and so on.)

Worksheet 6.6: Here are examples of students who were not good shoppers. Can you figure out why? Read each situation and write your answer.

Answers

1. Spent too much 2. Poor quality 3. Only bought one item 4. Wrong size
5. Not appropriate for all those places 6. Not appropriate for school 7. Too expensive
8. Wrong season

Extension Activities

1. *Catalog Shopping.* Give each student $100 in play money. Assign each the task of back-to-school shopping. What items did they buy through the catalog? How did each spend their money? What can you get for $100?

2. *Sneaker Survey.* Have students conduct an informal survey of members of the class, members in a certain grade level, all girls, and so on to determine which brand of sneaker is the most popular. You may also include a question concerning where most students purchase their shoes. Keep all respondents anonymous!

6.6   **Let's Go Shopping!**

These students were sent shopping for clothes. Why weren't they good shoppers? Write your answer in the space below each situation.

1. Beth's sister gave her $20 to buy a new skirt.

2. Ronald wanted some jeans that would last a long time.

3. Kate had $100 to get several outfits for school. This is what she came home with.

4. Fred really liked the color of this sweater.

5. Frank wanted to get some shoes that he could wear to school, at home, and on the football team.

6. Sally looked at three different dresses for school. She got the one in the middle.

7. Kris does not have a lot of extra money. She bought the shoes in the middle.

8. Ramon went shopping for some clothes that he could wear outside in the snow.

6.7 Final Inspection

Objective

The student will identify several areas of personal inspection of clothing that are important to consider before going out in public.

Discussion

Teacher: A lot of us are in a hurry before we step outside in public. Have you ever seen anyone get on the bus and look as though he just rolled out of bed? Was it you? Why do you think it is important to look in the mirror before you go outside? (To check over clothing details, see how you appear to others.) What are some things that you should check? (Hair, buttons, zippers, shoes, belt.) If you start at the top—your head—and go down, I bet we can make a list of a lot of important things to check.

Worksheet 6.7: What are some things that you need to remember to check on yourself before you go out? Add to the list.

Answers

(Answers will vary.)

Examples: check my nose, check my teeth, make sure everything that is buttoned is buttoned, pants pulled up, no underwear showing, belt buckled, socks match, shoes tied, and so on.

Extension Activities

1. *Head to Toe.* Have students work in groups to make a life-sized poster of a boy or girl who demonstrates poor dressing habits—messy hair, sweater buttoned the wrong way, and so on. Then have them make a second person with the details corrected.

2. *Before and After.* Have a student volunteer to portray the "before" and "after" look of a well-groomed person. Other students can critique the student and give hints to help him or her improve his or her appearance.

6.7   **Final Inspection**

What are some things that you need to remember to check on yourself before you go out? Add to the list below.

1. Comb my hair.

2. Check my zipper.

3. _____

4. _____

5. _____

6. _____

7. _____

Chapter 6: Clothing and Dressing   **155**

6.8 Fads

Objective

The student will identify whether a fad in dressing is appropriate or inappropriate for a given situation.

Discussion

Teacher: What are some popular ways that kids like to dress these days? (Spiked hair, earrings, certain brands of clothing.) Do you think it matters where you are or what you are doing when you get dressed? Why do you think something might be OK if you are with your friends, but might not be OK if you are in a different setting or with adults? (Guidelines for appropriate dress at a wedding, funeral, family reunion.) No matter what is popular or how you think you should look with your friends, remember that you have to think about where you are and who you are with to make sure you look right for that situation.

Worksheet 6.8: These students want to look cool! Write YES or NO if you think each student is doing the right thing.

Answers

1. YES   2. NO   3. YES   4. YES   5. NO   6. YES   7. NO   8. YES

Extension Activities

1. *How to Look Cool.* Have students bring in pictures from magazines that show popular clothing styles for their age group. Students can write a tongue-in-cheek description of a "style show" that describes what is currently "in."

2. *Fads of Yesteryear.* Bring in yearbooks from a decade or two ago and have students take a look at what was popular in days gone by. After having a good laugh with your students, remind them that someday their fads will be a good conversation piece as well.

6.8   **Fads**

The students below want to look cool! Write Yes or No if you think each student is doing the right thing.

1. Anna wants to get her ears pierced. Her mother gave her permission and took her to get an earring in both ears.

   _____

2. Jack is going to a funeral. He wants to wear his jeans very low around his hips so that his underwear shows.

   _____

3. Lauren wants to get a tattoo on her ankle. Her parents don't really want her to get a tattoo, so she will wait until she is older

   and ask them then if she can get one. _____

4. James likes to wear his shoelaces untied. When he went to gym class, the teacher said that everyone

   had to tie their shoes. James tied his shoes during the class. _____

5. Hailey wants to wear a really short skirt to school. Her mother said it was OK as long as she wore leggings under it. Hailey wore the leggings to school and then took them off when she got there.

   _____

6. Nicholas likes to wear his hat backward. There is a school rule that no one can wear a hat indoors, so Nicholas takes it off when he gets to school and puts it on as soon as he leaves.

   _____

7. Zoe loves bracelets. She has eleven bracelets that she likes to wear on one wrist. If she gets bored

   at school, she takes them off and puts them back on a few times. _____

8. Aiden came to school with his hair sprayed purple and spiked it so that it went straight up. He forgot that it was picture day. He decided that he would wash it out and have his picture taken and

   come with colorful hair on a different day. _____

Chapter 6: Clothing and Dressing   **157**

Chapter 7

Keeping Yourself Clean

PARENT LETTER #7

Dear Parents,

We will be working on the different skills involved in keeping yourself clean, including taking a bath or shower, caring for hair, cleaning hands and face, and brushing teeth. Your help is needed to reinforce these skills at home. Whatever method of maintaining cleanliness is used, it must be consistently followed every day. To a great extent, the way you want your child to look is influenced by you. Please allow your child lots of practice attempts to learn shampooing and taking a shower by himself or herself. Don't discourage your child by noticing only the mess that is left—praise the attempt!

Expect your child to wash his or her hands before eating, wash his or her face each night, and brush his or her teeth several times a day. We will be learning steps to complete these activities and will send home the list of steps. Please follow them carefully and help monitor your child's progress at home.

Thanks for your help!

Sincerely,

_____

Teacher

Skill Sheet #7: Progress Report

| + mastered |
| √ emerging |
| − not mastered |

Student Name	Taking a Bath or Shower	Hair Care	A Clean Face	Taking Care of Your Hands	Using a Mirror	Care of Teeth	Makeup	When You Are Sick	Comments

7.1 Taking a Bath or Shower

Objective

The student will state the appropriate sequential steps involved in taking a bath or shower.

Discussion

Teacher: What do you do when your dog rolls in the mud or gets dirt all over? (Bathe him.) Why? (Make him clean, look nice.) Why do you think people take baths? (Same reasons.) It's very important for people to be clean. Some people take a bath or shower every single day. Who can tell me everything you need to gather up before you take a bath or shower? Let's make a list. (Soap, towel, and so on.) Now, let's make a list of everything you would need to do to take a good bath or shower.

Worksheet 7.1: Carl is going to take a bath, but he got the list of instructions mixed up. The list is broken into four parts. Help Carl put the list in the correct order by numbering the parts 1 through 4 on the right side.

Answers

2, 1, 4, 3

Extension Activities

1. *Magic Soap.* Have students write stories about taking a bath with magic soap that would turn them invisible, give magic powers, and so on. Leave the vocabulary words pertaining to baths on the board.

2. *Rub-a-Dub-Dub.* Have students practice adjusting the temperature on a bathtub faucet, draining the water, scrubbing out a bathtub ring, and so on. These sound like simple skills, but they are important for independence and courtesy to the next user.

7.1   **Taking a Bath or Shower**

Carl is planning to take a bath, but he got his directions all mixed up. The left side shows what he did and how he looks now. Put the steps in the correct order by numbering them on the right side.

Get in the tub.
Rub soap and lather all over.
Scrub and rinse off soap _____

Get your washcloth, towel, soap and clean clothes. Turn on the water. Adjust the temperature. Take off your clothes. _____

Dry yourself off.
Put on clean clothes. _____

Rinse off the soap.
Get out of the tube.
Drain the water. _____

Chapter 7: Keeping Yourself Clean   **163**

7.2 Hair Care

Objective

The student will state the appropriate sequential steps involved in maintaining clean hair.

Discussion

Teacher: Part of looking your best has something to do with your hair. What do you think it is? (Washing, brushing.) No matter what style your hair is, it will look better if it is carefully taken care of. Some people wash their hair while they are in the shower; others wash it separately. However you do it, the steps are pretty much the same. First, let's list what supplies you'll need to get. (Shampoo, conditioner, towel, comb, dryer, and so on.) Now, let's list the steps for washing your hair: (1) wet, (2) shampoo, (3) rinse, and (optional) (4) conditioner and (5) rinse. After your hair is clean and rinsed, then what should you do to take care of it? (Style it, dry it, comb it.)

Worksheet 7.2: The students on this Worksheet tried to take care of their hair but had problems. Write what you think is the problem on the line next to each situation. Then we'll discuss what you think each student should do to help take better care of his or her hair.

Answers

Used too much shampoo   (Rinse it out.)

Left shampoo in hair   (Rinse it out.)

Didn't comb out hair   (Comb it.)

Left hair dryer on   (Turn it off.)

Dirty hair from not washing   (Wash it.)

Extension Activities

1. *Way-Out Hair.* Have students bring in pictures of exotic hair styles (punk rockers, weird styles, and the like). Discuss the importance of hair and what people think of you. Do people notice hair styles?

2. *Makeover.* With parent permission, have a student volunteer for a hair makeover if you can arrange this with a local beauty salon. Have the stylist explain the finer points of taking care of your hair and ways to make it more attractive. Hearing her express the importance of healthy, clean hair will, it is hoped, make an impact on your students too.

7.2   **Hair Care**

These students did not follow the steps for caring for their hair. What mistakes did they make?

7.3 A Clean Face

Objective

The student will state the appropriate sequential steps involved in washing and drying his or her face.

Discussion

Teacher: We've talked about a clean body and clean hair. What's next? Another important part to take special care of is your face. Why do you think a clean face is important? (First thing people notice, and so on.) Today we're going to talk about the steps for washing and drying your face and then go and practice!

Worksheet 7.3: Here are some directions that this student is correctly following to wash and dry her face. Let's read them and see if it makes sense; then we'll have a student volunteer come up and give it a try! When it's your turn, I'll help you check off each step that you can do correctly.

Answer

(A completed checklist.)

Extension Activities

1. *Clown for a Day.* To give students a reason to wash their faces at school, have a clown theme for one day, allowing students to use special facial makeup to decorate themselves. (Or simple face painting on the cheeks may suffice.) At the end of the day or activity, take students to the restroom or sink area and have them wash their faces for you. You'll easily be able to tell which students need additional practice.

2. *Practice, Practice, Practice.* Enlist parents' help to encourage students to wash their faces at home and maintain a chart at school for one week, applying a sticker each day that the student successfully washes his or her face. At the end of the week, reward the student(s) with a small bar of soap!

7.3   **A Clean Face**

Here are some directions for washing your face. Make sure you understand them and have everything you need. Put a check mark after you have done each step correctly.

Step 1. Pull your hair out of the way. You might use a head-
band or rubber band if you have long hair.

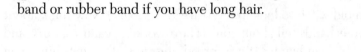

Step 2. Rinse all the surface dirt off your face with water.

Step 3. Cover your hands with soap. Then apply the soap to your face. You might want to use special face soap.

Step 4. Lather the soap all over your face in circular strokes. Really scrub!

Step 5. Rinse all the soap off your face. You might want to use a clean washcloth for this.

Step 6. Pat your face dry using a dry washcloth.

Chapter 7: Keeping Yourself Clean   **167**

7.4 Taking Care of Your Hands

Objective

The student will state and demonstrate procedures for washing hands, keeping fingernails short and clean, and awareness of health and safety procedures involving germs or disease.

Discussion

Teacher: What do you picture the hands of an old witch to look like? (Warts, long nails.) Now think about the hands of a doctor. (Very clean.) What do your hands tell about you? (Hard-working, calluses, dirty, and so on.) Why do you think it is important to have clean hands? (Stop spread of germs, don't get things you touch dirty.) What if the doctor was going to do surgery, but sneezed all over his hands before he started? It really is important to keep your hands clean, especially after you have touched something that may have germs on it. Can you give me any examples? (Be prepared for unsavory answers.) Today we're going to concentrate on ways to keep your hands clean and looking neat.

Worksheet 7.4: These students have been given some rules about keeping hands clean. Read the situations and decide which rule each student needs to follow. Write your answer on the line next to each situation.

Answers

1. Rule 3   2. Rule 5   3. Rule 1   4. Rule 4   5. Rule 2   6. Rule 5

Extension Activities

1. *Achoo Posters.* Have each student draw his or her face from the front. Attach a tissue by the nose on the picture. Have students write a rule or message on each poster such as "When you sneeze, please use me!"

2. *Handwashing Practice.* Pretend you are a robot and have students give instructions as to how to wash your hands. Do not assume that you will use soap, for example, if they don't specify to "pick up the soap." Then let students work in pairs and practice giving good directions to each other. Inspect their hands.

7.4   Taking Care of Your Hands

These students are trying to follow the rules about keeping their hands clean and safe. Read what each student is saying, and then write the number of the rule that each is trying to follow,

---

Rule 1. Wash your hands with soap.

Rule 2. Dry your hands completely on a clean towel or cloth.

Rule 3. Keep your fingernails short.

Rule 4. Keep your fingernails clean.

Rule 5. Wash your hands if they are dirty or if you have touched something unhealthy.

1. Look at my hands! I'm going to use his fingernail file to make them look better!

2. Wow, it's fun playing with these old rusty tools! But now I better do something...

3. There, I've gotten water all over my hands. They're clean now, aren't they?

4. Why does my mom complain about this? Oh well, I'll take care of the problem.

5. I'll just wipe my wet hands on my pants, my pants that I've just been playing football in.

6. Aaaaachoooo! I know which rule I have to follow now!

7.5 Using a Mirror

Objective

The student will give suggestions for improving the appearance of a student who is depicted looking at himself in a mirror.

Discussion

Teacher: How many of you have ever heard this: "Before you go out, check yourself in the mirror"? Why do you think someone said that to you? (So you wouldn't look bad going out, because there might be something you missed.) What kinds of things would a mirror show you? (If your hair was messed up, if your face was dirty.) Where do you have access to a mirror at school or at home? (Restroom, pocket mirror.)

Worksheet 7.5: These students are looking at themselves in a mirror to make sure they are clean. What advice would you give each of them to make them look better? We will discuss your comments.

Answers

(Answers will vary.)

1. Check your hair again.
2. Blow your nose.
3. Wipe the lipstick off your face.
4. You better wash your neck.
5. You missed a button.
6. There is something in your hair.

Extension Activities

1. *Mirror, Mirror.* Put up a large mirror in your classroom in a strategic spot—perhaps by the door? Have students use construction paper to make a pretty frame to go around the mirror. From time to time remind students to check themselves in the mirror.

2. *Positive Post.* Have students submit positive comments that you could stick on the mirror so that when students are checking their appearance, they are also reading a pleasant comment. ("Today, I can be my best!" "Don't forget to add a smile!") Change the comments periodically.

7.5   **Using a Mirror**

These students are looking at themselves in a mirror to make sure they are clean. What advice would you give each of them to make them look better?

1.

2.

3.

4.

5.

6.

Chapter 7: Keeping Yourself Clean   **171**

7.6 Care of Teeth

Objective

The student will brush his or her teeth in an appropriate manner and specify at least one purpose for visiting the dentist.

Discussion

Teacher: What would happen to me if I never brushed my teeth? (Rotten teeth, bad breath.) I'll bet every one of you did something to your teeth this morning. What was it? (Brushed them.) Tell me the name of the person who helps you take care of your teeth—what is he or she called? (Dentist.) Well, if you can brush your own teeth, why should you visit a dentist? (He can find cavities, pull teeth, correct teeth, and so on. Also, a hygienist uses special tools to check for decay and can clean your teeth.) Why do you think it is recommended to visit a dentist twice a year? (Cavity prevention, takes several months for cavity to form, regular cleaning keeps your smile bright.)

Worksheet 7.6: Today you are going to follow a girl, Flossie, as she takes care of her teeth. There are words missing from each part. Write the missing words on the lines supplied; then put the circled letters in order at the bottom of the Worksheet to form a word that has something to do with good dental care.

Answers

1. brush   2. miss   3. rinse   4. floss   5. dentist

Word: Smile

Extension Activities

1. *Visit from "Jaws."* Have a dentist, if possible, visit the class and explain current proper dental brushing procedures by using a model of a human jaw with teeth intact. If a dentist is not available, literature and a model can usually be obtained from your local dental society or dentist. A school nurse may also be able to help with this.

2. *A Tooth Speaks.* Have students pretend they are a tooth in their own mouth. Have the tooth describe what it feels like to be brushed, flossed, and possibly have a cavity forming.

7.6　　　　　　　　Care of Teeth

Flossie is taking good care of her teeth. Follow her through the day as she shows you what she is doing. Write the missing word on the lines provided. Then, when you're finished, put the circled letters in order at the bottom of the page to spell out a good word for you to remember to show off good dental care.

1. Flossie gets up in the morning and pulls out her

   green tooth ____ ____ ____ ◯ ____.

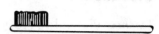

2. Then she puts toothpaste on the toothbrush and moves the brush up and down all over her teeth.

   She is careful not to ◯ ____ ____ ____ any spots; she gets them all!

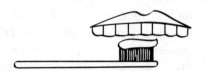

3. After the toothpaste is scrubbed all over her teeth,

   she uses clean water to ____ ◯ ____ ____ ____ out the toothpaste. She spits it into the sink and lets it drain.

4. Now she gets the dental floss and uses the string to get out any little bits of food that may be left or caught in between her teeth. Flossie thinks that

   ____ ◯ ____ ____ ____ ing is fun!

5. It's time for Flossie to visit the lady who can help her check for cavities and give her teeth an excellent cleaning. This person is

   Flossie's . ____ ◯ ____ ____ ____ ____ ____.

Now put the circled letters in order. How can you show off your good dental care?

____ ____ ____ ____

7.7 MakeUp

Objective

The student will state when use of makeup is appropriate.

Discussion

Teacher: Pretend you're getting ready to go out trick-or-treating for Halloween. You are dressed as a little green creature from Mars. What might you do to your face? (Use green makeup.) Now pretend you're going as a Native American from the Old West days. How might your face look? (Stripes, war paint.) How would wearing makeup change your appearance? (Make people look at you, cover or hide your own face.) Why do you think people wear makeup today for ordinary use? (Cover up blemishes or wrinkles, look attractive.) Lots of people, especially women and girls, like to wear makeup because they feel that it makes them look more attractive by covering up any blemishes they may have or adding colors to have attention drawn to them. But what kind of attention would I have drawn to me if I came to school looking like a strange creature or with war paint on my face? (People would laugh, think you look odd.) When you use makeup, make sure that you use it to make yourself more attractive, not to get attention for looking weird. Can anyone give me examples of too much makeup? (Models in magazines, fluorescent eye shadow, and so on.)

Worksheet 7.7: These students are using makeup, but some of them are not thinking where they are or how much makeup they should be using to look attractive. Write Yes or No if you think each is using makeup appropriately or not.

Answers

1. No (bad taste)   2. Yes   3. No   4. Yes   5. No   6. Yes   7. No

Extension Activities

1. *How Much Is Too Much?* Have students lood through magazines (particularly women's magazines) and discuss what products are shown that will make someone attractive. What about overdoing perfume? Or clothing? Or hair styles? Have students select pictures of people whom they think are quite attractive and discuss what features about them are interesting, unusual, or noticed.

2. *Makeover.* If you can get a cosmetologist to visit your class, have her take the girls aside and show them ways to use makeup to enhance their looks. Let the girls practice putting on makeup with each other and then make a "grand entrance" into the room. Take pictures—before and after. Emphasize that there is a happy medium to using cosmetics. (Some girls can benefit from using makeup just to make themselves feel pretty and by spending a little extra time taking care of themselves. Other girls may need to reduce the amount they use, mistakenly thinking that "more is better.")

Name _____ Date _____

7.7   **Makeup**

These students are using makeup for different reasons. Write Yes or No on the lines to say whether you think each student is using makeup appropriately.

1. _____ I'm going to a funeral, so I'm going to paint my fingernails black and use black eye shadow and black lipstick.

2. _____ I've got a pimple on my cheek. A little bit of this makeup should cover it up and maybe even help it heal.

3. _____ I want to look like I'm tan, so I'm going to put a ton of this dark makeup all over my face.

4. _____ I'm so pale—a little of this blush will make me look healthy.

5. _____ People will notice my pretty blue eyes if I use my eyeliner to make designs!

6. _____ My face has darker spots in places—this facial cover-up will even that out.

7. _____ I'm going swimming for P.E. first hour—but I'll just put all this makeup back on in the restroom after that class.

Chapter 7: Keeping Yourself Clean   **175**

7.8. When You Are Sick

Objective

The student will give a healthy suggestion when presented with situations in which a person is not feeling well.

Discussion

Teacher: When was the last time you were sick? How did it make you feel? (Not very energetic, tired.) Part of keeping yourself clean involves what you do when you are not feeling well. For example, if you have a runny nose, what would be a good way to keep yourself clean instead of wiping your nose on your sleeve? (Use a tissue.) It's always good to think about staying clean, but when you are sick you might have to think ahead a little bit.

Worksheet 7.8: What advice would you give to each of these students who is sick? Write your answer on the lines.

Answers

(Answers will vary.)

1. Get a tissue.
2. Don't share your utensils or personal items.
3. Stay home if you are contagious.
4. Let the teacher know.

Extension Activities

1. *Tissue Box Art.* Ask each student who is able to bring in a box of tissues for classroom use throughout the year. If the boxes are not colorful, have students design small posters or signs to glue on to the front (or largest face) of the box. Then when the box is available for use, students can be reminded to read the health suggestion.

2. *Extra Clothing Box.* Accidents will happen! Be prepared by having an assortment of boys' and girls' clothing in the classroom or at an appropriate site at your school. It might be important to have extra socks and shoes as well.

Chapter 7: Keeping Yourself Clean

7.8   **When You Are Sick**

What advice would you give to each of these students who is sick? Write your answer on the lines.

1. I can't stop sneezing. I just keep—ACHOO!—sneezing and sneezing!

_____

_____

2. I have a cold, but here—you can have the rest of my drink.

_____

_____

3. My mom thinks I might have the measles, but I didn't want to miss the party at school, so I came today anyway!

_____

_____

4. My stomach hurts and I feel like I might throw up. I wonder if I should let the teacher know. The restroom is two floors down.

_____

_____

Keeping Your Room Clean

PARENT LETTER #8: KEEPING YOUR ROOM CLEAN

Dear Parents,

Maintaining a clean bedroom is a task that we deal with pretty much every day of our lives! A bedroom not only serves as a place where your child sleeps, but it is also a toyroom, study, gymnasium, playground, and social activity center and whatever else might be a part of your lives. Though we want our kids to have privacy and enjoy their own space, we do need to teach them to accept the responsibilities of maintaining a room that might be open to the public.

Make your expectations clear and reasonable as far as how much you want your child to do. What do you want the child to do with his or her clothes after school? Where do you want books to be stored? Do toys have to be put away at the end of the day or can they stay out for continued use tomorrow? Convey your expectations to your child so that he or she knows the procedures.

If your child shares a room, there is the added aspect of sharing space, being considerate with belongings and privacy, and adjusting personalities to be compatible. To maintain fairness, talk with your children about who is responsible for which chores and the timelines for when they are to be completed.

It is a challenge (for any of us!) to keep things constantly organized, but it's never too early to learn the habits. Please allow your child to participate in the joys of cleaning up and being organized. Show him or her where the cleaning supplies are and how to run the vacuum cleaner (if appropriate), and don't forget to give a word of encouragement!

Sincerely,

_____

Teacher

KEEPING YOUR ROOM CLEAN

Skill Sheet #8: Progress Report

	+ mastered
	√ emerging
	− not mastered

Copyright © 2009 by John Wiley & Sons, Inc.

Student Name	Picking Up	Making the Bed	Floor Care	Dusting	"Too Much Stuff"/De-Cluttering	Organizing a Closet	Rules for the Room	Sharing a Room	Comments

8.1 Picking Up

Objective

The student will participate in keeping his or her room clean by picking up all items from the floor or other places where they do not belong and put the items in an appropriate place.

Discussion

Teacher: Think about your room at home. Now describe what it looks like. (Messy, organized, specific items named.) Today we're going to be talking about picking up your room. What does that mean? (Put things where they belong.) What kinds of things do you usually leave lying around in your room?

Worksheet 8.1: Dennis the Disorganized is a student who needs some help returning items from all over his room to their appropriate spots. Help him by matching the things that need to be picked up with the place where each should go.

Answers

1. b   2. d   3. f   4. g   5. j   6. h   7. e   8. i   9. a   10. c

Extension Activities

1. *A Peek into Your Room.* Have students use construction paper to make a large door (complete with door knob and signs or stickers that may be on their door). Arrange it so that the door can be "opened" with paper underneath. Have students draw the view that a visitor would see if they made a surprise visit to their room. (If students share a room with a sibling or someone else, they could include that person's belongings also.)

2. *Clean-up Math.* Have students write story problems involving items that are usually associated with having to be picked up. Exchange problems and have students solve them. (*Example:* George had three dirty plates in his room, each with four pieces of pizza on them. How many pieces of pizza were there in all?) Pictures are also welcomed!

8.1   Picking Up

Dennis the Disorganized was told by his father to "pick up the room." Help him match each item with its proper place. Write the letter of the place next to each item.

1. A dirty shirt _____

2. A clean shirt _____

3. A shoe _____

4. A pencil _____

5. A towel _____

6. School books_____

7. A bike tire _____

8. Skateboard magazines _____

9. A an empty soda can _____

10. A plate with cold pizza on it from last

    week's dinner_____

a. In the recycling bag in the garage

b. In the dirty laundry basket

c. To the dishwasher (after dumping out the food in the kitchen trash)

d. On a hanger in his closet

e. On his bike in the garage

f. Next to the other shoe on the floor of his closet

g. In the pencil can on his desk

h. Stacked neatly on his desk

i. In a magazine rack next to his desk

j. In the bathroom

8.2 Making the Bed

Objective

The student will follow appropriate steps to make a bed, including changing sheets, pillows, and bedspread.

Discussion

Teacher: Does this ever happen at your house? You find out that a guest is coming, and your mom or dad says that you have to help get the guest bed ready. What has to be done? (Prepare a nice-looking bed.) What's involved in making a bed? (Flat sheets, blanket neatly tucked in, pillow in place, bedspread smoothed out.) Why do you think a neat-looking bed is important? What if nobody ever comes in your room to see it anyway? (A good point! Stress that even if no one sees it, it's a good skill to know how to prepare a bed for visitors. And it feels good to get into a smoothly made-up bed at night rather than one with rumpled, balled-up covers.)

Worksheet 8.2: There are probably lots of different ways to make a bed. Some people just throw the blankets on; others take special care for each and every step. This Worksheet shows a step-by-step way that you could make your bed. Even if this is not the way you normally do it, let's go through the steps and make sure that you understand at least one way to do it. (You may want to send this sheet home as an assignment. Have a parent go through it with the student and initial it when completed.)

Answer

(A completed checklist.)

Extension Activities

1. *"I Did It" Chart.* Continue a cooperative effort with parents at home to monitor and reward bedmaking behavior. Encourage parents to let their child work on this task (even though it may be easier for the parent to do it instead at first).

2. *Step-by-Step Photos.* If you have access to a practice bed at school, use a camera to photograph students in various steps of the bed-making procedure. Have students arrange the pictures in sequential order on a poster and verbally explain what is involved in each step.

8.2   Making the Bed

Here are some directions for making a bed. Make sure you understand each step. Put a check mark next to each step after you have completed it correctly.

Step 1. Put the bottom sheet neatly on the bed. Make sure it is centered and tucked in.

Step 2. Put the top sheet over the bed. Fold back the top edge a little bit.

Step 3. Now put the blanket on top of the top sheet. Fold the top edge back.

Step 4. Put the pillow or pillows at the head of the bed. Fluff them up!

Step 5. Now you might want to tuck in the blanket and sheet all around the bed. Don't make it too tight or you'll have trouble getting in!

Step 6. If you use a bedspread, put that over everything and take extra care to tuck in part of it under the pillow. Then bring the top up to the head of the bed.

Step 7. You might want to put a stuffed animal on top!

Chapter 8: Keeping Your Room Clean   **185**

8.3 Floor Care

Objective

The student will specify what cleaning activity (vacuuming, sweeping) is most appropriate for the floor in his or her room and follow appropriate steps to clean the floor.

Discussion

Teacher: Look at our floor. Does anyone know how it is cleaned? (Vacuumed, swept.) Part of keeping your room clean is making sure that the floor is clean. Why do you think the floor gets dirty? (Shoes left on, walked on, stuff thrown on the floor.) Basically, there are two ways to clean a floor. If you have carpeting, you can vacuum it. If you have a hard floor, you can sweep it and mop it to keep it clean. Today we're going to learn how the different ways help keep the floor clean.

Worksheet 8.3: This Worksheet shows some tools that can help keep a floor clean. On the first part, you will match the name of the tool with the picture of it. On the second part, use the names from the top to complete the paragraphs of students explaining how they keep their floor clean.

Answers

  a. 2
  b. 3
  c. 1
  d. 2
  e. 3

Story

  1. Vacuum cleaner
  2. Broom, dustpan
  3. Mop, bucket, bucket

Extension Activities

  1. *Cleaning Extravaganza.* Have students collect pictures of different cleaning products. Categorize them into various functions, rooms they could be used in, types of procedures (mopping, dusting, and so on).

  2. *Floor Inventory.* Have students complete a simple chart indicating the type of floor surface in the various rooms of their home. Discuss why many kitchens are not carpeted or why people may use small rugs in certain areas or rooms.

Name _____ Date _____

8.3   **Floor Care**

These students are using different materials to clean their floors. Match each material with the method used.

1= vacuuming   2 = mopping   3= broom/sweeping

a. Bucket _____

b. Broom _____

c. Vacuum cleaner _____

d. Mop _____

e. Dustpan _____

Now use these words to complete the cleaning stories below.

1. My room is carpeted, so I am going to get the _____. I will plug it in to the outlet on the wall, turn it on, and move it all around the floor to pick up the dirt.

2. My floor is not too dirty, so I am going to get a long _____ and sweep all of the dirt from the corners and even under the bed into the

   center. Then I'll use the _____ to collect the dirt, and I'll dump it out.

3. My room is really dirty today, so I'm going to get a _____

   and put it in this _____ of soapy water. Then I'll move it

   back and forth all over the floor, rinsing it out in the _____ every once in a while. I'll let the floor dry—and it'll be nice and clean again!

8.4 Dusting

Objective

The student will dust a designated area with proper materials and in a safe and thorough manner.

Discussion

Teacher: AchOOO! There must be some dust in this room! Since we've been talking about keeping rooms clean, what do you think might need to be done to get rid of dust? (Dusting, cleaning dirt in the air.) What is dust, anyway? (Small particles of dirt or matter in the air.) How could we get rid of it? (Feather duster, fan, spray cleaner.) What happens when a lot of dust settles on something? (Covers with a fine layer.) What commercials have you seen that involve cleaning to get rid of dust? (Writing name on table, and so on.) Does anyone know some good materials to eliminate dust? (Rags, dusters, commercial sprays.)

Worksheet 8.4: The students on this Worksheet have been asked to dust, but only one is dusting in a manner that is going to get the job done properly. Circle the student who is dusting properly. Then we will discuss what the others are doing wrong.

Answers

1. Ineffective way to remove dust and probably unappreciated by neighbor.
2. Too much spray.
3. Didn't dust at all.
4. Deodorant doesn't substitute for spray cleaner.
5. Good job.
6. Broom is too large for small expensive knickknack cleaning.

Extension Activities

1. *Dust in the Room.* Have students focus on one room at a time and try to come up with five to ten places where they might find dust. Then take a look to see if they were right. Which rooms tend to be dustier? Why?
2. *Room Dusters.* Have students take turns being the room duster. Supply a colorful duster, clean rags, and spray, if desired. Be sure to evaluate the job done.

8.4   **Dusting**

Only one student below is dusting the right way. The others are doing at least one thing wrong. Circle the student who is doing a good job and explain why the others are not doing a good job.

1. I'll get rid of that dust! I'll blow it all at my neighbor's house!

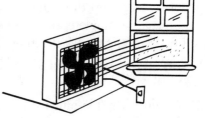

2. There, that should take care of the dust on that table!

3. No one will see the dust on top of the bookshelf, so I'll consider this job done!

4. I'll use this spray deodorant to clean off the top of this table. It looks just about like the spray stuff Mom uses when she dusts.

5. First, I'll spray this on the table, then I'll carefully wipe it with a clean rag until there aren't anymore streaks.

6. I can use this broom to dust the knickknacks on this shelf. I'll be careful since they are very, very valuable.

Chapter 8: Keeping Your Room Clean   **189**

8.5 "Too Much Stuff"/De-Cluttering

Objective

The student will sort items into a "keep" or a "get rid of" category.

Discussion

Sometimes people need to sort through their "stuff" and get rid of things that they won't use anymore or things that are broken, incomplete, or out of style. What are some examples of things in your room that you don't need or want any more? (Clothes, toys, games, broken items.) What are some things in your room that are very special to you; things that you know you will probably keep for a long time? (Photos, special gifts, jewelry.)

Worksheet 8.5: "Andrea has "too much stuff." Help her organize her room by marking the items that you think she should get rid of.

Answers

1. Yes, unless she has a younger sister
2. No; she probably can still use them
3. No; it will be winter again
4. Yes
5. No; it was a special gift
6. Probably yes
7. Yes
8. Yes
9. Yes
10. Yes
11. Maybe no if she likes to draw and will use it again
12. Yes
13. Yes
14. No, if she will wear them
15. No; special item

Extension Activities

1. *Pick Three.* Pretend that students have only sixty seconds to run into their room and choose only three items that they want to save. Set a timer, have students think for a bit, and then write down the three items that they value the most. Discuss why they picked the items that they chose.

2. *Collection for Others.* Many students probably do have a lot of items that they could discard. Set up a collection day in which students bring in an item of clothing, a book, or other item in good condition that your classroom could send to an agency that helps those in need.

Chapter 8: Keeping Your Room Clean

8.5   "Too Much Stuff"/De-Cluttering

Andrea has "too much stuff." Help her organize her room by marking with YES or NO the items that you think she should get rid of. Be prepared to discuss your answers.

_____	1.	A sweater that is too small for her
_____	2.	Sneakers that are a little bit worn
_____	3.	A winter coat, because now it is summer
_____	4.	Books that she read when she was little, but won't read again
_____	5.	A book that was given to her by her grandmother as a special gift
_____	6.	Some rocks from a picnic two years ago
_____	7.	A board game that she played with as a two-year-old
_____	8.	An old bathing suit
_____	9.	A jigsaw puzzle with missing pieces
_____	10.	A candle that is almost burned to the bottom
_____	11.	Some scrap paper for drawing
_____	12.	A glass that was under the bed for a long time
_____	13.	A computer game for a computer that she doesn't have anymore
_____	14.	Bright red socks
_____	15.	A picture of her family in a frame

8.6 Organizing a Closet

Objective

The student will sort items into an appropriate place within a "closet."

Discussion

Teacher: If I visited your home and opened your closet, what would happen? What would I see? (Probably a lot of interesting things!) If you have a lot of items, it can be very easy to just throw them onto a pile and not bother to put them in a specific place. What are some areas of a closet that help you know where to put things? (A shelf, a shoe rack, a pole for hangers, organizers.) Why do you think it is a good idea to keep a closet organized? (So you can find things, so your room will seem bigger.)

Worksheet 8.6: Help Logan organize his closet by showing where each item should go.

Answers

1. D   2. A   3. B   4. D   5. B   6. C   7. C   8. B   9. C   10. D   11. A   12. C

Extension Activity

Scavenger Hunt. Have students contribute suggestions for a closet scavenger hunt that they can complete at home. The list might include very specific items, such as a blue sock, a book about dogs, or a striped sweater. See how many students can locate these items in their closet. No cheating!

8.6   **Organizing a Closet**

Help Logan organize his closet by showing where each item below should go.

   A = in a storage box   B = on a hanger   C = on a shelf   D = on the shoe rack

1. Snearkers _____   7. Books _____

2. Off-season clothes _____   8. Pants _____

3. Suit _____   9. Football _____

4. Flip-flops _____   10. Slippers _____

5. Nice shirt _____   11. A shirt that is too big right now _____

6. Board game _____   12. A box of video games _____

8.7 Rules for the Room

Objective

The student will state a family rule that pertains to situations involving procedures for keeping one's room organized or maintained.

Discussion

Teacher: What do you do at home when your clothes are dirty? (Put them in a hamper, give them to my mom, throw them on the bed.) I bet that there are some specific procedures that your parents would like you to follow when you are at home. What would be a rule or procedure that happens at your house if you spill something on the floor? (You have to clean it up, tell an adult right away.) What about leaving things out? Do you have rules for when it is okay to leave things out and when you need to put them away? (Put away if there is no room, if there is company coming, if the dog can get it.) Why do you think there need to be rules for how to do things at home? (So one person doesn't always have to do everything, so you know where things go.)

Worksheet 8.7: You probably have your own system of rules for your house. Complete each sentence with the rules that you follow.

Answers

(Answers will vary.)

1. Put them in the hamper.
2. Put my dishes in the sink.
3. Have to take them off and put new ones on.
4. Get a paper towel and wipe it up.
5. Hang them up in my closet.
6. Turn them off.
7. Put the game on a table.
8. Make my bed.

Extension Activities

1. *Crazy Rules.* Have students divide a sheet of paper into two columns: on the left side, have students list situations for room activity similar to the ones on the Worksheet. On the right side, have students write their rule for each situation. Then separate all of the items on the right side, mix them up, and randomly put them next to the items on the left. It should result in a crazy rule such as: *When my clothes are dirty, I hang them up in my closet. If I spill something in the room, I am supposed to make my bed.* Enjoy!

2. *A Mixed-up Day.* Have students use the crazy rules from the above activity as a basis for a creative writing project in which they write about the day the rules got mixed up and the commotion that followed.

Name _____ Date _____

8.7   **Rules for the Room**

You probably have your own system of rules for your house. Complete each sentence below with the rules that you follow.

1. When my clothes are dirty, I . . .

   _____

   _____

2. If I eat in my room, I have to . . .

   _____

   _____

3. When my sheets are dirty, I . . .

   _____

   _____

4. If I spill something in my room, I am supposed to . . .

   _____

   _____

Chapter 8: Keeping Your Room Clean   **195**

8.7 (*Continued*)

5. When my clothes have been washed and dried, I . . .

_____

_____

6. If the lights are on in my room and I leave the room, I should . . .

_____

_____

7. If I have been playing with a game and have to leave to go somewhere, I . . .

_____

_____

8. When I get out of bed in the morning, I am supposed to . . .

_____

_____

Chapter 8: Keeping Your Room Clean

8.8 Sharing a Room

Objective

The student will provide a plausible solution for solving a problem involving having to share a bedroom.

Discussion

Teacher: How many of you have your own bedrooms? How many of you have to share a room? How many of you *wish* you had your own bedroom? Even though you might wish you had your own room, there are some good things about sharing a room. Any ideas? (You can talk, play, have fun with your roommate.) Unfortunately, when you have to share a bedroom, you also have to share the responsibilities for keeping it up, share the space, be concerned about different schedules, and other things. What are some things that are hard about sharing a bedroom? (Someone might be noisy, talk on the phone at night and keep you awake, spill things on your side.)

Worksheet 8.8: These students have to share a bedroom with other people. What advice would you give them to help them solve their problems? Write your answer on the lines.

Answers

(Answers will vary.)

1. Ask the sister to be quieter in the morning.
2. Do homework in another room.
3. Remind the sisters that she needs room too and to please clean things up before bedtime.
4. Ask if Micah could talk on another phone or stay in the room, and probably Micah will want to move to another place.
5. Ask a parent to help set rules for cleaning up.
6. List the chores, divide them up, switch every other week.

Extension Activities

1. *How We Share.* Have students who share bedrooms talk about how they divide the chores, deal with problems, and spend their time together with their roommates. Sharing a room can result in sharing a bond between family members.
2. *How Would You Like This Roommate?* Have students write creative stories in which they have a very unusual roommate with interesting qualities; for example, a kangaroo, a giant, an invisible friend, a twin, or a cousin from a foreign country. How would they address all of the situations discussed in taking care of a room shared with these new, special roommates?

8.8   **Sharing a Room**

These students have to share a bedroom with other people. What advice would you give them to help them solve their problems? Write your answer on the lines.

1. Samantha and her sister share a bedroom. Samantha says that her sister makes too much noise in the morning and wakes her up.

   _____

2. Jack shares a room with his grandfather, who is old and hard of hearing. When Jack is trying to work on his homework, his grandfather wants to talk and turns up the TV very loud.

   _____

3. Addison shares a room with two younger sisters. She came into the room to find that they were playing with their dolls and spread their toys all over the room so that she could hardly walk through.

   _____

4. Tyler and his brother Micah have a phone in their room. Micah is constantly talking to his girl-friend; this bothers Tyler when he wants to have friends over.

   _____

5. Isabelle's bedroom is very small and she has to share it with her cousin who never picks anything up. Isabelle gets very tired of picking up her cousin's clothes, toys, papers, books, and magazines.

   _____

6. Benjamin and Jackson are brothers. Neither of them likes to clean up their room. There are dirty clothes, leftover food, smelly shoes, and pieces of all kinds of things all over. Their mother said they have to work it out between them how they will keep their room clean.

   _____

Food and Eating Skills

PARENT LETTER #9: FOOD AND EATING SKILLS

Dear Parents,

Food and eating skills are skills that we deal with every single day, don't we?

This section of lessons centers around food—finding it, declaring it healthy, cooking it, serving it, and cleaning up afterward!

If possible, let your child accompany you as you shop for food and help pick out items that are healthy. Stop to look at the nutrition labels and explain why something might be a better choice than something else. Encourage the eating of fresh fruits and vegetables for healthy snacks.

When you go out to eat, use this as a teaching time to show your child how to use good table manners, show politeness to servers, say "no, thank you" when a food is not appealing, and keep the conversation nice at the table.

If you feel comfortable letting your child help you prepare a meal, this is also a good time to teach task completion—cleaning up! Perhaps you share the meal preparation chores, in which case your child can learn to participate however he or she is able.

While we all probably agree that nutrition is a wonderful thing, don't forget sometimes there is just nothing like a good chocolate candy bar. Let's be realistic!

Thanks again for helping to partner with us!

Sincerely,

_____

Teacher

FOOD AND EATING SKILLS

Skill Sheet #9: Progress Report

Student Name	Shopping for Food	Making a Shopping List	Simple Cooking, Easy Meals	Table Manners	Cleaning Up	Washing the Dishes	Eating Out	Food Groups	Healthy Snacks	When You Don't Like Something	Comments

9.1 Shopping for Food

Objective

The student will identify numerous items of food that can be obtained at a local grocery store.

Discussion

Teacher: I'm hungry. Is anybody else hungry? If we wanted to prepare a nice meal, where could we get the things we need? (Grocery store.) Who can help me list twenty things you can buy at the grocery store to help you with a meal? (Specify whether you want to include nonfood items, such as napkins, paper plates, and so on.) Most grocery stores now carry all kinds of nonfood items too. Can you list ten? (Games, cards, videos, toys.)

Worksheet 9.1: Here is a list of items that can be found in a grocery store. When you do this activity, I want you to check off each item that you found and write down what row or aisle or section you found it in. We'll see if there's a pattern in different stores.

Discuss with students why certain items may be grouped together, stored in refrigerators or freezers, or sold fresh.

Answers

(A completed checklist.)

Extension Activities

1. *Food Hunt.* When planning a school party, you may be able to take students shopping for needed items. Have students pair up and locate various items. This activity is not a race, but it should be carried out systematically. Instead of wandering all around the store, have students think about where it would most likely be found, then go there.

2. *Store Map.* If possible, have students draw a general map of the local grocery store, indicating where various items are located. Have them walk slowly around the store and come up with general categories (for example, "vegetables" instead of "corn, beans, peas").

9.1   Shopping for Food

Here is a list of items commonly found in any grocery store. Check off each one as you find it, and write down the location (row, aisle, section).

Item	✓	Where
1. Frozen green beans		
2. Can of corn		
3. Fresh carrots		
4. Box of cookies		
5. Tomato soup in a can		
6. Loaf of bread		
7. Frozen dinner		
8. Fresh hamburger		
9. Gallon of milk		
10. Box of cereal		
11. Paper plates		
12. Canned pop		
13. Potato chips		
14. Bacon		
15. Brownie mix		

9.2 Making a Shopping List

Objective

Given a situation or meal, the student will make a list of needed items.

Discussion

Teacher: Would it be fun to have a class party for another class, your parents, your pen pals, or class volunteers? What would happen if I dropped you all off at the door of the store and said, "Get what we need!" (Duplicate items, chaos in the store, run out of money.) What would be a good way to make sure none of that happened? (Make a list, be sure you have enough money before you start.) Would you need the same things if you were having friends over for dinner as you would if you were having people you didn't know over for snacks? Would you have to think about how many people were coming over too?

Worksheet 9.2: Help these students make lists of things that they need at a grocery store. Then we will talk about what things you all felt were important. Do you think everyone's list will be exactly the same?

(These are example.) Answers

1. Snacks (popcorn, soda)
2. Cake, ice cream, napkins, plates, balloons
3. Pizza mix, soda, garlic bread
4. Potato chips, popcorn, cookies, vegetables, dip

Extension Activities

1. *Class Party.* Begin planning an "event" that your class could host for another group. Have students make invitations, plan activities, and make a list of needed items. Really promote this.
2. *Helping at Home.* When parents need items at the store, have the students find the needed things on the list. Parents may want to divide their shopping list so that the student can get items located in a certain area, items that the student is likely to need, and so on. The sooner the student is familiar with the store, the more help he or she can be to the parent shopper.

Chapter 9: Food and Eating Skills

Name _____ Date _____

9.2   **Making a Shopping List**

These students are going to have a party or special event at their house. Help each make a list of needed items. Write your answers on the lines.

1. Ronald is having friends over to watch a basketball game at this house after dinner.

_____

_____

_____

2. Sandy is having a birthday party in the afternoon for a few friends.

_____

_____

_____

3. Alex wants to make pizza for his family.

_____

_____

_____

4. Kim is having a swimming party all day at her house and wants to have snacks for people to munch on.

_____

_____

_____

_____

9.3 Simple Cooking, Easy Meals

Objective

The student will follow directions for preparing a meal or particular part of a meal.

Discussion

Teacher: If I came over to your house and said that I'd like something to eat, what could you fix for me? What if I expected to stay for a whole meal? What would you like me to have? How would you prepare a dish if you weren't sure? (Ask someone, use a cookbook or recipe.) Today we're going to learn about preparing simple things to eat. By "simple," I mean there are just a few steps to follow. Can anyone name some things that are easy to prepare? (Sandwich, soup, and so on.)

Worksheet 9.3: Would you like to try cooking something? Here is a list of some foods that can be prepared quite easily. Your job is to find out how to do that. Then we'll compare our answers and give it a try!

(These are example.) Answers

Have students list all materials that need to be gathered.

List sequential steps for preparing the item (turn on the oven, cut up the fruit, flip the hamburger over, and so on).

Explain how the ingredients are combined.

Extension Activities

1. *Chef for a Day.* Have students try out a simple recipe at home, perhaps using something that their parents often serve or enjoy eating. They could tell about their experience and how it turned out—perhaps even bring in a bit of what they prepared, if possible.
2. *Class Cookbook.* Have each student bring in or contribute one simple recipe or procedure for preparing one item of food. Combine the directions into a class cookbook. Have students illustrate the steps and the final product. You may want to reproduce enough copies for each student to have his or her own.

9.3   # Simple Cooking, Easy Meals

Here are some items that are fairly easy to prepare or cook. Find out the different steps involved in each and list them on another sheet of paper. Circle one food item that you would like to try to make.

1. Peanut butter and jelly sandwich

2. Chicken noodle soup from a can

3. A cup of hot chocolate

4. Brownies from a mix

5. Fresh fruit salad

6. Hamburger patty (on a stove)

7. Macaroni and cheese from a mix

8. A frozen TV dinner

9.4 Table Manners

Objective

The student will demonstrate courteous table behavior when eating socially.

Discussion

Teacher: Who can describe for me what the lunchroom is like? Is it noisy, fun, or what? Why do people have to stand in line to get a hot lunch? (Orderly.) When you eat food or meals with other people, there are certain things that you should do to show that you have good manners at the table. What are some of the lunchroom rules that help make things orderly or show good manners? (Keep noise level down, don't all run for lunch at once, and so on.) Why do you think it's important to have good table manners?

Worksheet 9.4: Every home has its own set of rules or table manners. Here are some examples of students either following or not following a table rule. Circle the students who are showing good table manners; put an X the students who are not.

Answers

1. X, O   2. O, X   3. O, X   4. X, O

Extension Activities

1. *At Our House* . . . Have students draw an outline of a house and write a rule that is important for good table manners at *their* house (guests eat first, pray before eating, wash hands, and so on). Discuss why each rule is important.

2. *Party Time!* Have an event for which your students can play the part of "host" or "hostess" for visitors. Rehearse polite phrases (such as "Thank you for coming," "I hope you enjoyed it," "Would you like another brownie?") and actions (give everyone a napkin, make sure everyone has a nametag). This might also be a good opportunity to practice getting all cleaned up! Students will love getting compliments on their excellent manners. (Be sure to inform guests that the students are demonstrating good manners!)

Name _____ Date _____

9.4   **Table Manners**

Here are some examples of table manners. Circle the student in each pair who is showing good manners; put an X on the student who is not.

1. Wait until everyone at the table has his or her food before you start eating if you are sharing food.

2. Share the food with everyone.

3. Pass food politely.

4. Have nice topics of conversation at the table.

9.5 Cleaning Up

Objective

The student will specify the proper procedure for handling leftovers, removing dishes and tableware from the table, and cleaning up the eating area.

Discussion

Teacher: What happens after you've eaten a meal at home? (Leave the table, clean up.) What happens here at school when your lunch time is over? (Throw trash away, line up to leave lunchroom.) Because there's a proper procedure for everything else connected with eating and food, do you think there might be good things to do after you eat a meal to help clean up the area? What things need to be taken care of? (Dishes, leftovers, crumbs.)

Worksheet 9.5: Here is a story about a mixed-up girl who is trying to clean up. She made a few mistakes, however. Put an X on the pictures that show her mistakes.

Answers

1. X: Closet; Better: dishwasher
2. X: Blankets and towels; Better: aluminum foil or plastic wrap
3. X: Homework bag; Better: trash or garbage disposal
4. X: Vacuum cleaner; Better: paper towel or dishrag

Extension Activities

1. *Cafeteria Helpers.* Some schools allow students to help clean up in the cafeteria after meals in return for cookies, reduced rates on meals, or simply for vocational training. Often students enjoy being able and allowed to do this activity. It should not be perceived as a demeaning job; rather, view it as a vocational training task.

2. *Behind-the-Scenes at McDonald's.* McDonald's and other fast-food restaurants sometimes offer tours of the facilities to school groups. If you can, arrange for your students to hear about the standards of cleanliness required by many restaurants, specifically what happens to leftovers and trash. Does your community recycle? Do your local restaurants participate?

Name _____ Date _____

9.5   Cleaning Up

Molly is mixed up today. She is trying to clean up after a meal at her home, but in each thing she tried to do she has done one thing wrong. Put an X on her mistake and write a better choice on the lines next to each picture.

1. Everyone has finished eating, so Molly decided to take the plates, glasses, and silverware and put them in the closet so they would come out clean.

_____

_____

2. Molly took the leftover food and wrapped up the food that she wanted to save. She put blankets and towels around the food and put them in the refrigerator.

_____

_____

3. Some of the food was not worth saving. Molly scraped the food off of the plates and threw it into a bag that had her homework in it.

_____

_____

4. There were crumbs and water drops on the table, so Molly got a vacuum cleaner and sucked them up. Then she threw the vacuum bag into the trash.

_____

_____

9.6 Washing the Dishes

Objective

The student will demonstrate ability to wash, rinse, and dry tableware manually.

Discussion

Teacher: We already talked about cleaning up after you have a meal, but there's one task that we didn't talk about. It has to do with cleaning up the dishes. Can anyone think of it? (Washing the dishes.) Why can't you just brush off the food and put the dishes back? (Soap gets rid of any germs; promotes better health, sanitation.) Today we're going to work on washing dishes—and that includes glasses, bowls, and silverware.

Worksheet 9.6: Here are the steps for one way to learn to wash dishes. Remember, you might wash them differently at home, so the directions may not be exactly the same as you have heard before. That's all right—the important thing is that you learn at least one good method! When you work on this at home, be sure to have someone watch you to make sure you are doing it correctly. Then check off each step.

Answers

A completed checklist.

Extension Activities

1. *Kitchen Coupons.* Have students devise a "coupon book" containing coupons good for one washing of dishes. Have the students make several kinds—perhaps one would be good for breakfast dishes, another for Sunday dinner, and so on, depending on the family lifestyle. Have parents redeem the coupons from the student. Require signatures and a comment from the parent on the back of the coupon.

2. *Kitchen Assistant.* For students who may not be totally competent to wash dishes independently, assign only one or a few steps to be learned and demonstrated. Students may enjoy helping a parent or sibling with the dishwashing process, yet not be entirely responsible for the complete task.

Name _____ Date _____

9.6   Washing the Dishes

Here are some steps for washing dishes. Put a check mark next to each step after you understand it and have completed it correctly.

Step 1. Fill the sink with hot water. Be careful! Squirt in some dish detergent as you fill the sink. Turn off the water.

Step 2. Put the dishes, glasses, and silverware into the sink. Let them soak for a few minutes to loosen any food particles.

Step 3. Use a scrubbing pad or cloth to go over the dishes to make sure all of the food particles are off.

Step 4. Rinse the dishes. Be sure to get off all the soap!

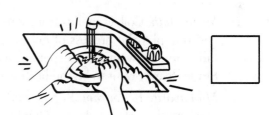

Step 5. Dry them with a clean towel or let them drip dry.

Step 6. Drain the water and clean out the sink.

9.7 Eating Out

Objective

The student will state the usual sequential steps involved in obtaining a meal at a restaurant, including seating, ordering, paying the bill, and tipping.

Discussion

Teacher: I'll bet all of you have had a meal recently that was not cooked by someone at your house or at a friend's house. Where else can you get food? (School cafeteria, restaurant, fast-food restaurant, convenience store.) What's different about eating at a restaurant from eating at someone's house? (Pay for it, are served, food may taste better or worse.) Eating out is fun to do, isn't it? Where are your favorite places to eat out, when you have the chance?

Worksheet 9.7: Randy is a student who eats some of his meals at home and sometimes eats out. You are to read over the sentences that tell about Randy and decide whether he is eating at home or out. Write the words HOME or OUT next to each picture.

Answers

1. HOME, OUT   2. OUT, HOME   3. HOME, OUT   4. HOME, OUT

Extension Activities

1. *Menu Math.* Collect menus from some local restaurants. Have students practice being the customers and role-play the process of entering the restaurant, ordering from the menu, and paying for the bill. You may want to incorporate math skills, calculator skills, and reading skills into this activity. Students may want to be the hostess or server in this role-play also.

2. *My Favorite Restaurant.* Survey students as to their favorite fast-food restaurant, item (French fries, chicken, dessert), or slogan. Combine responses and make a large graph. Also include containers with restaurant logos or ads to brighten up the graph. You could also survey students as to how often they eat out, how often they go to a particular fast-food place, or how many French fries a particular place includes in a regular order.

Name _____ Date _____

9.7   Eating Out

Randy ate one meal at home and another meal in a restaurant. Look at each set of pictures. Write HOME
if it took place at Randy's home; write OUT if it took place when he ate out. Write your answers in the
space next to the pictures.

1. Randy went to the table and sat
   down.

   Randy waited for the hostess to tell him
   where to sit.

2. Randy looked through the menu to pick out
   what he wanted to eat .

   Randy passed the dishes around the table and
   put some of everything on his plate.

3. Randy politely passed what other people
   wanted and waited until everyone was finished to leave the table.

   Randy politely passed what other people
   wanted and waited until the waiter gave
   them a bill before he got up.

4. Randy helped clear off the table and
   washed the dishes.

   Randy gave the cashier some money and left
   a tip on the table.

9.8 Food Groups

Objective

The student will identify at least two examples of a food from each of the six food groups.

Discussion

(*Note:* The following information is from the website www.keepkidshealthy.com.)

Teacher: People who study healthy eating and foods have developed what is called a "food pyramid." This contains six groups or types of food that people need to eat every day. We are going to take a look at the six groups and talk about some foods that would fit into each category.

First is the grain group. These are foods that come from grain products such as rice and oats. Some examples are bread, pasta, oatmeal, and crackers. Can you think of some others? (Breakfast cereals, tortillas, brown rice.)

The second is the vegetable group. Some vegetables include broccoli, sweet potatoes, carrots, and corn. Can you think of some others? (Spinach, kale, celery.)

The third is the fruit group. The fruits you choose can be fresh, canned, frozen, or dried. Can you think of some fruits that you like? (Apples, bananas, cranberry juice, frozen strawberries.)

The fourth is the oil group. You need only a little bit of oil each day and most likely it will already be in the foods you eat, such as nuts, fish, salad dressing, or cooking oil. You probably don't have to go looking for oil.

The fifth is the milk or dairy group. This includes milk, of course, but can you think of any other dairy products? (Cheese, yogurt.)

The sixth is the meat and bean group. These foods are high in protein. Examples include chicken, fish, and eggs. Can you think of others? (Peanut butter, nuts, beef.)

Worksheet 9.8: Circle examples of each type of food group listed.

Answers

1. bread, crackers   2. carrots, lettuce, broccoli   3. apples, glass of orange juice, grapes

4. nuts, salad dressing   5. yogurt, low-fat milk, cheese   6. fish, chicken, eggs

Extension Activities

1. *Food Pyramid Posters.* Have students draw and color posters similar to the food pyramid on www.mypyramid.gov, which depicts the food groups and the amount of each that should be consumed daily.

2. *Pyramid Card Game.* Write examples of each of the six food groups on individual cards. Be sure to code each example with the correct food group; for example, the item "apple" should also have "Fruit Group" written on the card. Put all cards in the center and have students take turns drawing one card at a time. The first student to obtain an example of all six groups is the winner. You can make the game a bit more complex by adding special cards such as "Give this card to the person on your left" or "Draw again."

9.8   Food Groups

Circle examples of each type of food group listed below:

1. **Grain Group:**

    bread   eggs   crackers   pineapple

2. **Vegetable Group:**

    carrots   lettuce   apple   broccoli

3. **Fruit Group:**

    cherry soda   apples   glass of orange juice   grapes

4. **Oils Group:**

    popcorn   nuts   salad dressing   cheese

5. **Milk Group:**

    yogurt   low-fat milk   cheese   pretzel

6. **Meat and Bean Group:**

    granola bar   fish   chicken   eggs

9.9 Healthy Snacks

Objective

The student will identify examples of healthy snacks.

Discussion

Teacher: How many of you have a snack when you get home from school? When are some other times you eat a snack? (On a trip, after a game, between meals.) What do you eat for a snack? (Apples, cookies, sandwich.) You probably have heard the term "junk food." These are food items that probably taste really good to you, but they have very little nutritional value. They might be very high in fat or sugar, which is not healthy. I bet you can give a lot of examples of junk food, can't you? (Candy, cookies, fried nuggets.) When you want a snack, it is better for you if you eat something that is healthy. Let's think of some examples of healthy snacks. (Fruit juices, fresh fruits, raw vegetables, yogurt, granola bars.)

Worksheet 9.9: Samantha is hungry and would like something to snack on. Which of the snacks would be a healthy choice for her? Circle each answer.

Answers

2, 3, 5, 6, 9, 10

Extension Activity

Healthy Snack Fair. As a class project, collect easy-to-prepare recipes for healthy snacks. (Remember "ants on a log"? Celery, peanut butter, and raisins!) Have students/parents bring in examples to share with the class. If possible, have a "Healthy Snack Friday" at which time students can prepare and sample nutritious snacks.

9.9   Healthy Snacks

Samantha is hungry and would like something to snack on. Which of the following snacks would be a healthy choice for her? Circle each answer.

1. Nachos with cheese

2. A bunch of grapes

3. A fruit cup with peaches and pears

4. A king-sized chocolate candy bar

5. Sunflower seeds

6. A granola bar

7. Chicken nuggets

8. A slice of pizza

9. Fruit juice popsicle

10. A cup of yogurt

9.10 When You Don't Like Something

Objective

The student will identify appropriate ways to refuse when he or she is offered something to eat.

Discussion

Teacher: Guess what's for lunch today? Barbequed eel! No, I'm just kidding; it's probably chicken tenders. But what if our cafeteria served something that you really didn't like? How would you react? (Say "no thanks," make a face or a comment.) You might find yourself in situations in which you are offered something to eat that you do not like. What are some foods that don't appeal to you? (Exotic foods, foods with strong tastes, individual ingredients.) How would people feel if they offered you something and you made a face or acted as though you were going to be sick? (Offended that you were rude, angry.) Not everyone likes all foods. But if you are in a place where you have the choice of taking something or refusing, it is much better to refuse as politely as possible. What are some ways that you could refuse some food that you don't like and still show good manners? (Say "No, thank you," ask for a very small portion, explain that you are allergic to a certain food, compliment something else that was served.)

Worksheet 9.10: Which of these students is refusing to eat something in an appropriate way? Circle the name of each student who is being polite.

Answers

2. Chloe   3. Nathan   5. Matthew

Extension Activity

Dee-licious Diner! Have students come up with unusual concoctions that they can pretend to serve at a fictitious diner (complete with an exotic name). Try not to offend any ethnic groups, but students might want to combine strange ingredients to name a "specialty of the house." (Example: Meatballs dipped in motor oil, covered with a light flaky topping of snail tails.) Role-play situations in which two students are the diners, one is the server, and the students practice politely handling this situation. (Some, of course, will ask for extra helpings!) Have other students in the audience critique how well it is handled.

9.10   When You Don't Like Something

Which of these students is refusing to eat something in an appropriate way? Circle the name of each student who is being polite.

1. **Jackson:** I hate mushrooms! Yuck! I'll throw them on your plate instead.

2. **Chloe:** No, thank you. I don't care for any anchovies.

3. **Nathan:** Just give me a small amount, please. (Then when I don't eat it, it won't look like so much!)

4. **Lily:** Oh my gosh! That is the weirdest looking salad I have ever seen! Don't give me any of that!

5. **Matthew:** Hmmm. I have never had eel before. I think I will just pass.

6. **Madison:** I refuse to eat vegetables without any ketchup. They can sit there all night—you can't make me eat them.

Chapter 10

Living a Healthy Lifestyle

PARENT LETTER #10: LIVING A HEALTHY LIFESTYLE

Dear Parents,

A healthy lifestyle includes taking care of oneself, getting enough exercise and sleep, and using common sense to avoid dangerous situations. These things seem pretty obvious to us as adults, but the roots of being healthy begin as a child. Encourage your child to get exercise (it can be a fun activity!) and find activities that they enjoy in their free time. You should not have to hear "I am bored. What is there to do?" if your child has projects, interests, and opportunities to become involved in healthy activities.

Remember that you are your child's most important teacher. Be a good example of living healthy. Perhaps there is something you and your child can do together or participate in as a family.

Good luck with your healthy living!

Sincerely,

_____

Teacher

Skill Sheet #10: Progress Report

	+ mastered
	√ emerging
	− not mastered

Student Name	Visiting Health Care People	Getting Exercise	Leisure-Time Activities	What About Drugs?	Avoiding Unhealthy Habits	Dangerous Situations	Following Safety Rules	Getting Enough Sleep	Comments

10.1 Visiting Health Care People

Objective

The student will state the importance of and purpose for visiting health care professionals.

Discussion

Teacher: During the next few weeks we'll be talking about ways to keep yourself healthy and safe. Why do you think that's important? (Live longer, live better.) I'll bet you can think of some people whose job it is to help you stay healthy. (Doctor, pharmacist, nurse, dentist.) Why don't those people come to your house to take care of you? (Don't know when you're sick, have offices to take care of many people.) So whose job is it to make sure you get to see someone when you need help? (Parents, self.) What could happen if you had a health problem and didn't do anything about it? (Might get worse.)

Worksheet 10.1: These students have some health problems and need to see someone who can help them. Match the student with the person who could best help him or her. Write the letter next to each student.

Answers

1. b 2. f 3. d 4. c 5. a 6. e

Extension Activities

1. *Doctor, Doctor.* As a vocabulary-building exercise, list some of the many specialties that doctors in your area practice. Common ones may include dermatology, ophthalmology, pediatrics, radiology, and anesthesiology. Students may have had experience in visiting one or more of these doctors.

2. *Health in the News.* Have students begin collecting magazine or newspaper articles dealing with health issues. Design a bulletin board that highlights "health in the news." Discuss vocabulary such as "cholesterol," "blood pressure," and "vaccination."

10.1   Visiting Health Care People

These students have some health needs. Match the student with the health care person who could help him or her. Write the letter next to each student.

_____ 1. John can't see the board in his classroom very well. Sometimes things look very blurry to him.

a. Doctor

_____ 2. Amy fell on the playground and cut her arm. It is bleeding a little bit.

b. Eye doctor

_____ 3. Sylvia needs to take medication for her allergies. If she doesn't, she feels very sick.

c. Dentist

_____ 4. Josh has a big tooth growing in his mouth, but the small tooth hasn't fallen out yet. Sometimes his teeth hurt.

d. Pharmacist

_____ 5. Mario needs to have a physical before he can play on the school football team.

e. X-ray techician

_____ 6. Ben had an operation on his leg and has to have X-rays taken every two weeks.

f. Nurse (school nurse)

Chapter 10: Living a Healthy Lifestyle

10.2 Getting Exercise

Objective

The student will indicate at least three ways to exercise that are personally interesting and possible for him or her.

Discussion

Teacher: Who knows what a "couch potato" is? (Someone who sits, does nothing.) What do you think you would look like if you never got any exercise? ("Like my dad," fat, flabby, tired.) Why is it important to exercise? (Get muscles, keep in shape.) There are lots of ways to get exercise—and many of them are a lot of fun.

Worksheet 10.2: These students want to get some exercise. Help them come up with an idea that will fit in with what they are interested in. There may be more than one good idea for each!

Answers

(These are suggestions.)

1. Walk the dogs, run the dogs
2. Bike riding
3. Jump rope
4. Hike
5. Swim
6. Ride horseback

Extension Activities

1. *Class Aerobics.* Borrow an exercise video for kids and have the entire class work on daily aerobics. Combined with music and laughter, this experience may turn out to be one that the entire class will look forward to.
2. *Exercise Quilt.* Have each student work on one square (paper, flannel, or the like) depicting a favorite exercise. Combine all squares to represent a "quilt" with lots of ideas for getting involved in exercise.

10.2   **Getting Exercise**

These students want to begin an exercise program. Each is thinking about how to have fun while exercising.

1. *I love to be outside. I also like to spend time with my two dogs.*

2. *My best friend just got a bike for his birthday. We like to do things together.*

3. *What could we do with this?*

4. *I live next door to a city park. There are lots of trails in the woods.*

5. *My neighbor has a swimming pool and said to come over anytime.*

6. *If I tell my dad that horses can help me keep in shape, do you think he will buy me one?*

10.3 Leisure-Time Activities

Objective

The student will identify and generate ideas for leisure activities.

Discussion

Teacher: Leisure time is when you can do pretty much whatever you choose—your own time. What are some things that you like to do when you have free time? (Play sports, talk on the phone, watch TV, read.) Think about what you are interested in and what you are good at. What activities does your community have that you could be a part of? (Park and recreation activities, library activities.) The next time you are tempted to say, "I'm bored!" think about what you could do instead!

Worksheet 10.3: Here are some leisure activities that children your age might enjoy. Add to this list with your own ideas!

Answers

(Answers will vary.)

Extension Activities

1. *Leisure-Time Quilt.* Have each student illustrate a different colored block or square with an example of a leisure activity. Assemble the squares to make a "quilt" for a bulletin board or hallway display.

2. *Give It a Try!* Have students from your own grade or an older grade or two talk to your class about a leisure activity that they have enjoyed. Perhaps someone has participated in a theater production or won a trophy for bowling. Expand students' interests by exposing them to activities that perhaps they have never thought about.

10.3   Leisure-Time Activities

Here are some leisure activities that children your age might enjoy. Add to this list with your own ideas!

1. Hiking

2. Joining the Girl Scouts or Boy Scouts

3. Checking out books at the library

4. Playing softball

5. Inline skating

6. Hooking a rug

7. Participating in a community theater play

8. Collecting coins or stamps

9. _____

_____

10. _____

_____

11. _____

_____

12. _____

_____

Chapter 10: Living a Healthy Lifestyle

10.4 What About Drugs?

Objective

The student will state appropriate usages of medication or drugs.

Discussion

Teacher: Have you ever had to take any medication? What? When? (Allergy pills, aspirin, and so on.) What's the difference between taking drugs that are written for you on a prescription and drugs that you can buy over the counter? (Doctor must order the prescription drugs.) Have you ever heard people say that drugs are bad for you or "don't do drugs"? Why? What do they mean? (Some will hurt your body, can overdose easily.) In general, if you take drugs that are prescribed for you and you follow the directions, you are taking drugs appropriately. You should never take any drugs that you can't identify or take drugs from someone you don't know. You should never take harmful drugs such as cocaine or acid. Only take drugs that are safe for you and are ordered by a doctor, and take them for only as long as you need them to help you become or stay healthy.

Worksheet 10.4: Sometimes it's hard to know when drugs are all right and when to stay away from them. Read these situations and write Yes or No to show if you think each situation is all right or not.

Answers

1. Yes   2. No   3. Yes   4. No   5. No   6. Yes   7. No   8. No

Extension Activities

1. *Instead of Drugs . . .* Emphasize to students that some people give the message that drugs will make them feel better or feel happy or make them feel good about themselves. Tell them that there are positive alternatives to "doing drugs" for that purpose. Have students list ways that they can feel good about themselves by doing positive things (playing basketball, painting a picture, singing with friends, and so on). Make posters to show their ideas.

2. *Good Drugs, Bad Drugs.* Students may be confused into thinking that all drugs are bad. Help inform students that many drugs (and vaccinations) have cured terrible diseases and keep people alive. Follow medicine reports in magazines and newspapers and have interested students follow up on researching some drug breakthroughs (such as polio vaccinations, measles and mumps shots) that have helped civilization.

10.4   **What About Drugs?**

Here are some situations involving drug use. Write Yes if you think this is a good or appropriate use of drugs. Write No if you think it is not.

1.   *I have a headache...
      I will take an aspirin.*

      _____

2.   *Here, take these pills.
      They will make you feel great.
      I will take an aspirin.*

      _____

3.   *The doctor gave me a
      prescription to take this
      medicine.*

      _____

4.   *The doctor wrote a
      prescription for this medicine for my
      brother, but I'll take it.*

      _____

5.   *My dad left some alcohol in is
      glass. I'll finish it for him.*

      _____

6.   *Ooooh...I feel so terrible. I'll have
      some of this medicine that my
      mother said I should take.*

      _____

7.   *My friend gave me some drugs to take.
      I know my friend really cares about
      me. He wouldn't give me anything that
      would hurt me.*

      _____

8.   *I heard that if I take
      a lot of these diet pills, I'll feel
      real good. I think I'll try it even
      though I'm not on a diet.*

      _____

Chapter 10: Living a Healthy Lifestyle   **233**

10.5 Avoiding Unhealthy Habits

Objective

Given an example of an unhealthy habit, the student will provide an example of a healthy alternative behavior.

Discussion

Teacher: Does anyone know what a habit is? (Something you do without thinking.) A habit is something that you do, usually without even thinking about it, because you get used to doing it over and over. What's the first thing you do when you get home from school? (Eat, change clothes, do homework.) Do any of you find yourself doing something while your brain is still asleep and then you suddenly realize that you just did it out of habit? Any examples? As long as your habit is a good one, it's no problem. But sometimes you find yourself involved in bad or unhealthy habits that can be hard to break. Today we're going to think about breaking bad habits by substituting good ones.

Worksheet 10.5: These students have been doing some things that they wish they could change. Help them change their bad habit into something positive. Draw or write about something that each student could do instead.

Answers

(These are suggestions.)

1. Read in bed, turn off the light
2. Start bicycling every day, chew gum
3. Organize books the night before, start getting up earlier
4. Order a smaller pizza, don't eat at pizza places
5. Put a bar of soap next to the sink by the door, wash hands every time you enter the house

Extension Activities

1. *Minor Behavior Modification.* Have students learn to become aware of their behavior by recording one simple behavior each day for several days. Choose a behavior that is relatively frequent (such as the number of times you brush teeth, wash hands, take the dog out). Were they surprised to find out how many times they engaged in the behavior without consciously being aware of it? Then train them to pair another behavior with the first behavior, such as cleaning out the sink every time they brush their teeth or check in the mailbox when they take the dog out, and so on. Is it easier to do the second behavior if you link it to the first?

2. *Smoking Survey.* Smoking is generally accepted as an unhealthy habit. Have students conduct a survey in which they poll classmates and adults to find out whether or not smokers wish they could quit, have tried to quit, have quit, or do not wish to change this behavior. Is smoking popular among students? Do students think more adults smoke or don't smoke? There are lots of informational questions that could be raised. (If smoking is an inappropriate topic, choose another habit or issue. Survey students to find out what they perceive is their worst habit, and so on.)

10.5 Avoiding Unhealthy Habits

These students have gotten into some unhealthy habits. Can you help them think of at least one way to break or change the habit by doing something that is healthy or different? Draw your picture or write your answer next to each situation.

Instead of: **Try:**

10.6 Dangerous Situations

Objective

The student will recognize potentially dangerous situations and state possible unhealthy outcomes.

Discussion

Teacher: Has anyone seen my black rattlesnake? I lost him somewhere in this room. Oh, I'm just kidding. But what if I really did lose a poisonous snake in this room? What could happen? (Could have bitten someone.) Part of leading a healthy life is being careful with dangerous things. Can you help me list some things that you think are pretty dangerous? (Bombs, guns, and so on.) What do you think is the best thing to do if you find yourself in a dangerous situation? (Leave, ask for help, find an adult.)

Worksheet 10.6: Here are students who are in some situations that could end up as pretty dangerous. Tell why each is dangerous and what the student in each situation should do. Draw or write your answers on the side.

Answers

(These are suggestions.)

1. Dog could bite   (Student should leave area, call for help)
2. Stranger   (Leave immediately, tell an adult)
3. Could start a fire   (Leave them alone, throw them away)
4. Troublemakers, could involve student   (Say no, have something else to do)
5. Could be loaded   (Don't touch it, tell an adult)

Extension Activities

1. *Role-Playing.* Have students act out the potentially dangerous situations, coming up with alternative endings. Have them practice saying no in many different ways!
2. *Super Student.* Create a "Super Student" superhero who comes to the rescue when students find themselves in dangerous situations. Students may wish to design a costume and draw a life-size figure. When discussing situations, refer to the figure and ask, "What would Super Student do?"

10.6   Dangerous Situations

These students are in some situations that could be dangerous. For each situation, list one reason why this is dangerous or what might happen. Then draw or explain what the student should do next.

1 SITUATION: **WHY?**

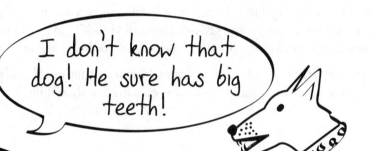

HE/SHE SHOULD:

2 SITUATION: **WHY?**

HE/SHE SHOULD:

10.6 (Continued)

3 SITUATION: WHY?

HE/SHE SHOULD:

4 SITUATION: WHY?

HE/SHE SHOULD:

5 SITUATION: WHY?

HE/SHE SHOULD:

10.7 Following Safety Rules

Objective

The student will explain and comply with rules that are intended to ensure safety.

Discussion

Teacher: How many of you have ever ridden on a roller coaster? Do they have a rule about keeping your hands inside and not standing up? Why? (Safety.) What might happen if you broke the rule? (Accident.) There are some rules that you should follow just because they are good ways to make sure you stay safe. Can anyone think of any safety rules around school? (No talking during fire drill, no knives.)

Worksheet 10.7: It seems like there are rules all the time telling you what you should and should not do. Here are some examples of rules you may have heard at home or at school. Some of them are silly rules. If the rule is a good safety rule, draw a smile on the face at the end of the rule. If it is silly, draw an X on it.

Answers

1. Smile   2. Smile   3. X   4. Smile   5. X   6. Smile   7. Smile   8. X   9. Smile   10. X

Extension Activities

1. *Old Rules.* Teachers' magazines often reprint rules from the early 1900s for teaching and keeping the school safe that now seem extremely humorous. Obtain such a list, or locate laws that are sometimes still on the books for some states that seem silly now. (Don't park your horse on the courthouse square after noon, and so on.) Discuss why the old rules were important even though they seem silly now. Will our rules seem outrageous in a hundred years?

2. *Safety Is Not Silly.* Have students compile a list of school rules. Although some (gum-chewing, quiet at lunch) may seem unfair or unnecessary, have students think about why they promote safety. Would an alien, visiting from another planet, think the school rules were silly? How would you explain to him/her/it why the rule was necessary?

10.7   Following Safety Rules

Some of these rules are safety rules; others are silly rules. If it is a safety rule, draw a smile on the face. If it is a silly rule, put an X on the face.

1. Wear your seat belt in the car.

2. Don't tell anyone where the key to your house is kept.

3. Don't brush your teeth while standing on your head.

4. Come home before it gets dark outside.

5. Only hitchhike with young drivers.

6. Don't talk during a fire drill.

7. Lock your bike when you leave it outside.

8. Don't put paper clips in your hair.

9. When strangers call on the phone, don't tell them if you are home alone.

10. Call the police if you oversleep and need a ride to school.

Chapter 10: Living a Healthy Lifestyle   **241**

10.8 Getting Enough Sleep

Objective

The student will identify situations in which a person may not be able to get enough sleep.

Discussion

Teacher: Why do you think it is important to get enough sleep? (So you can think clearly, get a lot of things done the next day.) What are some situations that might affect getting a good night's sleep? (Travel, doing something else instead, thinking about something, worrying.) How does it make you feel when you don't get enough sleep? (Crabby, can't think clearly or perform well.) Sometimes you don't have control over your sleeping opportunities, but whenever possible it is important to get enough sleep. You will think more clearly and feel better.

Worksheet 10.8: Are these students going to be getting enough sleep? (Remember that sometimes you can't control the circumstances affecting ideal sleep conditions.) Circle and discuss your choices.

Answers

(Answers will vary; be sure to discuss possible reasons for the responses.)

1. No—the next day is a school day.
2. No—but it is understandable.
3. Maybe—might not be a comfortable sleep.
4. Probably yes—if she has a good nap.
5. No—interrupted sleep is hard to overcome.
6. No—but worth it!

Extension Activities

1. *Sleep Statistics.* Have students keep a record of how many hours they sleep each night for a week. Discuss whether they have a regular bedtime, how much sleep they need to function well, and what events or situations affected their sleep routine.
2. *Dream Diary.* It is interesting to remember (if you can) and record your dreams. Some people dream vividly; others cannot remember anything that they dreamed about. If you have some "dreamers," have them keep a diary of their dreams for a week or two—with as much detail as they can remember. There may not be any profound meaning to the dreams, but it can be fun to try to figure out why certain people or events were triggered to make an appearance!

10.8   Getting Enough Sleep

Are these students going to be getting enough sleep? (Remember that sometimes you can't control the circumstances affecting ideal sleep conditions.) Circle and discuss your choices.

1. Angel is spending the night with some friends on a school night. They decided to stay up to watch the midnight movie.

   Yes   No   Maybe

2. Christopher is excited about his birthday party tomorrow. He is trying to sleep, but he is thinking about all of the fun he will have at the party.

   Yes   No   Maybe

3. Peter and his family are on a trip and they have been driving in the car for a long time. Peter is tired so his dad got him a pillow so he can sleep in the car.

   Yes   No   Maybe

4. Lily woke up early and was busy all day. She is supposed to go out tonight with her family, but she is really tired, so she is going to take a nap first.

   Yes   No   Maybe

5. Russell got a new puppy and wanted him to sleep in bed with him. Every few hours the puppy whines and wants to go outside. Russell has to get up and let him out several times during the night.

   Yes   No   Maybe

6. Kara's summer softball team traveled to a nearby city to play another team. It was late when the game was over, but her team won so they all went out for ice cream to celebrate.

   Yes   No   Maybe

Part Three

Community and Independence

Chapter 11

Community Places
and People

PARENT LETTER #11: COMMUNITY PLACES AND PEOPLE

Dear Parents,

Our next series of lessons is on developing independence within our community. The first step is to become familiar with places, people, and services that are available within our area. We will be discussing places such as local restaurants, parks, places of entertainment, sporting events, and community service places such as the post office, public library, zoo, and museums. If possible, we will try to visit some of these places or have individuals come to the class to give insight and instruction into what is available for students.

As you venture out into the community for shopping, entertainment, or errands, invite your child to come with you to see firsthand how these community places fit into your life. There are a variety of community helpers and services available for us to use and enjoy.

Thank you as always for your commitment to helping your child become independent!

Sincerely,

_____

Teacher

COMMUNITY PLACES AND PEOPLE

Skill Sheet #11: Progress Report

| + mastered |
| √ emerging |
| − not mastered |

Student Name	Restaurants	Shopping Mall	The Park	Houses of Worship	Movie Theater	Sporting Events	The Public Library	A Museum	The Zoo	The Supermarket	Barber or Beauty Shop	The Post Office	Comments

11.1 Restaurants

Objective

The student will be able to state the names, general locations, and general services of several restaurants in the area.

Discussion

Teacher: I'm going to describe a place where I had dinner last night, and you try to tell me where I was. (Describe the facilities, menu, and so on, of a local restaurant.) Where was I? (Restaurant.) What exactly is a restaurant? (Place where someone else cooks for the general public.) A restaurant is a public eating place. Who can help me name three of them? What is the same or similar about each? What is different? (Cost, service, menu items, location.) Who are some people or workers you would find at a restaurant? (Waiter, hostess, and so on.)

Worksheet 11.1: This Worksheet describes five restaurants that might be in a community. Then it describes five students who could get what they are looking for at the different restaurants. Match each student with an appropriate restaurant for him or her to eat at.

Answers

1. b   2. c   3. d   4. a

Extension Activities

1. *Restaurant Survey.* If possible, collect menus from several restaurants in your community. What is characteristic about each? Can the restaurants be grouped in several ways? (Appeal to young, appeal to adults; expensive, inexpensive; extensive menu, one main item.)

2. *Community Map.* Begin working on developing a community map, featuring items of interest in your community. Which restaurants would a visitor to your area be interested in? Draw a picture of the restaurant (or cut part of the menu and insert it in a drawing) and place it on the community map. Add to the map as the different community points are discussed in later lessons. Remember to plan this from a student's point of view—the most important restaurant in town may be the hamburger joint!

11.1   Restaurants

The numbered column describes several restaurants. Match the student on the right with a restaurant that he or she may want to visit. Write the letter of the student on the line next to the restaurant.

1. *Mexican Pete's Place* _____

   This is a fast-food restaurant that serves tacos, beans, and other Mexican-style foods.

2. *The Garden Spot* _____

   This is a sit-down restaurant with full-course meals, waiters, live music, and a very expensive menu.

3. *Millie's* _____

   This is a diner where you sit at a counter and order simple home-cooked meals, such as hamburgers, soup, and perhaps apple pie and ice cream for dessert.

4. *Carolyn's Cookin'* _____

   This is a sit-down restaurant that serves entire meals, has menus and waitresses or waiters, and lets you wear casual clothes, such as jeans.

a. Mike and his family want to go to a nice place with some friends, but don't want to spend a lot of money. They want to sit, talk, and not have to dress up.

b. Frank wants something quick to eat, but he doesn't have a lot of time and doesn't like hamburgers.

c. Allen and his parents are celebrating his sister's graduation from college. They want to go to a very nice place. Price is no problem.

d. Debbie and Darlene want a full meal, but don't want fast food or a big bill (but they have to eat dessert!).

Chapter 11: Community Places and People   **251**

11.2 Shopping Mall

Objective

The student will be able to state several stores that are likely to be found at a mall or at the local mall.

Discussion

Teacher: Let's say I wanted to get several things on my shopping day. I want to get some new shoes, a dress, a book for a birthday present for someone, food for my puppy, and some tennis balls. How many stores would I have to go to? (Lots.) Can you think of a place that has lots of stores close together? A mall, or shopping mall, is a place where there is a row of stores. Why do you think that's a good idea? (Easy to get to, park just once, might be enclosed and warm.) Who are some people or workers you would find at a shopping mall? (Clerks, store owners, cashiers.)

Worksheet 11.2: Here is an example of the stores in a mall. Sharon, who is shopping, wants to get several things at the mall, but she doesn't need to go to every store. Help her plan how she could get everything she needs by putting a number on each store that she should go to.

Answers

1. Pat's Pet Shop
2. Toys!!!
3. Photos While U-Wait
4. Polly's Plants
5. Beauty Boutique

Extension Activities

1. *Our Own Mall.* If possible, have students visit a local shopping mall and take a quick inventory of the different stores that are included. If they were the mayor for a day, what stores would they put in their mall? (Encourage creativity.) What's important? What's needed? What's wanted?

2. *Giant Mall.* Following the theme of the Worksheet, have students select mall stores that they would like to have or visit at a mall and then draw, find pictures, or otherwise create impressions of what would likely to found in the store. Maybe students would like to pair up to be jewelry shop proprietors, pet store owners, music or video store owners, or skateboard repair operators.

11. 2   Shopping Mall

Here is a map of a shopping mall called Parkway Plaza. Look at it carefully so you are familiar with the stores and how to get to them. Then help Sharon the Shopper plan how she would go to get everything on her list. Number the stores she would visit 1, 2, 3, and so on.

Sharon's List:

Doll

Plant for mother

Drop off film

Get puppy food

Hair spray

Chapter 11: Community Places and People   **253**

11.3 The Park

Objective

The student will identify several activities that can take place at a public park.

Discussion

Teacher: What's the name of a park in town? What are some things that people do there? (Play basketball, swing, walk on trails, and so on.) Why do you think communities have parks? (Provide public with clean, safe area to relax, and so on.) Most parks have some rules that go with the privilege of being able to use the park. Can you think of any? (Don't litter, keep your dog on a leash, and so on.) What people or workers would be at a park? (Park ranger, lifeguard.)

Worksheet 11.3: Here is a list of some things that could happen at a park. Write Yes if you think it should be done at a park; write No if you think it should not be done at a park.

Answers

1. Yes   2. Yes   3. Yes   4. No   5. No   6. Yes   7. Yes   8. No   9. Yes   10. Yes   11. No   12. Yes

Extension Activities

1. *Nature Walk.* Public parks sometimes offer guided tours for classes to point out interesting nature facts and teach students about ecology in action in your community. If not, plan to take your class on a walk, noting the various activities that are offered at the park.

2. *Park Rules.* Find out what specific rules are in effect at your local parks department. Discuss with your students why littering is harmful or why there is no swimming without a lifeguard, and so on. Also investigate what opportunities are available through the parks and recreation department, such as softball leagues, day-camping experiences, swimming lessons, and so on.

11.3   **The Park**

Here is a list of some activities. If you think it could be done at a public park, write Yes on the line. If you think it could not (or should not) be done at a public park, write No.

1. Swimming in a pool _____

2. Having a picnic _____

3. Walking on trails _____

4. Leaving soda cans and bottles

   _____

5. Shooting squirrels _____

6. Having a birthday party _____

7. Riding your bike _____

8. Driving a car on the baseball diamond _____

9. Swinging or using a slide _____

10. Playing Frisbee with a friend _____

11. Letting your dog run loose for a long time without watching him _____

12. Playing tennis _____

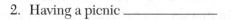

Chapter 11: Community Places and People   **255**

11.4 Houses of Worship

Objective

The student will identify and locate several houses of worship in his or her community.

Discussion

Teacher: I'm thinking of a community place that people might go to on a weekend day. Can anyone guess? (Church.) Many people go to church on Sunday, but some religions have their church services on Saturday. Does anyone want to tell us about the house of worship that they go to? Can you tell us where it is located? Besides listening to a sermon, what other activities happen at your church? (Youth group meetings, prayer meetings, softball practice, and so on.) In our country, we have the freedom to go to whatever church we want to go to, and worship the way we want to. This is a very important freedom that doesn't happen in every country. Let's think about the different houses of worship in our community and where they are. Can you help me with the names of the religious leaders? (Minister, pastor, priest, rabbi, choir director, and so on.)

Worksheet 11.4: There are many kinds of buildings of worship, but this Worksheet will show just a few of them. Match the number of each building with the student at the top who attends that place of worship. Write the number on the line.

Answers

Amy: 2   Adam: 4   Carolyn: 1   David: 3

Extension Activities

1. *Holidays.* Many holidays are religious (originally) in nature. Investigate the roots of these holidays and discuss the impact that each has on everyday life today. Why doesn't everyone celebrate Christmas? What is Hanukkah? In the midst of December festivities, you may want to have a person of the Jewish faith visit your class and explain the significance of this event.

2. *Historical Churches.* Many churches have an interesting history. Check out the church buildings in your area. When was each founded? Dig up some local historical trivia!

Name _____ **Date** _____

11.4   **Houses of Worship**

Here is a map of part of a small town. The houses of worship are marked with a star (*) and a number. Match the students below with the house of worship that they attend. Use the clues next to each student to help you match them. Write the number of the building next to the student who goes there.

1. **Amy** goes to a large church surrounded by many trees. She attends church early in the morning on Sunday. The service is called "mass." She is a member of a Catholic church. _____

2. **Adam** worships on Saturday at a building called a synagogue. Adam is Jewish. _____

3. **Carolyn** goes to a church on Sunday morning. She attends a Protestant church with a white fence around it. _____

4. David is also going to a Protestant church, but his is a different kind. His church has bricks on the side. _____

11.5 Movie Theater

Objective

The student will be able to state the location of the theater and procedure for attending a movie there.

Discussion

Teacher: Who here has seen a good movie lately? What did you see? If you wanted to see a movie, but didn't want to rent a video, where could you go? (Local theater.) Let's say I was new in town and I didn't know anything about getting to the movie or how to get a ticket or popcorn or anything! Could you help me? What people would you find working at a movie theater? (Usher, ticket-taker, counter clerk.)

Worksheet 11.5: Here is a scene from a typical movie theater. What are some things that you see? (Concession stand, restrooms, and so on.) I want you to look carefully at the picture and answer the questions about the situation. Write Yes or No on the line next to each statement.

Answers

1. Yes   2. No   3. Yes   4. No   5. No   6. Yes

Extension Activities

1. *Careful Questions*. Have students write additional questions about the picture requiring careful looking and thinking. Exchange the questions and discuss the clues. Were some more obvious than others?

2. *Ratings*. Use a local movie guide from the newspaper and discuss which movies the students have seen. What do the ratings G, PG, PG-13, and R indicate? Have students give movie reviews of pictures that they particularly enjoyed. Do they have to be violent to be enjoyed? Have students develop their own rating system; for example, Funny, Good Characters, Good Story, Exciting, and so on.

11.5   **Movie Theater**

These people want to see the movie *Mutant Frogs That Ate New York*. Look carefully at the picture and answer Yes or No to the questions about the moviegoers and the theater.

1. The frog movie is just about to start. _____

2. It will cost the 10-year-old boys $4.50 to get a ticket. _____

3. There are two movies playing at this theater. _____

4. The ticket-taker is a woman. _____

5. You can get hamburgers at the snack stand. _____

6. The frog movie is in Theater 2. _____

11.6 Sporting Events

Objective

The student will be able to determine location, times, prices, and other pertinent information about selected sporting events in the community.

Discussion

Teacher: Who here has ever been to a basketball game? Where? Has anyone ever watched a football game at the high school? Why do you think so many people are interested in sports and sporting events? (Fun, social, like to watch winners.) What sporting events are available in our community, either to participate in or to watch? What people or workers are connected with sporting events? (Coaches, players, ushers, broadcasters, and so on.) What is a spectator? (Someone who watches.) A spectator is a person who comes to a game to watch rather than to play. What games do you like to be a spectator at?

Worksheet 11.6: Here is an article that you might see in a newspaper, telling about a sporting event that you might want to attend. Read the article carefully and see if you can find the answers to the questions about the game. Write your answers on the lines.

Answers

1. Lakeside Lasers, Northside Rangers 2. Basketball 3. Lakeside gymnasium 4. 6:30 p.m.
5. $1.50 6. 7:30 p.m. 7. 50 cents 8. Yes

Extension Activities

1. *Sports Reading.* Have students bring in newspaper articles about their favorite teams. After reading the article, have them write comprehension questions about the article. Exchange questions among students.

2. *Sports Math.* Following the same ideas as sports reading, have students use sports statistics from games or player records to write math problems or story problems. Exchange problems among students.

11.6   **Sporting Events**

Here is an article telling about a basketball game in a community. Read it carefully, then try to answer the questions on the lines below.

The Lakeside Lasers are going to play the Northside High School Rangers in a championship basket-ball game on Friday, October 26, at 7:30 p.m. This will be a home game for the Lasers in the Lakeside High School gymnasium. Doors will open at 6:30 p.m., with tickets going on sale at both the front and side doors of the gym. Tickets are $2.50 for adults, $1.50 for students, and $1.00 for children under 12. Refreshments will be available at the concession stand throughout the game. Programs listing the players will be sold for 50 cents.

1. Which two teams are going to play? _____

2. What sport are they playing? _____

3. Where will the game be played? _____

4. What time can a person get into the gym to watch? _____

5. How much will it cost for a student to attend? _____

6. What time does the game start? _____

7. How much are the programs? _____

8. Will people be able to get something to drink there? _____

11.7 The Public Library

Objective

The student will be able to state the location of and general services provided by the local public library.

Discussion

Teacher: Who has been to the public library recently? What's a library for? (Reading and borrowing books.) Aha! I thought you'd say that! But I want you to think harder! Your public library can do a lot more for you than provide you with books to borrow for free. Start thinking of other things that you or your parents might have used the library for. (Copier machine, check out videos, computer searches for books or magazines, night courses for adults, summer reading clubs, phone books from other cities, newspapers, records, storytelling sessions for children.) Who are some workers at a library? (Librarian, researchers, audiovisual technician.)

Worksheet 11.7: A public library is a wonderful place to find out about a lot of things. On this Worksheet, I want you to list all the things a library can do for you and the community. We will try to visit the library soon to add to your list and learn about the things you can borrow, do, and learn there.

Answers

(Answers will vary.)

Check with your local library to find out what services are offered.

Extension Activities

1. *Library Visit.* Have your local librarian give your students a tour of the different sections of the library, classification of books, audiovisual products, tips on conducting research, and special events sponsored by the library. Conclude by making sure each student has a library card.
2. *Library Research.* Have students research how public libraries got started, how many books are in the local library, which are the most popular books, how many books are checked out each year, and so on. Have students pose questions that they are interested in and assign students in small groups or pairs to use the library to find some answers.

11.7   The Public Library

Your public library provides more for you than just letting you borrow books. Find out what else it can offer you! Can you find or think of at least seven things?

1. _____

_____

2. _____

_____

3. _____

_____

4. _____

_____

5. _____

_____

6. _____

_____

7. _____

_____

11.8 A Museum

Objective

The student will be able to state the location of and purpose for a museum.

Discussion

Teacher: I was wearing a necklace the other day, and someone came up to me and said, "Wow! That looks like something out of a museum!" What did he mean by that? (Old, interesting, valuable.) What is a museum? (Place to see things of interest and value.) A museum is a display of rare or interesting objects or things that people would like to learn about. Can you name any museums? (A local museum, natural history museum, wax museum.) How is a museum like a library? (Open to public, special collections.) How is a museum different from a library? (Can't take things home, museum might have books but mostly other items.) Who are some workers that you would find at a museum? (Caretaker/curator, custodian, archaeologist, other scientists.)

Worksheet 11.8: If you have never been to a museum, you might be interested to know about some of the different exhibits that might be there. This Worksheet lists some exhibits that could be at a museum. Circle the ones that sound interesting to you. Perhaps you'll get to visit a museum that has an exhibit like it!

Answers

(A completed checklist.)

Extension Activities

1. *Museum Ideas.* Many museums will send free information brochures or flyers publicizing special events. Check for displays of exhibits and call them to the attention of your students. If a local museum is featuring something special, arrange for a class tour.
2. *Museums A to Z.* If you can take a day for a field trip to a museum, have students at the end of the day make a list of the interesting things that they saw. You could go through the alphabet: A = ant farm, B = bug collection, C = Chinese jewelry, and so on.

Name _____ **Date** _____

11.8   A Museum

The following exhibits might be in a museum that you could visit. Circle the ones that you think would be interesting to see and learn about.

1. Ancient mummies from Egypt

2. Airplanes that were used in World Wars I and II

3. A giant heart that you can walk through

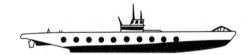

4. A submarine that was captured from the Germans in World War II

5. Chickens hatching from eggs

6. Sand paintings done by Navajo Indians

7. Dolls from around the world

8. A historic village that shows what life was like hundreds of years ago

9. A movie that shows what the Earth looks like from outer space

10. Uniforms and baseball mitts from famous baseball players

11.9 The Zoo

Objective

The student will use a map to match places with a description of services or animal housing.

Discussion

Teacher: What are some zoos in our area? (Local, petting zoo, larger state zoo.) Why do you think people want to have a zoo? (So you can see exotic animals, it is a nice way to spend time with your family.) What are some problems that a zookeeper or other zoo helpers have to think about when they deal with animals? (Keeping them in a cage, special diets, weather.) What are some jobs that zoo people do? (Maintain the animals, provide special events for people, safety concerns for people, health concerns for the animals.) What is your favorite zoo animal and why?

Worksheet 11.9: Look at the map of the zoo. Write the number of each description of what is going on next to each letter.

Answers

1. C   2. D   3. A   4. F   5. B   6. E

Extension Activities

1. *Zoo Animal Cards.* Have students each select an animal that interests them and prepare Zoo Cards that have pictures and facts about their selected animals. Have students exchange their cards and talk about what interesting facts they learned about their animals.

2. *Being a Zoo Vet.* Have students use books, the Internet, and resource people to help them learn about what is involved in taking care of the health needs of animals at a zoo. How much does an elephant eat? What shots does a rhino need? How do you keep a monkey happy? Students will find that there is a lot that goes on behind the scenes!

11.9   **The Zoo**

Look at the map of part of a zoo below. Write the number of each description of what is going on next to each letter.

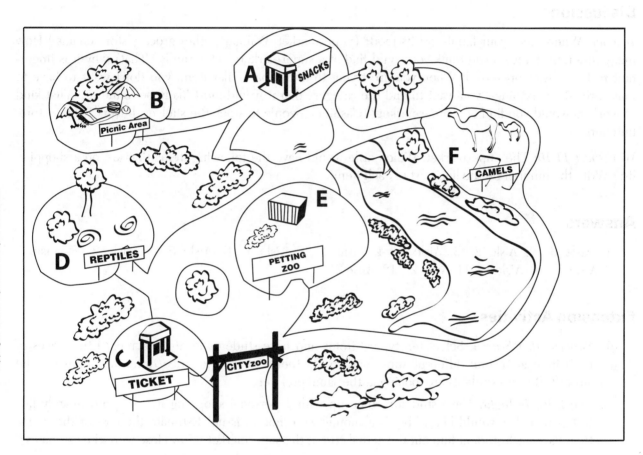

1. This is where you get your ticket to get in.

2. This is where you would see snakes.

3. This is where you can get something cold to drink.

4. This is where you can watch the camels being fed.

5. This is where you can have a birthday party.

6. This is where you can pet animals in the petting zoo.

Chapter 11: Community Places and People   **267**

11.10 The Supermarket

Objective

The student will identify typical items that would be located on labeled aisles at a supermarket.

Discussion

Teacher: Where does your family get its food? (Supermarket, Walmart, other grocery store chains.) How many different items do you think you could find at a supermarket? (Thousands.) That's why it is important to have aisles organized. When you are trying to find a particular item, you don't want to have to look through everything—you want to find the category that it would most likely be found in. What kind of workers would you find at a supermarket? (Cashiers, people to stock the shelves, buyers for the store, butchers.)

Worksheet 11.10: The Supermarket. Which aisle would have the following items that are on a shopping list? Write the number on the line next to each item.

Answers

1. Aisle 3   2. Aisle 2   3. Aisle 5   4. Aisle 4   5. Aisle 1   6. Aisle 5   7. Aisle 3   8. Aisle 5
9. Aisle 4   10. Aisle 1   11. Aisle 2   12. Aisle 3

Extension Activities

1. *Supermarket Search.* Select ten typical items and have students locate and record the prices of each item at several different supermarkets. Is there much of a price difference between the stores? (Be sure students are looking at the same product.)

2. *The Price Is Right.* Have students come up with a personal shopping list of approximately five things that they would like to buy—if money were not an issue! Estimate the cost of the items, then have each student find out the actual cost at the supermarket. How close were the estimates?

Name _____ Date _____

11.10   The Supermarket

Which aisle would have the following items on a shopping list? Write the number on the line next to each item

Aisle 1	Aisle 2	Aisle 3	Aisle 4	Aisle 5
Fresh Fruits and Vegetables	Paper Products	Canned Goods	Bread	Frozen Foods

1. A can of green beans _____

2. Napkins _____

3. A frozen pizza _____

4. Hot dog buns _____

5. A bag of carrots _____

6. Ice cream _____

7. Tuna fish _____

8. Popsicles _____

9. Rolls _____

10. Bananas _____

11. Paper plates _____

12. Baked beans _____

11.11 Barber or Beauty Shop

Objective

The student will use an advertisement about services to answer questions about a barber or beauty shop.

Discussion

Teacher: Where do you get your hair cut? (A beauty shop, barber shop, Dad cuts it.) Unless there is someone at your home who cuts your hair for you, you probably go somewhere to get your hair cut and perhaps styled. Can you name some of these places? (Answer will vary,.) What information would you need to know about a place before you went there? (When it is open, how much it costs, what services they provide.) What jobs would there be for people who worked at a hair salon? (Stylist, receptionist, designer for the store.)

Worksheet 11.11: Read the following advertisement for Joy's Haircuts. Then answer the following questions on the lines.

Answers

1. Yes
2. No, not open on Sunday
3. No, need at least $10
4. At least $35
5. No, walk-ins are welcome
6. Call or stop in
7. Either a bottle of shampoo or a bottle of conditioner
8. Yes
9. West Main Street
10. One week

Extension Activities

1. *Hair Styles of the Past.* Have interested students research hair styles that were popular in decades gone by for both men and women. Bring in pictures or old styling books (or even old yearbooks) to enjoy.

2. *Locks of Love.* Contact community hair care salons to see if they participate in the Locks of Love program, in which hair is donated from haircuts to make wigs for cancer patients. Perhaps a stylist would be willing to come in to talk about how they connect with their community—nursing home visits, children's first haircut, and so on.

11.11   **Barber or Beauty Shop**

Read the following advertisement for Joy's Haircuts. Then answer the questions below.

Grand Opening! Joy's Haircuts! Walk-ins Welcome!

2020 West Main Street

Phone: 222-3561

Open 9 a.m. to 6 p.m. Monday–Saturday

Haircuts: $10 and up

Perms: $35 and up

Color: $25 and up

Grand Opening Special: Free bottle of shampoo or conditioner with every haircut for first week only!

---

1. Could you get a haircut at 5 p.m. on Tuesday? _____

2. Could you get a haircut at noon on Sunday? _____

3. Could you get a haircut for $7? _____

4. How much would it cost to get a perm? _____

5. Do you need an appointment to get service? _____

6. If you wanted to make an appointment, what could you do?

   _____

7. What can you get for free with a haircut? _____

8. If you had $30, could you get your hair colored? _____

9. What street is this business located on? _____

10. How long does the Grand Opening special last? _____

11.12 The Post Office

Objective

The student will use resources to answer general questions about the post office and its services.

Discussion

Teacher: If you wrote someone a letter, how would they get it? (Put it in the mailbox and somehow they end up with it!) What is needed to get your letter all the way to whomever you sent it to? (Someone needs to sort it, deliver it.) The post office is a place where you can send mail, pick up mail, send out packages, get a passport, and use a lot of other services that you might not know about. What kinds of people work at a post office? (Mail carrier, people who sort the mail, office workers, truck drivers.)

Worksheet 11.12: How many of these questions can you answer about the post office and its services? You might need to do a little research or visit your local post office.

Answers

(Answers may vary as rates increase.)

1. (Wherever your closest local branch is located.)
2. (Varies.)
3. (Varies.)
4. A stamp that is issued one time to recognize a famous person or event.
5. A stamp that doesn't have a postage number on it; it is sufficient first-class postage no matter when the rates change.
6. At present, 44 cents.
7. Up to 13 ounces.
8. Upper left hand corner of a letter, on the front.
9. Drop a letter in a blue mail collection box, go to the post office, leave a letter in your home mailbox.
10. At present, $85.

Extension Activities

1. *Stamp Collecting.* Have students investigate what is involved in stamp collecting (www.usps.com). Students may be interested in reporting on recently issued commemorative stamps.
2. *Design a Stamp.* Have students design their own commemorative stamp for an event in their lives worth celebrating or perhaps to honor someone who is important to them. Use poster board to display the "stamp."

11.12   The Post Office

How many of these questions can you answer about the post office and its services? You might need to do a little research or visit your local post office.

1. Where is your closest post office? _____

2. What is your ZIP Code? _____

3. What is the abbreviation for your state? _____

4. What is a commemorative stamp? _____

_____

5. What is a Forever Stamp? _____

_____

6. How much does it cost to mail a first-class letter? _____

7. How much can a first-class letter weigh? _____

8. Where does the return address go on a letter? _____

_____

9. What are three ways that you can send a letter? _____

_____

10. How much does it cost to get a passport if you are under sixteen?

_____

Helpful Information

Parent Letter #12: Helpful Information

Dear Parents,

We want our children to become as independent as possible in the community, while keeping an eye on their safety and helping them develop common sense. The next set of lessons focuses on teaching children how to use information in the community, such as reading a menu, understanding a map, and interpreting schedules.

We also want our children to develop good thinking skills, such as what to do in a situation if they become lost, and how to use common sense regarding the Internet.

Whenever possible, use community trips as a teaching time to help your child read schedules, figure out money issues, understand where to look for information, and realize that you are very interested in what he or she is doing on the computer—and that you are in charge!

It may be hard to stop yourself from just doing things for them yourself—but take the time to let your child do some problem-solving and figure things out for him- or herself.

Sincerely,

_____

Teacher

Skill Sheet #12: Progress Report

+ mastered
√ emerging
− not mastered

Student Name	Pedestrian Safety	Bike Safety	Safety After Dark	Using a Menu	Tipping	Locating Restrooms	Reading a Map	Using a Mall Directory	Hours of Operation	Television Schedules	All About the Newspaper	Using a Catalog	If You Get Lost	Safe Computer Sites	Computer Common Sense	Comments

12.1 Pedestrian Safety

Objective

The student will identify safe procedures for getting around on foot.

Discussion

Teacher: Where are some places that you could get to "on foot"? (Local shops.) What does "on foot" mean? (Walking.) Does anyone know what a "pedestrian" is? A pedestrian is simply someone who is on foot. Whenever you are out walking on the street, you are a pedestrian. What are some situations that might be dangerous for a pedestrian who is trying to get around town? (Traffic, being lost.)

Worksheet 12.1: This Worksheet shows students who are walking around. Each picture shows a good safety rule that the student should follow. Let's discuss a good rule for each picture.

Answers

1. Walk facing traffic.
2. Cross at "walk" signal.
3. Stay on the sidewalk.
4. Look where you're going.
5. Ask an adult for help.
6. Look both ways before crossing.

Extension Activities

1. *More Good Rules.* Have students list more pedestrian safety rules (don't dart out between parked cars, don't play in the street, keep your purse or wallet close to you, and so on) and illustrate them on posters.
2. *Walking Tour of the Town.* From a central point, have students devise (and go on) a walking tour of the town or main area of interest in the town. As they write out the directions to the various destinations, have them indicate "safety spots" where they, as pedestrians, should take care to follow safety rules for crossing a street, being careful of footing, or whatever. Students may want to publish a walking tour map for others to use and follow.

12.1 Pedestrian Safety

These students are walking around town. What is a good safety rule that is shown in each situation?

12.2 Bike Safety

Objective

The student will identify safe procedures for getting around on a bicycle.

Discussion

Teacher: Sometimes people don't want to get around by walking. Why not? (Too far, too long.) What are some other ways that students could get around? (Bike, skateboard, horse.) Today we're going to concentrate on bicycles and bicycle safety. Do you think that bike safety rules are similar to pedestrian rules? (Yes—have to watch out for others; No—more like traffic vehicle than walking.)

Worksheet 12.2: I bet you know a lot of bike safety rules already. Write one rule in each space around the bike on the sheet. You can use the clues if you need help thinking of some. Then we'll compare answers.

Answers

(These are examples.)

Don't ride at night without a light.

Don't ride on the sidewalk.

Ride single file in a group.

Use proper hand signals for turning.

Stay on the side of the street; don't zigzag.

Wear reflective, light-colored clothes at night.

Keep your bike in good working condition.

Follow all road signs, including stop signs and yield signs.

Cross railroad tracks perpendicular to the rail

Wear a helmet.

Put a flag and reflectors on your bike.

Extension Activities

1. *Obstacle Course.* Set up an obstacle course in the parking lot of the school or another large, flat surface. Arrange pylons so that students must demonstrate control over their bikes by staying within the designated lanes, stopping at a certain place, using hand signals correctly, and so on. You may want to have students act as observers and raters for other students who participate by riding their bikes through the course.

2. *Bike Trip.* Weather permitting (and if all students have access to a bike), arrange for a group bike outing to a nearby destination, perhaps resulting in a picnic lunch. Parents should be invited to help supervise and ride.

12.2   **Bike Safety**

What are some rules that a biker should follow? Write one rule in each space around the bike. There are some word clues to help you if you can't think of many!

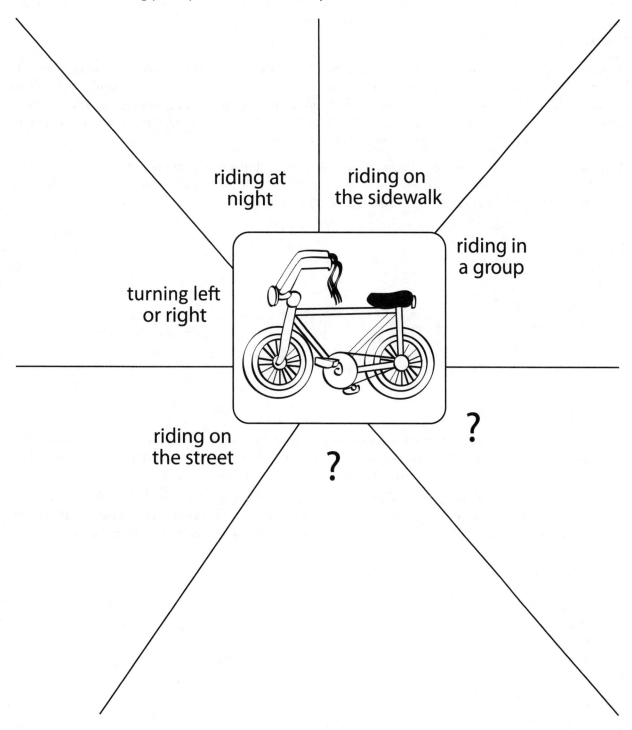

riding at
night

riding on
the sidewalk

riding in
a group

turning left
or right

riding on
the street

?

?

12.3 Safety After Dark

Objective

The student will identify ways to ensure personal safety after dark.

Discussion

Teacher: We've been talking about how to get around to places in the community and finding people to help you. We've also been talking about safety in the community—being careful when you're out walking or riding a bike. Here's a new slant on things—how does darkness make things different? (Have to be in early, can't see as well.) What times do you have to be in the house at night? Why do you think parents and adults give you a time limit or curfew? (Want you to be safe.)

Worksheet 12.3: On this Worksheet, there are five pictures of students who are out at night or in the evening. In each picture there is someone or something that is helping to make that student a little safer. Circle the person or object that is helping the student be safer.

Answers

1. Adult
2. Being in a group
3. Flashlight
4. Phone call home
5. Light-colored clothes

Extension Activities

1. *Night Watching.* Have students assigned to observe other people in an evening hour. What colors are easily seen at night? What safe—or unsafe—behaviors have they seen? Have each record his or her observations and participate in class discussion the following day.

2. *Halloween All Year Long.* People become conscious of night safety usually on Halloween when children go trick-or-treating. What rules or safety tips are publicized then? Which could be followed all year long? (Dressing for visibility, staying in groups, carrying a flashlight, and so on.)

12.3   **Safety After Dark**

There is something in each picture below that shows how the student is being careful to be safe at night.

1.

2.

3.

4.

Hi, mom! I'm just leaving Kara's house right now. I'll be home in about 10 minutes.

5.

12.4 Using a Menu

Objective

Given a menu, the student will identify prices of specific items and information pertinent to ordering.

Discussion

Teacher: I'm thinking of something that helps you choose food when you're in a restaurant. What is it? (Menu.) What information is on a menu? (Price, descriptions of food, and so on.) How are the items grouped? (Entrées, desserts, children's selections, and so on.) Why do restaurants have menus? (So server doesn't have to say everything over and over, to advertise specials, and so on.)

Worksheet 12.4: Here is part of a menu from a restaurant that shows some items you might be interested in ordering. Look it over carefully and answer the questions.

Answers

1. 95 cents   2. Sandwiches   3. Two   4. Include more   5. Roast beef   6. Drinks

7. Entree, potato, salad   8. Desserts   9. Hot dog   10. Answers will vary

Extension Activities

1. *Menu Math.* Using different menus from local restaurants, write items to make a meal on index cards. Have students use the menus to locate and total the price of the suggested meal. You could use duplicate copies of menus to have "food races," with competing teams racing to figure out the total first.

2. *Ordering.* Although students may go out to eat with family or friends, they may not actually practice ordering their food, but rather allow others to order for them. In class, have students form groups and take turns being the server and customers, using clear voices, eye contact, and decisiveness to place a food order. If possible, enlist parent support to take students out to eat at a restaurant, make decisions about meals, and order on their own.

12.4   Using a Menu

Here is part of a menu. Use the information to help you answer the questions below. Write your answers on the lines.

WELCOME*TO*JOHN'S HOME COOKING'

Beverages
coffee...75¢
soft drinks.................................95¢,65¢

orange juice...................................55¢

Sandwiches
hamburger.....................................$1.35
cheeseburger................................$1.65
hot dog..$1.25
bacon, lettuce, tomato...................$1.40

Main Meals (all dinners include entree, choice of potato, and salad)

roast beef..$6.95
pork chops......................................$7.35
baked ham.......................................$8.75
meat loaf...$6.35

Desserts
cheesecake......................................$2.50
hot fudge sundae............................$1.99

1. How much would a large soft drink cost? _____

2. Where would you look for a hamburger on the menu? _____

3. How many desserts are featured? _____

4. Why do the main meals cost more than the sandwiches? _____

5. Which costs more, a roast beef or a meat loaf dinner? _____

6. What are beverages? _____

7. What is included in the main meal? _____

_____

8. If they added chocolate cake, where would it be listed? _____

9. What is the least expensive sandwich on the menu? _____

10. What is something you would like to order? Figure out the total of the meal:

12.5 Tipping

Objective

The student will identify types of services for which tipping is appropriate and be able to compute an approximate amount for the tip.

Discussion

Teacher: When you're done with your meal at a restaurant, what do you usually get? (Bill.) You have to pay for your meal, but people usually leave some money on the table. Why? (Tip, for waitperson service.) A tip is extra money that you give to someone who has done some service for you, such as a waitperson. Can you think of other people who receive tips? (Taxi drivers, hair stylists, delivery people.) Most people tip about 15 percent for good service. An easy way to figure out the amount of the tip is to take the approximate total and multiply by .15 with a calculator, or figure out 10 percent and then add half as much to that. For example, if the bill was $40.00, 10 percent of that is $4.00, and half of that is $2.00, so $4.00 + $2.00 = $6.00.

Worksheet 12.5: On this Worksheet are some examples of people whom you might tip if they perform a service for you or your family. After reading each situation, write who the person is (their role or occupation) and how much you would probably tip them. (Use 15 percent as a guide.)

Answers

1. Waitress, $1.50   2. Delivery person, $1.80   3. Car wash attendant, $1.20

4. Beautician or stylist, $3.00

Extension Activities

1. *It Costs That Much?* Have students use the menus from a previous lesson and tally the amount of the meal. Add to it the sales tax (whatever percentage is used in your area) and the tip. How much does it really cost you to eat out?

2. *Good Service, Bad Service.* Have students interview adults to find out what they expect insofar as service from those whom they tip. What would a good waitress do that would warrant a larger tip? (Friendliness, efficiency.) What about a good worker for lawn care? (Showing up on time, not taking too many breaks.) Use the activity to teach a larger lesson that good work habits may pay off for them in terms of tips when they work for others.

12.5   Tipping

Here are some people who have done a service for you or your family. If you were going to tip each one 15 percent, how much money would you give to each? (You might want to use a calculator.) Write the type of job or service occupation that the person is doing and how much tip you would leave.

Here is your bill for $10. Thank you for coming to our restaurant.

Person: _____
Tip: _____

Here's your pizza! It costs $12!

Person: _____
Tip: _____

We're finished washing and waxing your car. Have a nice day! It comes to $8.

Person: _____
Tip: _____

Oh, I love the haircut! Here's $20 for that, and a tip for you!

Person: _____
Tip: _____

12.6 Locating Restrooms

Objective

The student will be able to locate public restroom facilities in public or community buildings.

Discussion

Teacher: Let's say you just had a quick lunch with some of your friends at the local fast-food hamburger place. You drank a large cola and a glass of water, and now you have to find a—what? (Bathroom.) Why do many public places provide bathrooms? (Lots of people, too far to go home.) Help me list as many places as you can think of that have public restrooms. (Should be a long list!) How are they labeled or how could you find them? (Men's Room or Women's Room signs, RESTROOM signs.)

Worksheet 12.6: Here are two students, Sandy and Randy, who are looking for restrooms while they are at the mall. Read each suggestion surrounding them that gives an idea for how they could locate the restrooms at the mall. Circle the good ideas and put an X on the ones that aren't good ideas.

Answers

Good ideas are 2, 3, 4, 6.

Extension Activities

1. *Sign Collection.* Different places sometimes use different terminology to indicate restrooms, especially theme restaurants (such as Sailors and Mermaids at a seafood restaurant). Have students be on the lookout for lots of different signs, wording, or pictures that depict restrooms for each of the sexes. Don't forget the international symbols, without words.

2. *What Would They Be Called.* Playing along with the idea of cute, creative ways to indicate men's and women's rooms, have students come up with restroom door signs for horse lovers (Stallions and Mares), Hollywood people (Actors and Actresses), hunters (Bucks and Does), and so on.

12.6   **Locating Restrooms**

Sandy and Randy are looking for a restroom at the mall. Circle each way shown below that could help them. Put an X on the ways that probably would not help them find a restroom.

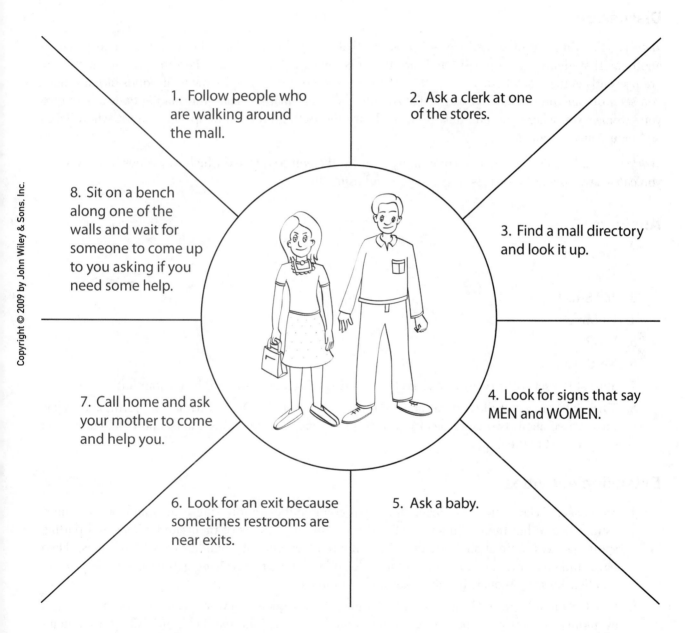

1. Follow people who are walking around the mall.

2. Ask a clerk at one of the stores.

3. Find a mall directory and look it up.

4. Look for signs that say MEN and WOMEN.

5. Ask a baby.

6. Look for an exit because sometimes restrooms are near exits.

7. Call home and ask your mother to come and help you.

8. Sit on a bench along one of the walls and wait for someone to come up to you asking if you need some help.

12.7 Reading a Map

Objective

Given a map of a specific area, the student will identify features of the key and will be able to locate places on the map.

Discussion

Teacher: I'm thinking of something—an object—that can help you find your way from one place to another. (If students say "compass," indicate that a compass points out only the direction in which they are presently going, not whether that is the correct way or not.) It's a map! How many kinds of maps have you seen or can you think of? (Road maps, state maps, world maps.) What information does a map give you? (Shows you where you are, tells what roads are there, the direction of specific places, where lakes and mountains are, and so on.)

Worksheet 12.7: This is a map of a community. Look at the compass to see which way is north. Now see if you can answer the questions about getting around using this map.

Answers

1. 1st Street
2. Three
3. 2nd Street
4. 1st Street
5. North
6. North Lake
7. Start at the school, go west past Lake Drive and Zoo Lane; the zoo will be on your left.
8. Turn right or east at the zoo entrance, go two blocks to Lake Drive, turn left or north, and follow Lake Drive about two more blocks until you see Pine Avenue. Go left and follow the curvy road until you get to the airport.

Extension Activities

1. *Mapmakers.* Have students create their own communities by drawing a map and placing interesting sites within them. Students will enjoy naming the streets of their subdivisions and putting sports centers, animal shelters, or other important community buildings on their maps. Then have students write directions or problems for other students, involving getting from one place to another. Be sure students include a key and a compass.

2. *Our Community Map.* Using a community map, have students solve realistic map problems, such as finding the best route from their home to the high school football field, or locating class members' homes on the map and determining who is the farthest north, south, and so on. You may want to make up a thinking game, giving students clues as to which destination you are thinking of. Students will enjoy listening for clues that lead to their own house!

12.7   **Reading a Map**

Use the map shown to answer the questions about this community. Write your answers on the lines.

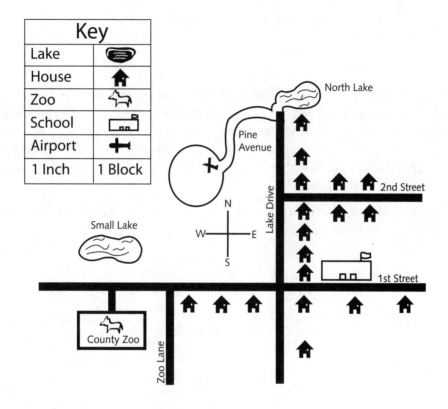

Questions

1. On what street is the entrance to the County Zoo? _____

2. How many houses are between Zoo Lane and Lake Drive _____

3. Which street is the north of First Street? _____

4. What street is the school on? _____

5. Is Small Lake north of or south of the zoo? _____

6. If you went north on Lake Drive until it ends, where would you be? _____

7. How would you go from the school to the zoo? _____

_____

8. How would you get to the airport from the zoo? _____

_____

Chapter 12: Helpful Information

12.8 Using a Mall Directory

Objective

The student will locate various stores or mall areas by using a directory.

Discussion

Teacher: How many of you have been to a mall recently? How many stores would you guess are there? If someone was new in our town and wanted to find a store there quickly, what could he or she do? (Ask someone, use a directory.) Sometimes when there are many stores close together or stores that have several floors for you to shop on, they will put up a directory. A directory is a sign that lists all of the stores and services and where they are located. How do you think that might be helpful? (Saves time, makes it easier to plan where you're going to go.)

Worksheet 12.8: Many malls put a large directory close to the entrance. This Worksheet shows an example of a directory. Use it to answer the questions.

Answers

1. Two
2. Fashions and More
3. Bert's Flowers
4. Furry Friends Pet Store
5. Silverman's Cafe
6. Designs by Denny
7. Johnson's Shoe Repair, Furry Friends Pet Store

Extension Activities

1. *Other Directories.* Similar activities can be created by using office building directories (indicating different floors), department store directories (which list departments by category), and even a school directory, which may list the location of the various offices and classrooms. If your school does not have a directory, offer to make one. (It will be helpful for conferences and open houses!)

2. *Directory of My Bedroom.* Have students complete a tongue-in-cheek activity organizing the items in their bedroom by location. Perhaps this could be hung on the outside of the bedroom door to assist parents who want to locate socks, yesterday's newspaper, important papers, pencils, and so on. Have students decide whether they are going to divide the room into quadrants, enumerate items according to the perimeter of the room, use north-south-east-west directions, and so on.

12.8   Using a Mall Directory

Here is an example of a mall directory. Read it carefully and use it to answer the questions below.

WELCOME to SPRINGVILLE MALL

B
  Bert's Flowers   ...1-A
  Big and Tall Clothes 3-B

D
  Designs by Denny 2-A

F
  Fashions and More 3-A
  Furry Friends Pet Store 1-B

J
Jenny's Cookies and Fudge.....3-B
Johnson's Shoe Repair 5-A

R
  Restrooms   ....RR

S
  Silverman's Cafe 2-B

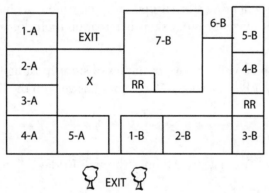

X= you are here

N

1. How many sets of restrooms are there? _____

2. What is the name of the store at 3-A? _____

3. What store could you go to get flowers? _____

4. Which store has pets? _____

5. Where can you get something to eat? _____

6. Which store is closer to the directory: Designs by Denny or Big and Tall Clothes? (Circle your answer.)

7. If you were meeting your friends at the south exit, what two stores would you be near?

_____

12.9 Hours of Operation

Objective

The student will be able to determine what hours a store will be open by reading an "hours of operation" sign.

Discussion

Teacher: What stores can you think of that are open twenty-four hours a day? (Gas station, convenience store.) Why aren't all stores open all of the time? (People need to sleep, may not be busy at night.) If you wanted to find out if a store was open or was going to be open at a certain time, how could you find out? (Yellow Pages, call the store, ask a friend, sign on door.) There are lots of good ways to find out that information—let's focus on one. What kind of a sign do many businesses put on their door? (Sign that tells when they're open.) A sign that tells when the store is open may be called an "hours of operation" sign or a "business hours" sign. Why do you think stores put signs like that on their doors? (So people know when to come back.)

Worksheet 12.9: On this Worksheet, you will find two examples of stores posting their business hours. Use the information on the signs to answer the questions. Write your answers on the lines.

Answers

1. Thursday   2. No   3. Monday, Tuesday   4. Monday through Friday   5. 8 p.m.

6. Saturday   7. Sunday   8. Jewelry store

Extension Activities

1. *When Are You Open?* Assign students to pick two businesses nearby and copy their hours of business. Analyze the information from the class. When are most businesses open? Do the weekend hours differ from weekdays? Do most stores have evening hours? Which stores? Arrive at some conclusions!

2. *Retail or Service?* Group local businesses into product/retail stores and services (dentistry, beauty salon, dog grooming). Assign students the task of interviewing the owner of the store or the provider of the service (by phone or in person). Develop a set of questions, including "How were the hours of operation determined?" "Are there more customers during the day or evening?" "How many employees does it take to keep the business running smoothly?" and so on. You may also wish to have a manager-owner of a retail store come to your classroom and answer questions about running a business.

12.9   Hours of Operation

Here are some "business hours" signs from two stores. Use the information to answer the questions below. Write your answers on the lines.

THE JEWELRY STORE

WE ARE OPEN.....

MONDAY   8 A.M. TO 5:00 P.M.
TUESDAY   8 A.M. TO 5:00 P.M.
WEDNESDAY   8 A.M. TO 4:30 P.M.
THURSDAY   8 P.M. TO 9:00 P.M.
FRIDAY   CLOSED
SATURDAY   8 A.M TO NOON.
SUNDAY   CLOSED

PRESTO PRINT SHOP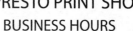

BUSINESS HOURS
DAILY   7:30 A.M.- 4:30 P.M.
SAT.   NOON-8:00 P.M.

CLOSED SUNDAYS

1. You want to shop for a necklace, but you have to go at night. Which day could you shop at the

   jewelry store? _____

2. You wanted to get your ring cleaned, so you got to the store at 10 minutes before 8 on a
   Wednesday. Was the store open? _____

3. Which two days have the same hours at the jewelry store?

   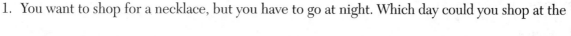

4. On what days does the print shop open at 7:30 A.M.? _____

5. What time does the print shop close on Saturday? _____

6. On what day does the print shop have evening hours? _____

7. Which day is not a day of business for either store? _____

8. If you wanted to visit both the jewelry store and the print shop on Saturday, which store would you

   go to first? _____

12.10 Television Schedules

Objective

The student will use a listing of television programs to determine the times when programs will be broadcast, their duration, and the channels.

Discussion

Teacher: What are your favorite TV shows? When do they come on? Why is it that you know those times so quickly? (Watch them regularly.) What if I told you that a special show was going to be on featuring [someone interesting], but I wasn't sure what night or what time it was on? How could you find out? (Use TV listing, call a friend, check newspaper.) Most newspapers publish information that highlights the regular shows and special shows that are going to be on each day. What information is given in this type of listing? (Time, channel, information about it.) We are going to practice looking up particular TV shows using a guide.

Worksheet 12.10: This Worksheet shows a partial listing of what's on television on a certain day. The left side tells what programs are on; the right side explains a little about some of those programs. Use that information to help you answer the questions.

Answers

1. Four
2. "The Day the Principal Went Away"
3. 18
4. 7:00
5. One-half hour
6. Famous places in Europe

Extension Activities

1. *What's On Here?* Use a local television listing to have students answer questions about what's going to be on. Make a game by awarding teams one, two, and three points for correct answers to questions about the listing; for example, "For two points, find out what channel has baseball on at 8:30 on Thursday," and so on.

2. *Movie, News, and Other Reviews.* Assign students (perhaps in teams) to view designated programs on certain nights during the week and report on them. Questions could be formulated beforehand, such as (1) How long did the program last? (2) Was it funny? (3) Was it interesting? (4) How many commercials were there? Make sure students circle their assignment on the TV listing and complete a report/summary of the show. Students may think that the news is "dull," but they should give reasons why (after watching the news).

12.10   Television Schedules

Here is an example of a television listing for a community. Use the information given to answer the questions below. Write your answers on the lines.

TUESDAY, Nov. 13

Evening

6:00

(2)   "Nightly News"

(4)   "Local News"

(18) "Cartoon Friends"

(22) Movie Time

6:30

(2)   "News "(Continued)"

(4)   "Local Happenings"

(18) "Cooking with Fred"

(22) "Movie (Continued)"

7:00

(2)   "A Tour of Europe"*

(4)   "Adventures with Math"

(18) "The Three Goofs"

(22) Movie (Continued)

∗Special

(2)   7:00 "A Tour of Europe"—famous places to visit in Europe are shown in this program.

Movies

(22) 6:00 "The Day the Principal Went Away" (comedy). A high school goes crazy when the principal decides to take a day off to go fishing.

(18) 9:00 "Return of the Slimeman" (science fiction). A town is terrorized by an alien who resembles slime.

---

1. How many television channels are given in this listing? _____

2. What movies is on at 6:00? _____

_____

3. What channel has cartoons at 6:00? _____

4. What time does "The Three Goofs" come on? _____

5. How long does "Local Happenings" stay on? _____

6. What is "A Tour of Europe" about? _____

12.11 All About the Newspaper

Objective

The student will be able to use the newspaper directory to locate various types of information within the paper.

Discussion

Teacher: How did the newspaper help you when you were trying to find out what shows were on television? (TV listing.) What other information does the newspaper give you? (Weather, local events, classified ads.) For the next few days, I want you to bring in a copy of the newspaper so we can practice finding things in it and discovering all the different things that are available to us through the newspaper. (Students whose families do not get a newspaper can share, or you can make sure extra copies are available.) Why do you think communities print up newspapers? (Information that applies to the area.) Why wouldn't a newspaper from Japan help us find out what movies are playing down the street? If I wanted to know which stores were having a sale on shoes, how would a community paper help me?

Worksheet 12.11: For this activity, you will need to use a real newspaper. Before we start, let's look through the different parts of the newspaper to get a general idea of what's inside. Then I want you to complete the Worksheet, looking for answers in the news paper.

Answers

(Answers will vary.)

Extension Activities

1. *Newspaper Tour.* Most newspaper companies willingly provide educational tours for school groups, including brief descriptions of the jobs of the many people who are involved in reporting, writing editing, and printing the paper. This is a fascinating experience for students.

2. *Letters to the Editor.* Select a pertinent local topic—for example, "Should a skateboard park be designated for the community?" "Why aren't there more 'G' movies at the local theater?" Have students write letters to the editor expressing their viewpoints. Send them, with a cover letter explaining the project, to the local paper. Watch to see if some show up in print.

12.11   All About the Newspaper

Use your local newspaper to find the answers to the following questions.

1. What is the name of your newspaper?

2. How many sections are in the paper? (Usually indicated at the top)

3. Where would you find the local weather? (Section, page)

4. What does the headline say?

5. What is on television at 8:00 Thursday night?

6. How many cartoons are featured?

7. What pictures are on the front page?

8. How many classified ads are there for cats?

9. What movies are playing in your area?

10. What coupons are in the newspaper? What products? Which stores?

12.12 Using a Catalog

Objective

The student will use a catalog to locate information about items within the catalog and will complete an order form.

Discussion

Teacher: I know a way that I can go shopping at a store that is a thousand miles away—and I'll be back in ten minutes. How could I do that? (Catalog, phone order, TV shopping.) You have some good ideas! What I'm thinking of is a special kind of book that lists all sorts of products. What is it called? (Catalog.) A catalog is a special book that contains a list of all the items that a store has or can get for you. How many different kinds of catalogs (or stores that have one) can you think of? (Toy store, chocolate products, department stores, and so on.) How is buying from a catalog different form buying from a store? (Send away for product, might have to wait to get it, don't have to leave your house.)

Worksheet 12.12: This is part of a catalog from a made-up store called Crazy Joe's Weird Stuff. Can you figure out why it's called that? Read the descriptions about the items for sale and pick two that you would like to order. Fill out the order form at the bottom, including sales tax (assume that it's 5 percent) and the handling fee. Total up your order on the very last line.

Answers

(Answers will vary; make sure students correctly specify any color, size, or other features for the ordered items.)

Extension Activities

1. *More Orders.* Have students bring in catalogs from several different kinds of stores. Practice filling out order forms, perhaps giving each student a $100 limit to spend on another member of the class. How much can they buy for their dollars?

2. *Our Class Catalog.* Have students draw or design an item or product, complete with a brief description of its features, colors, price, and ordering information. Compile the items into a "class catalog" and draw up an order form. What information needed to be standardized for the catalog? What numbering or coding system is used? How can they best describe their product in only a few well-chosen words? What makes a write-up appealing to a customer? Students will have fun creating and promoting their own "weird" inventions or ideas.

12.12   **Using a Catalog**

Here is a sample page from a catalog. Pick two items that you would like to receive and complete the order form.

Item No. 107-A Chocolate Monster This is a 2-pound edible Monster..........$15.00	Item No. 124-c Remote control plane Comes in red, blue, or yellow. $150.00	Item No. 174-F Pet Boa Constrictor Live! Cage is not included. $29.95
Item No. 274-F Deluxe Roller Skates Come in white or black. Specify size................$39.00	Item No. 643-H Motorized skateboard Comes in red or black $290.00	Item No. 860-A World's Largest Pizza This is 6 feet in diameter. Mushroom or Pepperoni. $237.00

CRAZY JOE'S WEIRD STUFF
New York, New York   Payment by: check____ credit card ____
                                                          Please do not send cash!

Buyer information
Name _____   Street Address _____
City _____   State _____   Zip _____

Product Information		Price Each	Color/Size/Etc.	Total Price
Item No.	How Many			

Order Subtotal _____
Sales Tax (5%) _____
Shipping and Handling:
$3.00 for orders under $20.00
$5.00 for orders over $20.00 _____

Order Total _____

12.13 If You Get Lost

Objective

The student will identify a safe procedure to follow if someone is lost.

Discussion

Teacher: How many of you have ever been lost? What was the situation? (Wandered away from group, parents moved too fast, took a wrong turn, forgot to watch where they were going.) How did you feel? (Scared, confused, nervous.) Obviously, you are here so you were found by someone, but what did you do? (Talked to an adult, waited to be discovered, used a cell phone.) It can be a very frightening experience to realize that you are lost. What are some things that might help someone who is lost? (Get directions, know where you are, look for street signs and landmarks, talk to someone at a public place, look for an adult who is outside.) What are some things that are probably *not* safe? (Go into someone's house to get directions, wander around hoping you will be found, get into a stranger's car.)

Worksheet 12.13: These students have gotten lost. Pick the best answer that tells what they could do.

Answers

1. b   2. a   3. b   4. b   5. a

Extension Activities

1. *Community Helper.* If possible, have a local police officer visit your classroom to talk about safety procedures for your community. Are there some safe houses or places where a child could go? Where is the nearest library or public building? Talk about whom to ask and where to go for help.

2. *Safety Plan.* Have students talk with their families about making a safety plan in case they are lost or separated. Share ideas about how to locate each other if family members are separated. You might come up with some creative ideas!

Name _____ Date _____

12.13   If You Get Lost

These students have gotten lost. Pick the best answer that tells what they could do.

1. Jose was on a field trip with his class at a park. He realized that he has become separated from his group. What could he do?

   a. Scream, "I'm lost!"

   b. Look for an adult and ask for help.

2. Ashley was at the mall with her parents. She was looking at some shoes and looked up, but couldn't see her parents. They were there just a minute ago. What could she do?

   a. Stay where she is and wait for them to find her.

   b. Move on to the next store and keep shopping.

3. Angel was riding his bike and took a wrong turn. He is now on a street that he doesn't recognize. It is beginning to get dark. What could he do?

   a. Knock on the door of a nearby house to get directions.

   b. Ask at a gas station or convenience store for directions.

4. Andrea was taking her dog for a walk when he got loose! She chased him for a few blocks and finally caught him, but now she isn't sure where she is. What could she do?

   a. Let the dog lead her back to her house.

   b. Ask someone who is outside for directions.

5. Miguel went to a soccer game with a friend after school. The friend left the game early, but Miguel wanted to stay until the end because it was very exciting. He has a cell phone, but he doesn't know where he is. His mother is waiting for him to call. What could he do?

   a. Find out what street the soccer field is on and give her directions.

   b. Start walking toward where he thinks his mother will be coming.

12.14 Safe Computer Sites

Objective

The student will visit and comment on selected supervised Internet sites.

Discussion

Teacher: How many of you have access to the Internet at home? What are some good sites that are fun, educational, or just plain interesting? Why do you think it is important for your parents to know that you are on a safe site? (There are some sites that are not appropriate for kids, parents need to know what their kids are looking at.) There are a lot of good things on the Internet for kids, but just like movies, you have to know what is appropriate for you and what is not. We are going to look at some good sites for kids.

Worksheet 12.14: Here are some computer sites that have games, jokes, study help, and interesting things for kids. Put a check mark next to ones that you have visited. Your teacher may have more sites for you to add to the list.

Answers

(Answers will vary.)

Extension Activities

1. *Internet Referral Board.* Have students "review" selected Internet sites and write up a brief report on each. Include information that would appeal to other students, such as what is fun or interesting about the site. Collect and arrange the information on index cards and post them by category (games, educational, jokes, other, and so on) on a wall or bulletin board.

2. *Student Challenge.* Pick a "site of the week" and have students become familiar with the features. If the activity includes a game, have students challenge each other or try for a personal best score.

12.14   **Safe Computer Sites**

Here are some computer sites that have games, jokes, study help, and interesting things for kids. Put a check mark next to ones that you have visited. Your teacher may have more sites for you to add to the list.

☐ www.iknowthat.com   ☐ www.factmonster.com _____

☐ www.bigfishgames.com   ☐ www.pics4learning.com _____

☐ www.funschool.kaboose.com   ☐ www.thinkquest.org _____

☐ www.spellingcity.com   ☐ www.kidsclick.org _____

☐ www.learninggamesforkids.com   ☐ www.askkids.com _____

☐ www.funbrain.com   ☐ www.kids.yahoo.com _____

12.15 Computer Common Sense

Objective

The student will evaluate computer-related activities as appropriate or inappropriate.

Discussion

Teacher: Why do you think adults are so concerned about what you are doing on a computer, especially if you are on one at home by yourself? (They want to make sure kids aren't getting into trouble on chat sites, looking at adult sites, or spending too much time on the computer instead of doing homework or getting exercise.) How much time do you think you spend each day on a computer at home? What rules do your parents have for you at home regarding the computer? (Limit the time, share with siblings, turn the sound down, no sites that aren't approved.) We are going to talk about some rules that make sense for being on a computer.

Worksheet 12.15: When you are using a computer or are on the Internet, you should use common sense. Do these behaviors show common sense? Write Yes or No on the blanks.

Answers

1. No   2. Yes   3. Yes   4. No   5. No   6. No   7. Yes   8. Yes   9. Yes   10. Yes

Extension Activities

1. *Computer Time Bar Graph.* Have students keep track of their time on a computer at home for one week. Plot the number of minutes and hours that students are using the computer, on average, by making a bar graph. Have students write questions for each other using the graph; for example: Who is on the computer the most? What is the class average time for computer use? (Note: You might want to have students plot their information anonymously or by number. Be sensitive to students who do not have a computer at home.)

2. *Parent/Student Contract.* Have students and parents work together to develop a contract that will apply to their own situation regarding computer use at their homes. This might include items such as e-mail dos and don'ts, password locations, privacy issues, and time limits.

Name _____ Date _____

12.15   Computer Common Sense

When you are using a computer or are on the Internet, you should use common sense.
Do these behaviors show common sense? Write Yes or No on the blanks.

1. I will stay on the computer for hours playing games even if it is a

   school night. _____

2. If someone is waiting to use the computer, I will finish what I am

   doing and let someone else have a turn. _____

3. I will check with my parents or teacher before going on the

   Internet. _____

4. If I can't get the computer to work right, I will hit the keys harder. _____

5. If I have to pay to download a game or music, I will find my parents' credit card and use it.

   _____

6. If someone e-mails me with a mean message, I will send a mean message right back to them.

   _____

7. If I get an e-mail from someone I don't know, I will show it to my parents. _____

8. If my parents have favorites or personal messages, I will not open them or change their settings

   without permission. _____

9. If I am supposed to set up a password for a game or site, I will write it down and show it to my

   parents. _____

10. If someone on line asks me for my name, address, phone number, or other personal information

    and I don't know the person, I will check with my parents first. _____

Chapter 12: Helpful Information   **307**

Part Four

Getting Along With Others

Being a Good Citizen

PARENT LETTER #13: BEING A GOOD CITIZEN

Dear Parents,

Our life skill unit begins with the focus on being a good citizen. This includes skills such as being polite to others, helping others by volunteering, demonstrating appropriate behavior in community places (the movies, the bowling alley, and so on) and avoiding vandalism or pranks that will get someone in trouble.

As we think about the community, it would be helpful for you to talk with your child about places you like to visit, some resources that are available in your community (such as the library or a community center), and possibly some events that your community sponsors (a book drive, a parade, and the like). Help your child see the positive things about living in your town.

Volunteering to help on a community project is an excellent way for your entire family to become connected to your town as well. If there is a town event, fair, or specific need that you can help out with, do so. Let your child see the importance of belonging to a group such as your neighborhood or town.

Sincerely,

_____

Teacher

BEING A GOOD CITIZEN

Skill Sheet #13: Progress Report

| + mastered |
| √ emerging |
| − not mastered |

Student Name	Being Polite to Others	Having a Good Attitude on a Bad Day	Speaking Up	Lending a Hand	Volunteering	Being Courteous	At the Movies	Helping Others	Rudeness in Others	Vandalism and Pranks	Comments

13.1 Being Polite to Others

Objective

The student will provide an example of a way that someone could show politeness to others.

Discussion

Teacher: Part of being a good citizen means being polite to other people. What do you think it means to be "polite"? (Show good manners, let others go first.) Why should you be polite to someone you don't even know? (Shows that you can initiate good behavior, shows respect.) Who are some people you are polite to every day? (Bus driver, teacher, lunch people.)

Worksheet 13.1: Here are some people who might be part of your daily life. How could you show that you are a polite person to each of them? Write something that you could do or say on the lines next to each person to show politeness.

Answers

(Answers may vary.)

1. "Good morning." 2. Let the other person go first. 3. Open the door. 4. "My name is _____."

Extension Activities

1. *Politeness Award.* Look for students who are demonstrating politeness to other people, and recognize their efforts with a small ribbon, special certificate, or other tangible award. Be sure to mention what was done and why this showed politeness.

2. *Practice Politeness.* Choose one specific example of being polite to others and put it into practice for a day or even a week. You might start out with something as simple as saying "thank you." Discuss when you could sincerely thank someone for something, and look for examples that will come up throughout the day.

13.1   **Being Polite to Others**

Here are some people who might be part of your daily life. How could you show that you are a polite person to each of them? Write something that you could do or say on the lines next to each person to show politeness.

Looks like you got something special today.

Hi. We are your new neighbors.

13.2 Having a Good Attitude on a Bad Day

Objective

The student will identify the character in each pair who is showing a good attitude.

Discussion

Teacher: Sometimes things just don't go your way. Maybe it's your turn to read and the teacher accidentally skips over you. Or perhaps your mom was late picking you up and you got caught in the rain. These things can make you feel like you're having a bad day. Is it still important to have a good attitude? (Yes.) Why? (You don't want to cause someone else to have a bad day by making them feel bad, it might be disruptive to call attention to yourself.)

Worksheet 13.2: Each of the characters on this Worksheet is in a situation in which something went wrong. Circle the one in each pair who is showing a good attitude, even though something went wrong.

Answers

1. first (a)   2. second (b)   3. second (b)   4. first(a)

Extension Activities

1. *Turn It Around.* Role-play the situations on the Worksheet by having the student first demonstrate the bad attitude, then spin around and "replay" the situation showing a good attitude. When this happens in a real situation, cue the student to "turn it around" and try a new response.

2. *"You get what you get. . . ."* There is a little poem that goes like this: "You get what you get, and you don't throw a fit." This can be useful in situations in which you (the teacher) might pass out something randomly to students (colored pens, paper, games, books) and students are to accept what they get without pursuing their personal preferences. ("But I wanted *that* one!") Randomness is a fact of life—and school! By having students recite this little poem at opportune times, they can be reminded that sometimes they just have to accept what they are given.

13.2   **Having a Good Attitude on a Bad Day**

Each character below is in a situation in which something went wrong. Circle the one in each pair who is showing a good attitude, even though something went wrong.

1. The last ice cream bar was sold just before Tommy got to the front of the line.

   a. I really wanted an ice cream bar, but I like popsicles too, so I'll take one of those.

   b. It isn't fair! I really wanted an ice cream bar! Someone has to trade with me!

2. The teacher asked students to raise their hand to tell what they did over the weekend. Alicia had an exciting weekend to talk about, but the teacher called on Karla instead.

   a. Why didn't the teacher call on me? I raised my hand like she said!

   b. Maybe I can tell her about my weekend during recess.

3. The students were going to play kickball at recess, but it started to rain, so they have to stay indoors.

   a. It always rains when we are going to play kickball!

   b. I think it will be nice tomorrow. We can play then.

4. James forgot to finish his homework, so the teacher didn't give him a check mark in her book.

   a. Could I still get points if I remember to bring it in tomorrow?

   b. It's not my fault. My mother forgot to make me do my homework.

Chapter 13: Being a Good Citizen   **317**

13.3 Speaking Up

Objective

The student will identify a situation that needs to be addressed and supply an appropriate response.

Discussion

Teacher: What would you do if you walked into the kitchen and noticed that the faucet was running? (Turn it off, see if someone was around.) If there was no one in the kitchen and you saw that the sink was going to overflow, you would probably turn the water off. If you see something going on that doesn't seem right to you, you should think about telling someone about it.

Worksheet 13.3: Here are some examples of situations that might turn into a problem for someone. Show how a good citizen would speak up about this problem by drawing a picture or writing what you could do.

Answers

1. Call the animal shelter.
2. Tell an adult about the graffiti.
3. Ask the lady if she is okay.
4. Stay with the child and get an adult.

Extension Activities

1. *Good Citizen Poster Contest.* Have students illustrate and color a poster that shows a child doing something in the community that promotes good citizenship. Display the posters in the school or community building. Give awards as appropriate.
2. *Peer Stories.* Have older students speak to your class about why it is important to be a good citizen. Perhaps they could tell the younger students about specific incidents in which they did something that helped someone else.

13.3   Speaking Up

Here are some examples of situations that might turn into a problem for someone. Show how a good citizen would speak up about this problem by drawing a picture or writing what you could do.

1. There is a big dog running around the neighborhood. He doesn't have a collar and he is chasing some of the children.

   _____

   _____

   _____

2. Some older children are writing bad words on the side of a building in your neighborhood.

   _____

   _____

   _____

3. A lady slipped on some ice while walking on the sidewalk and fell down.

   _____

   _____

   _____

4. A small girl is walking around the park, crying for her mother. She seems to be alone.

   _____

   _____

   _____

13.4 Lending a Hand

Objective

The student will match people who need help with a way to meet that need.

Discussion

Teacher: There are times when a person needs somebody else to help out or lend a hand. Can you think of a time when you helped someone? (Opened a door, helped clean up a room.) Can you think of a time when someone helped you? (Helped with homework, gave a ride to a game.) Being a good citizen means helping someone if you can.

Worksheet 13.4: The people on the left side of the Worksheet need some help. Match the people on the left with the people on the right who are trying to help them out or lend a hand.

Answers

1. c   2. a   3. d   4. b

Extension Activities

1. *Match Game.* Prepare a deck of cards with ten pairs. On ten of the cards, write a situation in which someone needs help. (Example: I need a pencil.) On ten other cards, write a matching, appropriate response. (Example: I have a pencil.) Have students place all twenty cards face down and try to match the pairs by turning over two at a time. Keep it simple enough that students can match the pairs by reading a short phrase or using picture clues.

2. *Lend a Hand.* Have students draw the outline of their hands on a piece of construction paper. Then have students complete the sentence: "I can lend a hand by . . ." (Fill in something that each student is able to do.) Display the hand posters around the room.

13.4   **Lending a Hand**

The people on the left side need some help. Match the people on the left with the people on the right who are trying to help them out or lend a hand.

1. I need help mowing my lawn.

2. I am going on vacation for a week.
   I need someone to water my garden.

3. Oh no! My dog got out again!

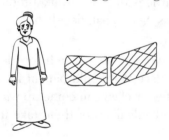

4. The wind knocked over my garbage can.
   What a mess!

a. I will come over to take care of your flowers.

b. I'll get a new bag and help pick up the trash.

c. I know how to mow.

d. Here, Ralph! Come here!

Chapter 13: Being a Good Citizen   **321**

13.5 Volunteering

Objective

The student will identify ways to volunteer his or her services in the community.

Discussion

Teacher: Every community has opportunities for people to volunteer. What is a volunteer? (Someone who gives time without pay to help support a cause.) Why would someone work without getting paid? (The idea is service, not profit.) Can you think of some places where people volunteer to help out in our community? (Habitat for Humanity, Meals on Wheels, and so on.)

Worksheet 13.5: Think of some organizations or places in our community that use volunteers to help. On the lines, write down as many ideas as you can think of.

Answers

(Answers will vary. Some suggestions: local hospital volunteer opportunities, visit nursing homes, pack items for the troops, join a bake sale to help the homeless, and so on.)

Extension Activities

1. *Class Project.* Involve the class in a worthy project such as writing letters to a local services person who is overseas, collecting canned goods for a food pantry, participating in a walk-a-thon for a disease, or any community event that is appropriate for your class. Set a goal, decide how you will participate, and involve everyone in some aspect of this project.

2. *Researching Needs.* Collect issues of your local city or town newspaper and search for ideas for volunteering. Have students ask their parents if they work at a place that could benefit from volunteers (a hospital, a clinic, envelope-stuffing, and so on). See if your class can come up with fifty different ways that they could volunteer, either as a group or individually. Let them take it from there!

13.5   # Volunteering

Think of some organizations or places in our community that use volunteers to help. Write down as many ideas as you can think of on the lines. Two are given to help you get started.

Organization/Place   **What It Does**

1. U.S. Post Office Food Drive   Collects canned goods for the needy

2. Animal Shelter   Uses volunteers to clean cages, walk dogs

3. _____

4. _____

5. _____

6. _____

7. _____

8. _____

13.6 Being Courteous

Objective

The student will identify situations in which courteous or discourteous behavior has been displayed.

Discussion

Teacher: During the next few lessons we will be talking about being courteous. Does anyone know what that means? (Being kind to others, good manners.) Being courteous means being considerate and polite to others. The opposite of courteous is discourteous. When you are in the community, that's different from being alone or with just your friends. How? (Other people are around.) Can you think of some community places in which you might be noticed by other people or have to talk to others? (Library, playground, and so on.) Why is it important to be courteous? (Don't get kicked out of the place, don't annoy others.)

Worksheet 13.6: This Worksheet shows some students who are in community places. Some of them are showing courteous behavior; others are not. Write Yes or No on the lines to show what you think. Then we will discuss your answers.

Answers

1. X; noisy and rude   2. X; mean remarks   3. Yes   4. X; pushy   5. X; inconsiderate   6. Yes

Extension Activities

1. *Observations in Public Places.* Have students look for and report examples of courteous behavior that they have noticed in public places. You may want to put smiley stickers or faces on their drawings of good examples of good behavior.

2. *Today I Will...* Have students discuss and commit to performing one specified courteous act at some community place that they will be visiting in the near future. It may be as simple as a polite comment, or a nonverbal act of unselfishness, or a secret card to cheer someone, but have them specify and predetermine what that act will be. Afterward discuss how it made the students feel about themselves and how it made others feel. If it went unnoticed, was it worthwhile anyway?

Name _____ Date _____

13.6   Being Courteous

Look at the following pictures of students in community places. Are they being courteous? If yes, leave the picture alone. If no, put an X on the picture and explain why.

13.7 At the Movies

Objective

The student will state ways that he or she could demonstrate good manners while at a movie theater.

Discussion

Teacher: Has this ever happened to you? You go into a movie theater, have to jump over four people who won't move their legs for you to pass by, and then end up sitting on a seat where there are popcorn and spilled drinks. How would that make you feel? (You wouldn't want to go back to that place.) What's the point of going to a movie? (To watch the show.) What are some ways that people can show good manners while at a movie theater? (Be quiet, don't throw things, and so on.) Why do you think some people don't care about their manners at the movies? (It's dark, no one will know who did it, takes too much effort to throw things away, and so on.)

Worksheet 13.7: I want you to think about what behaviors are acceptable or not acceptable at a movie theater. Read through the list and write Good or Bad according to what you think. Then we'll discuss your answers.

Answers

1. Bad   2. Good   3. Bad   4. Bad   5. Good   6. Bad   7. Good   8. Bad   9. Bad   10. Good

Extension Activities

1. *Class Movie.* Practice simulating good movie behavior by arranging the room in rows, providing popcorn (if desired), and showing an entertaining movie to the class. You may even want to have a ticket-taker, lines, and a refreshment counter. Practice good manners!

2. *Movie Behavior Review.* If students attend movies, have them fill out a "movie review"; they should rate the behavior of the other moviegoers, though, not the movie itself! Was the audience polite as a whole? What behaviors did they observe that showed good manners as well as discourteous manners?

Name _____ Date _____

13.7   **At the Movies**

Read the following list of behaviors that could happen at a movie theater. On the line next to each example, write Good or Bad to show what you think about that behavior.

1. Getting up six times during the movie to go to the bathroom or
   use the phone

2. Saying "excuse me" when you step over people to get to your seat

3. Laughing loudly during the movie, even when something happened
   that wasn't funny

4. Throwing popcorn on people who are sitting a few rows
   ahead of you

5. Passing your popcorn or candy quietly to your friends next to you

6. Letting your friends jump in line ahead of the crowd

7. Throwing your empty cup and popcorn container in the trash can

   on your way out

8. Putting your feet up on the seat in front of you   _____

9. Pushing through the crowd of people at the end of the movie so
   you don't have to wait to get out   _____

10. Sitting behind little kids instead of in front of them so they can
    see the screen   _____

13.8 Helping Others

Objective

The student will identify specific ways to assist someone in a situation in which a person needs help.

Discussion

Teacher: If you saw someone with a heavy bag and he or she was coming to a door, what could you do to help? (Open the door.) Do you think that person would say, "Get out of my way, I can do that myself"? (Probably not.) What would they say? ("Thanks for helping.") Do you think people appreciate it if you help them when they need it? (Yes—even though they may not say it.) What are some ways that you have helped someone recently? Why is it good manners to do that? (Shows you care about someone other than yourself.)

Worksheet 13.8: There are lots of ways that you could show good manners by helping someone in need. On the left side of this Worksheet are examples of people who could use help. Match them with a person on the right who could help them. Write the letter on the line.

Answers

1. d   2. c   3. g   4. f   5. b   6. a   7. e

Extension Activities

1. *Finish the Picture.* Have students draw a picture of someone in need of assistance, but without drawing a helper. Have students exchange pictures and complete each other's drawings by putting a person helping the first person in the picture (for example, someone raking leaves, tying a shoe, and so on). The problem should be fairly clear before exchanging pictures.

2. *Good Manners Tickets.* Pay extra-close attention to students helping each other in the classroom. Surprise students by awarding them a small ticket (exchangeable for a small prize or candy) that says I NOTICED! and tell them why you presented it to them.

13.8   Helping Others

Match each person on the left who could use some help with the person on the right who could help them. Write the letter of the helper on the line.

1. Mr. Jones is very sick. The grass around his house is getting very tall.

 _____

2. Jenny is having trouble with her math homework. She has a big test on Monday.

 _____

3. The Kellers are going on vacation for a week. They have two cats and a big dog to leave at home.

  _____

4. Rick made an out while playing softball, and his team lost. He feels very had about the game.

 _____

5. Grandma O'Brien has two bags of groceries to carry up to her second-floor apartment.

 _____

6. A man you don't know dropped a wallet while he was walking past the school.

 _____

7. A little girl has a letter to mail, but she can't quite reach the mailbox opening.

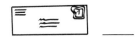 _____

a. Frank could pick up the wallet and give it to the man.

b. Randy could carry the two bags up the stairs.

c. Alice could help go over how to do math and review the problems on the weekend.

d. Bob could borrow his dad's lawn mower and cut the grass.

e. David could take the girl's letter and put it into the box for her.

f. Jon could tell the person that everybody messes up sometimes, so don't worry about it, and then help him with batting practice.

g. Sandy and Megan could feed and walk the pets until the family comes back.

13.9 Rudeness in Others

Objective

The student will state appropriate behaviors that could be followed when someone is rude to him or her.

Discussion

Teacher: Even though you may have good manners, what should you do about people who don't? If you are courteous to someone, and they are nasty back to you—well, what could you do? (Never be nice again, say nothing, tell them they don't have good manners.) Let's think about some ways that you could handle a situation where other people are rude or don't show good manners.

Worksheet 13.9: In this activity, you are going to pretend you are with the person in each picture who is being rude to you. What would you do or say without losing your own good manners? Write or draw what you would say or do.

Answers

(Answers will vary; these are suggestions.)

1. "I'm sorry if you thought I had it too long. Thanks for letting me borrow it."
2. "I guess purple isn't everyone's favorite color, but I thought the dress was cute."
3. Smile and say nothing.
4. "You certainly can borrow it if you need it, but please don't grab it out of my hand."

Extension Activities

1. *TV Examples.* Have students watch a show on television and pick out examples of people being rude to each other. On some shows it is done to be humorous; be sure to point out that real life and television can be quite different. Even though on television it might be funny for someone to be put down for something about themselves, discuss why it could be cruel in real life.

2. *Good Examples of Bad Examples.* A quick response does not come naturally when someone has been rude to us; collect examples of rudeness in the classroom and make examples (anonymously) of how to respond to those situations (such as students rushing to cut in line, making fun of another student, taking items without asking).

13.9   **Rudeness in Others**

Pretend that you are the student in each situation shown here. Write what you would say or draw a picture showing what you would do. Remember to use good manners, even though the other person may not.

1.

2.

3.

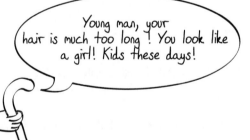

4.

Chapter 13: Being a Good Citizen   **331**

13.10 Vandalism and Pranks

Objective

The student will identify examples of vandalism or pranks and state reasons why such activity is harmful to others.

Discussion

Teacher: Have any of you ever gotten a phone call and heard the person on the other end give a silly message? Or heard of anyone calling a wrong number on purpose and trying to tell the people that they have won a million dollars? Those kinds of phone calls might sound funny, but they can be mean, too. Why? (Might scare the other person, older people might fear they will be robbed, wastes time.) What are some other jokes or pranks you have heard about? What's vandalism? Vandalism is hurting someone else's property on purpose. It could also refer to public property. Can you give some examples of vandalism? (Writing on walls, knocking over headstones in cemeteries.) Why is that harmful to others? (Someone has to pay for it, take time to repair it.) Vandalism and pranks are not only bad manners, they can lead to seriously hurting or scaring other people as well as getting someone in trouble with the law. A joke is one thing, but when you tease someone to the point of possibly hurting them or scaring them, that is going too far. Today I want you to think about why these things are wrong and how they could hurt others.

Worksheet 13.10: This Worksheet shows some examples of people who are playing pranks or—worse—being vandals. This is a very serious subject, and we are going to talk about these examples together today. In each situation, tell how the people are being harmful to others and, second, what you would do in each situation if you were part of the group or knew about what was happening.

Answers

(These are examples.)

1. The city will have to pay to have the graffiti removed, or people will have to look at the defaced bridge (also, the boys might be caught by police, especially if they write their own names!).

2. Mike will be in trouble for not having his work; he is worried about losing the papers.

3. Jane will probably feel very bad that she was made fun of.

4. The smaller boy probably needed the dollar for something at school; now he won't have the money for it.

5. Susan is being made fun of and is excluded from the group; by going along with the main girl's idea, the other kids are following a bad leader (and might find themselves being made fun of if they continue to obey her).

6. Stealing is a crime, and the boys could be in trouble with the police, getting a criminal record.

Extension Activities

1. *Police Visit.* This is an excellent opportunity to have a local police officer visit and explain the consequences of vandalism for the individual, the family, and the community. Shoplifting is another area that should be addressed. Students should be made aware of what "breaking the law" means.

2. *Breaking Away from the Group.* Students should be aware that pranks and vandalism usually occur because more than one student or person is involved. Why? Why is it easier to do something in a group that you would never do alone? Discuss ways that you could pull out of the group or activity when you know it is wrong.

13.10   Vandalism and Pranks

These people are involved in vandalism or pranks against other people. In each situation, tell (1) how it is harmful to others and (2) what you would do in each situation.

Working with People

PARENT LETTER #14: WORKING WITH PEOPLE

Dear Parents,

The next set of skills in our unit on Getting Along with Others is that of working with people. It would be great if everyone we worked with was polite, understanding, patient, helpful, and had a sense of humor, wouldn't it? However, whenever there are leaders and followers, deadlines, incomplete instructions, different personalities, and factors such as good days and bad days—whew! It's amazing we get along as well as we do!

Whether your child is in school, at home, in the community, or on a job, it is very important to have the skills to get along with others. Some of the activities in this section focus on understanding the task, using your skills, expressing an opinion appropriately, using common sense, and basic communication between people.

When talking with your child about others, be sure to emphasize that sometimes we feel emotions in the heat of the moment (anger, annoyance, frustration, and so on) that later will go away. Rather than be angry and regret it later, try to keep your feelings in check until you understand the situation. Use moments at home to encourage your child to ask questions about things he or she does not understand, use common sense to figure things out, and be prepared to "give in a little" on issues that are not crucial.

Sincerely,

_____

Teacher

WORKING WITH PEOPLE

Skill Sheet #14: Progress Report

| + mastered |
| √ emerging |
| − not mastered |

Student Name	Working as a Team	Understanding the Task	Understanding Your Role	Matching Skills with Jobs	Expressing Your Opinion	Being Trustworthy	Knowing When to "Let It Go"	Another Point of View	Having a Discussion	Having an Argument	Defining Terms	Common Sense	Comments

14.1 Working as a Team

Objective

The student will identify several tips that can be useful when working in a team.

Discussion

Teacher: Today we are going to talk about working with other people; specifically, working as part of a team. What are some teams that you know about? (Baseball team, cheerleading team, and so on.) Why is it important to have more than one person on a team? (Need lots of people to get the job done, to compete, and so on.) How would a leader help with teamwork? (That person can supervise the whole job, see the big picture, tell people what to do, and so on.)

When people work together as a team, it is important that everyone in the group plays their part. For example, what would happen if everyone on the team decided to be the boss? (It would be a mess.) What if there were no leaders in the group—if everyone waited for someone else to take charge? (Nothing would get done.) Think about this: What if the leader asked people to do things that they didn't know how to do? (Another mess.) We are going to learn about a few tips that will help people work together as a team. They are: 1. Use your strengths. 2. Follow the leader. 3. Include everyone.

Worksheet 14.1: The tips for working together are at the top of the page. Read the examples and write 1, 2, or 3 to indicate which tip is being followed by members of the group.

Answers

1. 3   2. 1   3. 2   4. 1   5. 3   6. 2

Extension Activities

1. *Leader/Follower Trade.* Choose a task that several students can work on together. (Examples: Putting a puzzle together, drawing a poster, sorting small toys by color/function.) Assign one student to be the leader, with instructions that the others are to follow his or her instructions without comment. Have students take turns being the leader for a few minutes or until a logical break in the activity. Discuss what was hard or easy about being the leader. Discuss being a follower. Was it hard to take directions from someone if the instructions seemed wrong or inefficient? Would each student prefer to be a follower or leader?

2. *Leader for the Day.* Let students have a turn at being the "leader for the day" for several routine tasks, such as line leader, lunch count runner, or leading the pledge of allegiance. Emphasize that a good leader demonstrates how to do something well.

Name _____ Date _____

14.1   Working as a Team

The tips for working as a team are at the top of the page. Read the examples and write 1, 2, or 3 to indicate which tip is being followed by team members.

Tip #1: Use your strengths.
Tip #2: Follow the leader.
Tip #3: Include everyone.

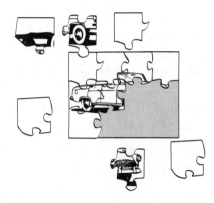

The students were given the job of putting a large classroom puzzle together. Juan was the team leader. The other team members were Maria, Steven, Pete, and Kelly.

_____ 1. Juan emptied all of the puzzle pieces from the box. Maria and Steven turned the pieces right-side up. Pete cleared a space on the floor of the room. Kelly began looking for edge pieces.

_____ 2. Maria is really good at matching colors together, so she worked on all of the puzzle pieces that had red on them.

_____ 3. Juan suggested that they look for the corner pieces first, so everyone began looking for corner pieces.

_____ 4. Steven notices tiny details and likes to find small clues, so he worked on putting together one section of the puzzle that had the same pattern.

_____ 5. Kelly's eyes were getting tired after working on the puzzle for a few minutes, and she wanted to quit, but the others said that she could hold the puzzle box up so that everyone could see what the finished puzzle should look like.

_____ 6. Pete was sure that a piece was missing from the puzzle, but Juan said that they should keep working on it anyhow and maybe the piece would show up later. Sure enough, the piece was under another piece on the floor.

Chapter 14: Working with People   **339**

14.2 Understanding the Task

Objective

The student will identify the end result of a task and several steps that are required to complete the task.

Discussion

Teacher: When people work together on a task or project, it is really important to keep the goal in mind. If everyone understands what the purpose is and stays on track, it will be easier to accomplish the goal. What would happen, for example, if you got a group of people together to make pizzas to sell and half of them decided that they wanted to go watch TV instead? Or if they decided to make hamburgers instead after you had purchased all of the ingredients for pizza? (Time and money would have been wasted, it doesn't follow the original goal, and so on.)

Worksheet 14.2: Here are some examples of tasks and the purpose of each. Write down several steps that might be needed to accomplish each task.

Answers

1. *Making cookies:* buy the ingredients, make sure you have bowls and spoons, make sure you have an oven (and that it works), have boxes or baggies to put the cookies in

2. *Having a car wash:* make sure you have a place to hold the car wash; advertise; have soap, towels, and water available

3. *Painting a mural on a wall:* design the picture(s) first, have the right colors of paints, have cleanup supplies, allow time for it to dry

Extension Activities

1. *Get-R-Done.* Check the local newspaper or community bulletin board for sources of projects that groups of people have worked on together. Have students list the project (picnic, fund-raiser, theater, building project, and so on) and brainstorm to come up with a list of subtasks that people might have had to work on to accomplish the goal.

2. *Class Project.* Adopt a class project for the purpose of working toward a goal. Select an appropriate task for your age and interest of students and break it down into smaller steps or tasks. Some ideas might include writing to a service, raising money for the animal shelter, cleaning up the school playground, or hosting a breakfast to celebrate Grandparents' Day. When you have finished, talk about how many people worked together to accomplish one goal.

14.2   Understanding the Task

Here are some examples of tasks and the purpose of each. Write down several steps that might be needed to accomplish each task. One is given for each to help get you started.

Task #1 Making Cookies

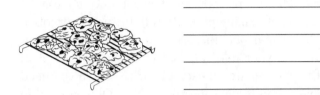

_____
_____
_____
_____

Your group is going to make several kinds of cookies to sell at a bake sale.

You need to:

• Decide what kinds of cookies we will make.

Task #2 Car Wash

_____
_____
_____
_____

Your group is going to hold a car wash to raise money for a class project.

You need to:

• Decide what day we will have it—Saturday? Sunday? Both days?

Task #3 Painting a Mural

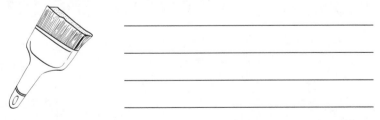

_____
_____
_____
_____

Your group is going to decorate a wall by painting pictures of things kids like to do.

You need to:

• Find out what colors of paint we need.

14.3 Understanding Your Role

Objective

The student will be able to identify characters who understand their role in a group task.

Discussion

Teacher: Once you have a task that you are working on with other people, you can then get down to business and figure out what your role is. Let's go back to the example of making pizzas to sell. It is not your job to do *everything*, but your role in reaching this big goal is to do *your part* the best you can. You are responsible for doing your share when you are working together. If your role is to put price tags on the pizza boxes, do you need to worry about how many pieces of pepperoni are on each pizza? (No.) Do you need to be concerned about answering the phone when people call in to give an order? (No.) Do you need to focus on getting the right tags on the pizza boxes? (Yes.) If you have a clear idea of the goal—getting the pizzas ready to sell—and of your job—putting the price tags on the boxes—then you can focus on doing the best job you can on *your* job.

Worksheet 14.3: These students are organizing cookies for a bake sale. Each student has a role or job to help accomplish this goal. Write Yes or No on the line to show whether each student is doing his or her job.

Answers

1. No   2. Yes   3. No   4. Yes

Extension Activities

1. *Help Me Out.* Discuss why Julie and Eduardo did not understand their role in the cookie task. Choose students to act as "supervisors" and demonstrate by role-playing how they would explain to the characters what they were doing wrong and how they could advise them to do their jobs better.

2. *Cookie Tester.* Who wouldn't want to be a cookie tester to see how delicious the cookies that are for sale really are? Have students volunteer to explain why he or she is best qualified for this very important role!

14.3   Understanding Your Role

These students are organizing cookies for a bake sale. Each student has a job to help accomplish this goal. Write Yes or No on the lines to show if each student is doing his or her job.

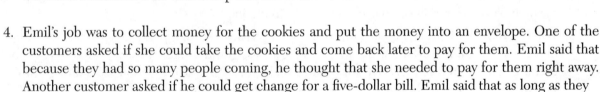

1. Julie's job was to put up signs around the school to let people know when and where the cookie sale will be held. She got some bright yellow paper and wrote COOKIE SALE! in big letters. She went all around the school and taped a sign in every hallway so that people would come to the

   cookie sale. _____

2. Carmella's job was to separate the three different kinds of cookies on a big table. She put the chocolate chip cookies on one end, peanut butter cookies on the other end, and snickerdoodles in the

   middle. _____

3. Eduardo's job was to put price tags on the baggies of cookies. He put a sticker with "25 cents" on some of the baggies, but when he ran out of stickers he wasn't sure what to do, so he stopped. Then he thought it looked like it would be fun to help separate the cookies, so he went over to

   Carmella and asked if he could help her. _____

4. Emil's job was to collect money for the cookies and put the money into an envelope. One of the customers asked if she could take the cookies and come back later to pay for them. Emil said that because they had so many people coming, he thought that she needed to pay for them right away. Another customer asked if he could get change for a five-dollar bill. Emil said that as long as they

   had enough money to make change that would be fine. _____

14.4 Matching Skills with Jobs

Objective

The student will match skills with a task or job that would use those particular skills.

Discussion

Teacher: Remember how we talked about working as part of a team with everyone contributing something? Today we are going to focus on using specific strengths and skills to fit in with a particular task. For example, if a job called for having a sign made, would you look for someone who was good at writing letters? (Yes.) What kind of skills would be helpful if you wanted someone to sew a costume for a play? (Someone who could sew.)

Worksheet 14.4: These students have the task of planning a Grandparents' Day party for their class. Take a look at the skills that these students have and match them with a possible way that they could help out at the party.

Answers

1. b 2. a 3. c 4. f 5. e 6. d

Extension Activities

1. *I Could Help!* Have students pretend that they are planning a Grandparents' Day party or program for their class. What skill could each contribute to the job?

2. *What's My Skill?* Have students pair up and take turns suggesting possible skills that the other has demonstrated while working with others. Make a class graph or table to show the different abilities that are represented in the class. Make sure that every student is given at least one example of a skill or ability, even if it is general, such as "is friendly," "is willing to clean up," and so on.

14.4   Matching Skills with Jobs

These students have the task of planning a Grandparents' Day party for their class. Take a look at the skills that these students have and match them with a possible way that they could help out at the party.

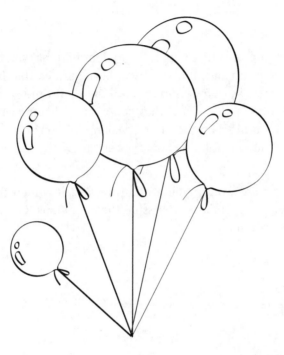

Student Skill

_____1. Has good handwriting

_____ 2. Loves to draw

_____ 3. Good organizer

_____ 4. Takes pictures with a camera

_____ 5. Loves to decorate

_____ 6. Can make balloon animals

Job for Grandparents' Day

a.   Draw pictures of grandparents playing with their grandchildren.

b.   Write the information about Grandparents' Day on a poster.

c.   Put the food and games in the best places around the room.

d.   Blow up balloons and make them into funny animals for the grandparents.

e.   Hang streamers and balloons around the room.

f.   Take a picture of each grandparent with his or her grandchild.

Chapter 14: Working with People   **345**

14.5 Expressing Your Opinion

Objective

The student will identify appropriate and inappropriate ways to express opinions for a given situation.

Discussion

Teacher: When you are working around other people, you might find that you have something to contribute. Maybe you are working with a group and think that you have an idea that is better than someone else's. What would be a good way to express your opinion? (Find the right time and way to tell your idea, and so on.) What could you do if you offer an idea and other people don't like it? (Accept their opinion, try again later, try it on your own, and so on.) It is important to speak up for yourself if you think that you truly have something to contribute to a situation. You don't always have to be the one holding the poster if you have the ability to draw it!

Worksheet 14.5: These students are working on a group project in which they are planting flowers in a planter in the city center. Some of them are expressing their opinions. Circle the ones who are using an appropriate way to express their opinions.

Answers

1. Yes   2. Yes   3. No   4. Yes   5. No   6. Yes

Extension Activities

1. *Just My Opinion.* Give students opportunities to offer their opinions on many different matters. It is really an important skill for students to be able to formulate an opinion and express it. Use opportunities to ask students questions such as: "What do you think about _____?" "David, do you agree with Sarah? Why or why not?" "Allen, what do you think I should do about _____?" (providing an appropriate example).

2. *Opinion Plus.* As you talk about what an "opinion" is, discuss how it is important to back up your opinion with careful thought, experiences, appropriate delivery, and factual basis as much as possible. As you discuss opinions with students, encourage them to add more by asking questions such as: "That's an interesting idea. What makes you think that?" or "Wow, that's a pretty wild idea. Did you have an experience that helped you get that idea?"

14.5   Expressing Your Opinion

These students are working on a group project in which they are planting flowers in a planter in the city center. Some of them are expressing their opinions. Circle the students who are using an appropriate way to express their opinions.

1. **Alyvia:** I think we should plant flowers that require a lot of sun, because the planter will be in a place where there is not a lot of shade.

2. **Jorge:** We should make a sign-up sheet of who will be responsible for watering the flowers every week.

3. **Ellen:** I think we should plant only red flowers because that's my favorite color. If you disagree with me, then you are pretty dumb.

4. **Gilbert:** I don't really like red flowers, but I know that you do, Ellen. So maybe we could plant some red flowers but also some that are other colors. That would be fair, wouldn't it?

5. **Stephanie:** I think we are spending too much money on the plants. We should take all of the plants back and get our money back and try something cheaper. Like plastic plants. Then we don't have to water them at all.

6. **Vic:** Stephanie, it's too late for that. We already went over the budget and decided that this was what we were going to do. But if you have other ideas, bring them up before we have our vote next time and I know we'll consider everything.

14.6 Being Trustworthy

Objective

The student will identify examples of trustworthy behavior.

Discussion

Teacher: If I told you that I was going to bring you something you needed tomorrow, would you expect me to do it? Why? (Past experience of being trustworthy.) I hope that I would not let you down—that if I said I would do something, I would do it. When you are working with other people, being trustworthy means doing something you say you will do or living up to expectations of what someone expects of you. Have you ever had someone let you down by not doing what they said they would do? (Ask for examples, but do not use specifi names.) How did it make you feel? Would you trust that person again? (Examples.)

Worksheet 14.6: Which of these students are showing trustworthy behavior? Write Yes or No on the line next to each one.

Answers

   1. No   2. Yes   3. No   4. Yes   5. Yes   6. No

Extension Activities

1. *Excuses, Excuses.* Discuss the examples on the Worksheet. How did the student in each example demonstrate trustworthiness? For example, in 1, 3, and 6, what excuse was given? What could the student have done to solve the problem in each case?

2. *Track Record.* Sometimes students are unaware that someone is holding them accountable for their promises. Give students opportunities to "practice" being trustworthy by allowing them to borrow books, take home class treasures for the weekend, and so on, but have them sign a log book that records their borrowing. As always, do not send home something that belongs to someone else or has value that would cause a problem if it is lost or forgotten. When students ask to borrow something, go to the log book and have them check their record.

Name _____ Date _____

14.6   **Being Trustworthy**

Which of these students are showing trustworthy behavior? Write Yes or No on the line next to each one.

1. I know I said I would bring paper bags to school, but I forgot. Sorry. _____

2. Here are the books we are going to repair. I brought them in early so we have plenty of time to work on them. _____

3. I was supposed to come in early today to help decorate, but my mother needed me to watch my little sister. I guess I should have called someone, but I got really busy. _____

4. Here is my list of the times I came over to feed the cat. _____

5. My homework is all done, Dad! Now can we go get ice cream? _____

6. I changed my mind about giving you my sweater. I'm sure you can find someone else who will let you borrow one for the party. Or you have time to go shopping for another one. _____

14.7 Knowing When to "Let It Go"

Objective

The student will give reasons why it is a good idea to let go of an issue in some circumstances.

Discussion

Teacher: You probably don't expect to hear a teacher tell you that it is a good idea to give up on something, but when you are working with people you have to know when it is time to stop. Stop what? Stop arguing, stop trying to make your point about something, or stop focusing on something that doesn't matter, so you can move to something else. Why do you think it might be better to stop and "let it go," rather than win an argument? (Hard feelings, people stop listening anyway, wasting time, and so on.)

Worksheet 14.7: The characters need to "let it go." Circle the answer that gives a reason why.

Answers

1. It's not that important.
2. Nothing can be done.
3. The person stopped listening.

Extension Activities

1. *Role-Playing.* Have students write skits or act out the examples on the Worksheet. By demonstrating how some things can be minor, rather than major issues, students may be able to put these kinds of issues in perspective.
2. *"Let It Go."* Keep a record of issues that come up during a week that you would categorize as "let it go" issues. At the end of the week, discuss each one and have students give reasons why. When similar issues arise, try using the phrase "let it go" and refer back to the issue that has already been discussed in class.

14.7 **Knowing When to "Let It Go"**

These children need to "let it go." Circle the answer that gives a reason why.

1. MARLISSA: I need an eraser. I want to write my name in cursive.

    ADELE: No, it's fine. Just leave it.

    MARLISSA: No, I want to write my name in cursive. I don't like the way I wrote it.

    ADELE: You already erased the numbers. It's fine.

    MARLISSA: I need an eraser! I want to write my name again!

    Let it go. It's not that important. ***or*** Erasers cost money.

2. CHILD: I hit my finger on the desk. I need a bandage.

    TEACHER: The nurse isn't here today.

    CHILD: I need a bandage. My finger hurts.

    TEACHER: There is no blood. A bandage won't help you.

    CHILD: I can't work unless I have a bandage.

    Let it go. There aren't any bandages. ***or*** Nothing can be done.

3. CALEB: That marker is *red*.

    MARIA: No, it's *dark pink*.

    CALEB: I said, it's *red*.

    MARIA: Well, what difference does it make?

    CALEB: It's not pink, it's *red*.

    MARIA: Big deal, OK, it's red.

    Let it go. The person doesn't know her colors. ***or*** The person stopped listening.

Chapter 14: Working with People   **351**

14.8 Another Point of View

Objective

The student will be able to state at least two points of view for a given situation.

Discussion

Teacher: Have you ever been in a situation where you saw something differently from how your parents or a brother or sister saw it? Can anyone give an example? (Allow time for sharing.) Sometimes people have a different point of view. That means they "see it differently" from you, but it doesn't mean either one of you is wrong. It just means there is a different side to look at. To understand others, it helps you see things from their side or their point of view.

Worksheet 14.8: This Work sheet lists some topics that not everyone feels the same about. For example, some people like these things; others don't. On this Worksheet you will practice thinking two different ways to try to understand another point of view. Write what you think each person might be saying.

Answers

(Answers will vary.)

1. Cats can be friendly and funny.
2. I am old enough and brave enough to ride.
3. I think that hair style looks great.
4. Bikes are safer in the street than on a sidewalk.
5. I eat lots of chocolate without getting fat.
6. It's mean to play phone tricks on people.

Extension Activities

1. *"Yes, But . . ." Game.* Have students sit with a partner (back to back) and take opposite sides of a controversial topic. Others watch and give each side thirty seconds to state their side.
2. *Two Sides.* Have students fold a sheet of paper in half. On one side they should illustrate the "pro" side of a topic; on the other, the "con" side, or an alternate point of view. Students should discuss and select topics they wish to portray.

14.8   Another Point of View

Each of the people here has a different point of view about the subject. One point of view is given. Write what the other person's point of vew might be.

1. I hate cats because they scratch!

CATS

2. Riding A ROLLER COASTER

You are too small to ride. It will scare you!

3. That looks WEIRD!

Hair STYLES

4. RIDING IN THE STREET

Bikes should get out of the road! It's dangerous!

5. Chocolate will make you fat!

EATING CHOCOLATE

6. Crank PHONE CALLS

It's fun to call people and hang up on them!

14.9 Having a Discussion

Objective

The student will identify and explain key elements of a discussion between two parties.

Discussion

Teacher: In an interview, one person asks most of the questions and the other person answers. In a discussion, both people talk and ask questions and try to understand each other. Let's make a list of some topics that you would like to discuss or talk about. What are your favorite things to talk to friends about? (Allow time for sharing, and list on the board.)

Worksheet 14.9: Here are three examples of students trying to have a discussion. What should you look for in a discussion? (Read over the four rules.) Decide whether or not the students are having a good discussion.

Answers

1. Yes—Topic: monster movies
2. No—No single topic, both sides talked, but didn't listen to each other
3. No—Topic: baseball game, but only one side talked

Extension Activities

1. *Let's Talk.* Have students list interesting topics and randomly assign them to pairs. Have them carry out a discussion for one minute in front of the class. Go through the four rules to evaluate how good their discussion was. Also have the class evaluate the discussion. Did both sides talk and listen? Can each person accurately summarize what was said?

2. *What Do You Think?* Tape examples of discussion from TV programs using a VCR. Have students evaluate different types of discussions. (Examples may be from soap operas, talk shows, situation comedies, and so on.)

14.9　　　　　　　Having a Discussion

Rules for having a discussion:

> 1. Pick a topic.
> 2. Both sides talk.
> 3. Both sides listen.
> 4. Each side understands the other side.

These students are trying to have a discussion. Go through the four rules for having a discussion and decide which groups are having a good discussion. Write Yes or No for each one.

1.

2.

3.

14.10 Having an Argument

Objective

The student will identify how an argument differs from a discussion between two parties.

Discussion

Teacher: In a discussion, both sides try to understand how the other feels and listen to what each has to say. The term "argument" can mean different things, and not all of the meanings are bad. For our purposes in getting along with others, though, we will use the word "argument" to describe a situation in which there is not good listening and good understanding going on, or there is disagreement without good reasons. What are some things that you might argue about with a friend? With a parent?

Worksheet 14.10: On this Work sheet you will find some examples of people having arguments. Let's read some characteristics of arguments. (Read the four points.) Decide which of them are involved in the arguments. Each may have more than one correct answer.

Answers

1. 1, 4
2. 1, 2
3. 1, 4
4. 1 (although the mother may not be involved in the argument), 3 (discuss whether or not they think this is an argument)

Extension Activities

1. *Discuss, Don't Argue.* Have students role-play the arguments on the Worksheet, only change them into discussions. Help students demonstrate how the issues can be thought through by listening and communicating.
2. *Good Reasons.* Have students select "hot" issues that they find themselves arguing about with others and list various reasons why they feel strongly. Go through the reasons and clarify whether or not the group feels the reasons are valid or irrelevant.

14.10   **Having an Argument**

In an argument . . .

> 1. Someone disagrees.
> 2. Reasons may not be very good.
> 3. Each side may not listen to the other.
> 4. Each side may not understand the other side.

These students are having arguments. Which of the four reasons explains why it is an argument? Write the numbers of your answer next to each picture.

14.11 Defining Terms

Objective

The student will demonstrate the ability to clarify specified terms so that they are objective, not subjective.

Discussion

Teacher: Many arguments start or grow out of discussions because the two sides involved aren't really talking about the same thing. If someone says, "You can have my old shirt," but later says he only meant that you could borrow it, could that lead to an argument? If that person said, "I don't want it back, you can keep it," does that make it clearer? Does the word "have" mean forever or just for a little while? What are some instructions that people give you that aren't always very clear? When you define something, it means you say it clearly so that everyone understands what you mean.

Worksheet 14.11: You will see four examples of people who are talking but not really understanding each other. You will rewrite what the first person in each example is saying to make it very clear to both sides what they mean. (You may wish to do the first example together.)

Answers

(Answers will vary; these are suggestions.)

1. "Come inside in one hour."
2. "Ask your aunt how her trip was and sit quietly in the chair for at least fifteen minutes."
3. "Play with your own toys. No hitting."
4. "Don't take anything or even touch it!"

Extension Activities

1. *What I Mean Is.* Continue listing instructions that may not be clear (such as dress nicely, clean your room, take a bath), and have students specify exactly what is involved in each instruction for them.
2. *What Happened Next.* Using the four examples, have students write or draw the next logical event that could happen based on the misinterpreted instruction.

14.11   **Defining Terms**

These people are using words that don't mean the same thing to each side. How could you rewrite the instructions to make them clearer?

14.12 Common Sense

Objective

The student will demonstrate ability to use common sense to resolve conflicts.

Discussion

Teacher: Listen to this little story and tell me at the end what the boy should have done:

> *It was raining very hard one morning. A boy got up, got dressed, and was getting ready to go to school. He walked past his umbrella, went out into the rain, and got all wet. Then he got to school, all drenched, and told his friend it was his mother's fault that he was wet because she didn't give him an umbrella.*

Whose fault was it that he got wet? If he knew about the umbrella, what do you think he should have done? What does the term "common sense" mean? We will use it to mean figuring out what to do without being told.

Worksheet 14.12: This Worksheet shows some ways to use common sense. (Read over the list.) Circle the person in each situation who is using common sense, and write the number of the reason in the box.

Answers

1. Second student, 3
2. First student, 1
3. Second student, 3
4. First student, 2

Extension Activities

1. *Silly Stories.* Have students write stories in which the main character does not use common sense. Exaggerations of this can be quite humorous (for example, wearing a sweater in 90-degree heat, playing in the mud with wedding clothes on, and so on).

2. *But You Didn't Say So.* For a set time limit (ten to fifteen minutes), require students to say specifically everything they mean, allowing others to misunderstand and not use common sense. They will find that having to specify everything can be time consuming, ridiculous, and funny.

14.12   **Common Sense**

These are ways to use common sense:

> 1. Think the situation through to what will probably happen next.
> 2. Look around you and see if the answer is clearly there.
> 3. Think about how this type of situation was handled before.

Which of these situations show a student using common sense? Circle the student. Write in the box the number of the way he or she used his or her common sense.

Chapter 15

Having a Social Life

PARENT LETTER #15: HAVING A SOCIAL LIFE

Dear Parents,

We all want our children to have friends. We want to see them playing together, exploring, laughing, and spending time with peers. All children can benefit from good relationships. However, sometimes special children do not understand how they are perceived by others, nor are they able to evaluate themselves in terms of how appropriate their behavior is. Are they talking too much? Are they being brutally honest, when tact is important?

Some of the skills in this section deal with knowing how to treat friends, having something to bring to a friendship, having good hygiene, knowing how to start a conversation, and being willing to try new things.

You can help your child by helping him or her get to places where child-friendly activities are offered, such as the local YMCA classes, sports, 4-H, and other groups in which your child will meet peers. If possible, invite children over to your home or to a park so they can interact with your child in a safe and entertaining setting. Help your child understand what it means to include others and to say nice things.

Cue your child to know when he or she needs to "back off," share, listen, or be more outgoing. Prepare your child for events so that it is not a surprise if suddenly there is a clown, or a cold swimming pool, or competitive games. The best way to have a friend is to be one—a time-honored cliché, but true! Help your child develop friendship-making skills as much as possible!

Sincerely,

_____

Teacher

HAVING A SOCIAL LIFE

Skill Sheet #15: Progress Report

+ mastered
√ emerging
− not mastered

Student Name	Meeting People	Understanding That Friends Are Important	Knowing How to Treat Friends	Having Something to Offer	Saying Nice Things	Having Good Hygiene	Using Conversation Starters	Trying Something New	Going Places	Comments

15.1 Meeting People

Objective

When meeting a person for the first time, the student will show eye contact, shake hands properly, and state an appropriate greeting.

Discussion

Teacher: Who is someone whom you would really love to meet? (Rock star, sports figure, the President.) If he or she walked into the room right now, what would you do? (Run up, ask for autographs.) Usually when you meet someone or are introduced to someone for the first time, it's good manners to tell him or her who you are, shake hands, and say something like—like what? (Examples: nice to meet you, how are you?) Today we're going to practice showing good manners when meeting someone—whether it's someone famous or just an ordinary person, you should show the same good manners. We're going to look for: (1) eye contact, (2) shaking hands, and (3) something appropriate to say.

Worksheet 15.1: This Worksheet shows some examples of students meeting other people. You are going to circle the good examples and put an X on the examples that could be improved. Then we'll discuss your choices.

Answers

1. Circled   2. X   3. X   4. Circled   5. X   6. Circled

Extension Activities

1. *Handshaking.* Have students practice shaking hands with each other while maintaining eye contact. Teach them to grasp the other person's right hand (extended) and give a firm, sincere clasp for a second or two. Students will probably act a little silly at first, but insist on this exercise when someone visits the room. You as the teacher might want to greet each student with a handshake as they enter the classroom each morning for a few days.

2. *Students Meeting Students.* When students meet others of their own age, handshaking is probably not an accepted form of greeting. Some students might make up their own special handshake. Discuss how kids can be friendly to each other and make a newcomer feel welcome to a group in other ways.

Name _____ Date _____

15.1   **Meeting People**

These students are meeting someone for the first time. Circle the students who are showing (1) eye contact, (2) handshakes, and (3) something appropriate to say. Put an X on the students who need to improve in some way.

15.2 Understanding That Friends Are Important

Objective

The student will state at least three reasons why it is important to have friends.

Discussion

Teacher: I want you to think about something for a minute. If you were going to go roller skating or to the water park with just one friend, who would it be? Don't say the name out loud, just think it in your head. Now think about being scared or maybe lost somewhere and wanting to be with someone. Think of who you would talk to, someone other than your family. Are you thinking of the same person for both situations? Now, one more time, pretend that you are laughing really hard about something funny. Think about what you might be laughing at and who you would be laughing with. Is it the same person again? There are many reasons why people want and need friends. We are going to spend some time in the next few lessons thinking and talking about friendship.

Worksheet 15.2: Read the comments by each person on the left. Draw a line to match the person with the reason why that person would like a friend on the right. Discuss your answers.

Answers

1. b (*or* b)   2. e   3. a   4. d (*or* b)   5. c

Extension Activities

1. *You and Me!* Have students bring in photos of themselves and a friend. Decorate a bulletin board with the pictures. You might have a theme such as CELEBRATE FRIENDSHIP!
2. *F-R-I-E-N-D-S-H-I-P.* Using the letters of "friendship," have students come up with words that begin with each letter to describe some aspect of friendship. Examples: *Funny, Really nice, Interesting, Enjoyable, Nice, Devoted, Special, Happy, Into roller skating, Pleasant!*

15.2   Understanding That Friends Are Important

Read the comments by each person on the left. Draw a line to match the person with the reason why that person would like a friend on the right. Discuss your answers.

1. I am tired of sitting by myself. I wish there was someone who would go walking with me.

a. To have someone to laugh with

2. I want to tell someone about this great book! But who would be interested?

b. To have someone to do things with

3. That was the funniest movie! I want to see it again and laugh out loud!

c. To have someone who can help

4. This is a great game. But it would be more fun with a partner.

d. To have someone to share things with

5. I just don't know how to put this model together. I can't figure it out.

e. To have someone to talk to

15.3 Knowing How to Treat Friends

Objective

The student will identify examples of treating friends appropriately in a variety of situations.

Discussion

Teacher: Having a friend is a wonderful gift. It means that someone has chosen *you* to spend time with or to care about. That means that you need to take care of your friendship as well. What are some ways that you can take care of your friends? (Listen to them, don't talk behind their back, and so on.) If you want to keep your friends, you need to be sensitive to what is going on in their lives as well.

Worksheet 15.3: Some of these friendships are in trouble! Write the examples of friends treating each other appropriately. Write NO next to those friends who are not treating each other appropriately. Discuss your answers.

Answers

1. NO (she is ignoring her friend)
2. YES (he is including the friend in the game)
3. NO (he is "too busy" to help his friend)
4. NO (she is gossiping)
5. YES (she is trying to understand her friend)

Extension Activities

1. *Storybook Friendships.* Read some grade-appropriate books to your students and list the friendships that you find. Discuss why the characters are friends and how they show their friendship. (Frog and toad, twin stories, and so on.)

2. *Friend versus Friendly.* Discuss the differences and similarities between having a friend and being simply "friendly" to someone. Not everyone you meet will end up being a friend, but you can certainly act in a friendly manner to almost everyone you meet. Being "friendly" can often lead to having a friend, however, so it should not be overlooked.

15.3   # Knowing How to Treat Friends

Some of these friendships are in trouble! Write YES next to the examples of friends treating each other appropriately. Write NO next to those who are not. Discuss your answers.

1. "Hey, I thought we were going to ride bikes!"

   "No, I decided to go skating with Julie."

2. "Want to join us?"

   "Sure!

3. "Can you help me paint this birdhouse?"

   "I don't have time. I'm going to take a nap."

4. "Bye, Veronica!"

   "Did you hear that she got a D on her report card in math? She is really going to get in trouble at home!"

5. "I don't know why Stella won't talk to me."

   "Don't feel bad. She is really busy with cheerleading right now and doesn't have a lot of time for anything else. It's not you!"

15.4 Having Something to Offer

Objective

The student will identify some personal things that would be interesting for someone to know in order to become a friend.

Discussion

Teacher: If I asked you to tell me about a friend of yours, what would you say? (Might describe what he looks like, things you do together.) If you have a friend, you know some things about him or her that maybe not everyone else knows. Why is that? (Because you spend time with a friend, you share ideas and thoughts.) If someone asked you if you were a good friend, what would you say? (Ideally "Yes.") You have probably heard the saying, "If you want to have a friend, be a friend." Think about some things about yourself that would make you a good friend. In other words, what do you have to offer to someone who might be looking for a friend?

Worksheet 15.4: Make a list of things about yourself that show you would be a good friend.

Answers

(Answers will vary.)

Extension Activities

1. *Yellow Pages Ad.* If appropriate for your class, have students compose a short "ad" that features a picture or drawing of themselves and some comments about their qualities as a good friend. Display the ads around your room. (You might have to explain that the "Yellow Pages" is a term used by a phone book to represent businesses!)

2. *Guess Who?* Using the responses on the Worksheet, lead a class game in which you have the students guess whose paper you are reading. Keep the comments positive and affirm the qualities whenever possible. Even guessing "wrong" can be a compliment to students who may be surprised to find that they are perceived as funny, friendly, nice to others, and so on. Save the most unique comments for the end, as some students can be identified right away by personal comments.

15.4

Having Something to Offer

Make a list of things about yourself that show you would be a good friend. Two examples are given to get you started.

I am a good listener if someone has a problem.

I don't forget to return things when I borrow something.

_____

_____

_____

_____

_____

_____

_____

_____

_____

_____

_____

_____

15.5 Saying Nice Things

Objective

The student will identify some positive comments that could be made in various situations to help them make a friend.

Discussion

Teacher: One way to come across as a good friend is to say nice things about others. But you have to be sincere about what you say. For example, if I told every single person that I came across whom he or she was the smartest, nicest, funniest person I had ever met—well, do you think they would believe me? (No.) Why not? (After you hear something repeated often, it doesn't seem true anymore; some of the comments might not even be accurate.) Look at the person next to you and think of a nice, true comment that you could say.

Worksheet 15.5: Read each of the situations. Write something nice that you could say in each situation.

Answers

(Answers will vary; these are examples.)

1. I really like your sweater.
2. You did a good job on that test.
3. I think your hair is really pretty.
4. Nice try—you'll get it next time.

Extension Activities

1. *I Wish I'd Said That.* Help your students collect general "nice" comments that they could say to someone and write them on "speech balloons" (like in comic books). Have students draw or find pictures of children's faces and attach the comments so it appears that the child is talking. Then, if someone in your class ever runs out of nice things to say, direct them to the wall or board where are displayed.

2. *Turn it Around.* Collect examples of impolite or unflattering comments and write them on one side of a Paper Ping-pong paddle. Have students read and edit them so that the comments are "turned around" to say something positive or at least neutral. Glue or attach them to the opposite side of the Ping-Pong paddle. If possible, display them on mobiles so students can read both sides. (Example: You are really slow. / You take your time on things.)

15.5   Saying Nice Things

Read each situation below. Write something nice that you could say in each situation.

1. I just wents hopping!

_____

_____

_____

3. I'm not sure I like this haircut. What do you think?

_____

_____

_____

2. Look!

4. I didn't make the team.

_____

_____

_____

_____

_____

_____

Chapter 15: Having a Social Life

15.6 Having Good Hygiene

Objective

The student will identify at least five ways to maintain good hygiene.

Discussion

Teacher: One sure way to turn people off is to have poor hygiene. That means not taking care of the way you look, smell, or appear to others, especially regarding being clean. No one really wants to be around someone who smells bad, doesn't brush his or her teeth, or doesn't take care of personal things such as washing hair or trimming nails. What are some other examples of ways that a person can make sure that he or she has good hygiene? (Take a bath or shower regularly, wash your hair, clean under your fingernails, change your clothes.)

Worksheet 15.6: What could each person do to improve his or her hygiene?

Answers

1. Wash his hair.
2. Change her sweatshirt.
3. Clean the wound with medicine.
4. Take a bath(or shower).
5. Brush her teeth.

Extension Activities

1. *Soap and Toothpaste Contest.* Have students name as many brands of soap or toothpaste as they can within two minutes. You may want to divide students into teams of small groups. Who can list the most?

2. *Special Event.* Create or use an already-scheduled parent event to encourage students to clean up and really focus on their appearance. Whether the students are performing something or just greeting adults, they can use this opportunity to practice their hygiene skills, ideally in time to be well turned out!

15.6   Having Good Hygiene

What could each person below do to improve his or her hygiene? Write your answer on the blank next to each item.

1. Jeremiah spray-painted parts of his hair bright red for a weekend party. He liked the way it looked, so he didn't wash his hair for two weeks even though the red dye was beginning to fade.

   _____

2. Ashley wore her favorite sweatshirt to school. After school, she wore it while she played soccer with her friends. She wore it to the movies that night with her family. The next day, she put it on again. At lunch, she spilled ketchup on a sleeve. On her way home from school, she tripped and got some dirt on the elbow. The next day, she wore the sweatshirt again.

   _____

3. Joshua was riding his bike without holding onto the handlebars. He hit a rock and was tossed off onto the street. His leg was cut and bleeding from a gash. He wiped off the blood a little bit and then got back on the bike to ride some more.

   _____

4. Natalie went to visit her uncle's farm. She got to ride a pony, then helped clean out chicken cages, and finally helped dig holes to plant some flowers. Her face, hands, and clothes got covered with all kinds of farm smells and dirt.

   _____

5. Jasmine loves garlic. When her family went out for pizza and garlic bread, Jasmine helped herself to several helpings of her favorite food. When it was time to kiss her parents good-night, her mom and dad both said, "Whew!"

   _____

15.7 Using Conversation Starters

Objective

The student will identify suggested conversation starters as appropriate or inappropriate.

Discussion

Teacher: If you want to get along with others socially, you might want to prepare some good conversation starters that would interest others around you and get them involved in a conversation. Of course, you have to make sure that you are in a good place and at a good time before you strike up a conversation. Some people may not want to be bothered with small talk or chit-chat if they are doing something else. However, most people welcome a friendly comment. Can you think of some examples of ways to start up a talk with someone? (Hello, my name is . . . ; Good morning; How's your day going?)

Worksheet 15.7: Which of these are appropriate conversation starters if you were in the following situations? Circle YES or NO.

Answers

1. YES   2. NO   3. NO   4. YES   5. YES   6. YES   7. YES   8. NO   9. NO   10. NO   11. YES   12. NO   13. YES   14. YES   15. NO

Extension Activities

1. *Community Conversation Quest.* Put forth a personal challenge to each student to engage someone in the community in conversation by (a) preparing a general, positive, and interesting comment, and (b) targeting a person who is in an appropriate setting. Have students report how their conversations went!

2. *Eavesdropping—One Time Only!* While students are in public places—such as the cafeteria, on a bus, at the grocery store, at a meeting—have them try to pick up on beginnings of conversations between people who are around them. Although eavesdropping is generally impolite, in this case (for research and discussion) students should try to observe what type of greetings, questions, and comments lead to polite conversations.

Name _____ Date _____

15.7   **Using Conversation Starters**

Which of these are appropriate conversation starters if you were in the following situations? Circle YES or NO.

At a party . . .

1. "Do you like to play Ping-Pong?"   YES   NO

2. "Where did you get that awful shirt?"   YES   NO

3. "I'm so bored."   YES   NO

4. "Hey, why don't you come with me to get some cake?"   YES   NO

5. "I like to play games. Do you?"   YES   NO

At a club or meeting . . .

6. "Were you at the last game?"   YES   NO

7. "I just joined this club/team. Can you tell me what it's like?"   YES   NO

8. "I am sure I am the best player here. I hope this team doesn't have too many nerds on it."
   YES   NO

9. "That sure is a dumb coach."   YES   NO

10. "We did things a lot better at my other school."   YES   NO

In the community . . .

11. "Good morning, my name is Victoria."   YES   NO

12. "What a boring day. I hate rain."   YES   NO

13. "Did you happen to hear any news about the new
    museum/zoo/park in town?"   YES   NO

14. "Hi, Chris. We are walking to the pond. Would you like to
    come with us?"   YES   NO

15. "I'm in a bad mood. Leave me alone."
    YES   NO

15.8 Trying Something New

Objective

The student will match interests with a likely activity that would incorporate that interest.

Discussion

Teacher: Another way to get to know other people is to try something new. If you do the same thing all the time, you are probably doing it with the same people. If you expand your interests a little and look for opportunities to try something new, you might meet some new people as well as have a chance to learn something you might enjoy. If you were interested in animals, for example, what is something that you could do? (Work at an animal shelter, help care for a neighbor's pets.)

Worksheet 15.8: These people would like to try something new. Match each person on the left with the new thing that they could try or do on the right.

Answers

1. b   2. e   3. a   4. f   5. c   6. d

Extension Activities

1. *Interest Wheel.* Have students cut out two circles of different sizes. Divide each circle into four equal parts. On the smaller circle, have students write four interests that they have. Now put the larger circle behind the smaller circle and attach them at the center with a brad or pin that will allow them to spin separately. On the larger circle, have the student write a corresponding activity that they could try that would involve the interest on the smaller circle. Have students randomly turn the circles and exchange them with others. Try to match up the interests and the activities.

2. *Match Game.* Develop and play a simple match game in which an interest is on one card and a corresponding activity is on another. Make a pool of at least twenty cards and have students take turns flipping over two at a time until they make a match.

Name _____ Date _____

15.8　　　　　　　Trying Something New

These people would like to try something new. Match each person on the left with the new thing that they could try or do on the right.

1. Andrea likes to work with her hands. She likes to draw pictures and doodle cartoons.

a. Take swimming lessons.

2. Brandon is pretty good at sports. He played on a baseball team and a soccer team.

b. Design, write, and draw a comic book.

3. Vanessa moved into a neighborhood that has a large public swimming pool. She is not afraid of the water, but she doesn't know how to swim.

c. Make a cake in the shape of a dinosaur.

4. Bryan heard that the public library just opened a new section for kids that has a lot of books on things that kids are interested in.

d. Get some friends together and play music for the neighborhood.

5. Jayla sometimes helps her mom cook after school. She found a book that has recipes for cakes and how to decorate them.

e. Find friends who like to play sports and organize a contest.

6. Jordan likes to pretend he can play the drums in a band. He thinks it would be fun to really make music with a group someday.

f. Get a library card.

15.9 Going Places

Objective

The student will identify several places that are available in the community to visit with friends.

Discussion

Teacher: Every community has places where you can go with friends to have a good time. If you and your friends like to bike ride, where could you go? (School parking lot, bike trails.) If you wanted to go swimming, what are some choices? (High school pool, community pool, beach, park.) Let's find out about the things our town has to offer.

Worksheet 15.9: Put a check mark in front of the places in your community that you would like to visit with friends. Add some ideas of your own at the bottom.

Answers

(Answers will vary. *Note:* If your community does not have some of these places, have students cross out the item. Add items that reflect your own town or city.)

Extension Activities

1. *Kid's-View Map.* As a class project, have students make a map of their town depicting the places that are of particular interest to kids. Where is the local pool? Where is the library? Where are the parks? Where is the best ice cream in town? Have students decorate the map.

2. *Reverse Field Trip: Bringing the Community to **You!*** If your class or school is limited on field trips, try to arrange a person from community places to visit your class as a guest speaker. A librarian, nature center volunteer, or even the person who feeds the birds at the zoo would make a great guest and should inspire some interest in visiting community places with friends.

15.9   **Going Places**

Put a check mark in front of the places in your community that you would like to visit with friends. Add some ideas of your own at the bottom.

☐ Zoo   ☐ Beach

☐ Water park   ☐ Museum

☐ Movie theater   ☐ Community airport

☐ Bowling alley   ☐ Hiking trails

☐ Arcade   ☐ _____

☐ Community pool   ☐ _____

☐ YMCA   ☐ _____

☐ Skate park

Chapter 15: Having a Social Life   **383**

Place Words

Community:
airport
apartments
bank
barber shop
beauty salon
car dealer
church
court house
dentist's office
fire department
florist shop
football field
funeral home
gas station
golf course
government office
hardware store
hospital
jewelry store
Laundromat
library
motel
newspaper office
nursing home

park
police station
print shop
school
shoe repair
sporting goods store
travel agency
YMCA

State:
Tourist attractions,
historical sites,
the capital city,
other noteworthy places

United States:
the Alamo
Churchhill Downs
Disneyland
Grand Canyon
Monticello
Niagara Falls
states
Washingon, D.C.

Object and Thing Words

Animals:
antelope
bear
elephant
goat
horse
iguana
jackal
kangaroo
llama
mouse
octopus
pony
quail
rooster
squirrel
zebra

Tools:
chisel
drill
hammer
level
nail
saw
screwdriver

Toys and Games:
baseball
basketball
crayons
dartboard
marbles
model car
modeling clay

Furniture:
bed
chair
couch
desk
dresser
lamp
table

Clothing:
bathing suit
belt
jacket
mittens
shoes
socks
underwear
vest

School Items:
book
eraser
lunch box
markers
paper
pen
ruler

House:
attic
basement
bathroom
bathtub
bedroom
carpet

closet
dishwasher
door
kitchen
living room
oven
porch
refrigerator
rug
stove
telephone
television
toilet
typewriter
VCR
window

Food:
apple
banana
bread
butter
carrot
cereal
cheese
cookies
crackers
hamburger
hot dog
lettuce
macaroni
pizza
tomato

Sign and Safety Words

Information Signs:

elevator

entrance

exact change needed

men/women

no trespassing

open/closed

out of order

ohone

please pay cashier

please wait to be seated

push/pull

quiet

rest rooms

self-serve

up/down

use other door

caution- wet floor

danger- keep out

do not enter

don't walk

emergency exit

exit

fire alarm

fire extinguisher

flammable

hot/cold

keep off

no smoking

on/off

poison

police

stairs

watch your step

Safety Words:

beware of dog

caution